EL SEGUNDO PUBLIC LIBRARY
3 5156 00536 5753

W9-BNQ-783

THE AGE OF GENIUS

BY THE SAME AUTHOR

An Introduction to Philosophical Logic
The Refutation of Scepticism
Berkeley: The Central Arguments
Wittgenstein
The Long March to the Fourth of June (with Xu You Yu)
China: A Literary Companion (with Susan Whitfield)
Philosophy 1: A Guide through the Subject (editor)
Russell
The Future of Moral Values
Philosophy 2: Further through the Subject (editor)
The Quarrel of the Age: The Life and Times of William Hazlitt
Herrick: Lyrics of Love and Desire (editor)
What is Good?
Descartes: The Life and Times of a Genius

The Meaning of Things
The Reason of Things
The Mystery of Things
The Heart of Things
The Form of Things

The Continuum Encyclopaedia of British Philosophy (editor)
Among the Dead Cities: Was the Allied Bombing of Civilians in WWII a Necessity or a Crime?
Against All Gods
Towards the Light: The Story of the Struggles for Liberty and Rights that Made the Modern West
The Choice of Hercules
Truth, Meaning and Realism
Scepticism and the Possibility of Knowledge
Ideas That Matter
To Set Prometheus Free
Liberty in the Age of Terror
Thinking of Answers
The Good Book
The God Argument
The Challenge of Things
A Handbook of Humanism (editor, with Andrew Copson)

THE AGE OF GENIUS

The Seventeenth Century and the Birth of the Modern Mind

A. C. Grayling

BLOOMSBURY
NEW YORK • LONDON • OXFORD • NEW DELHI • SYDNEY

Bloomsbury USA
An imprint of Bloomsbury Publishing Plc

1385 Broadway
New York
NY 10018
USA

50 Bedford Square
London
WC1B 3DP
UK

www.bloomsbury.com

First published in Great Britain 2016
First U.S. edition 2016

Plate section images sourced from Getty Images.

ISBN: HB: 978-1-62040-344-0
ePub: 978-1-62040-345-7

Library of Congress Cataloging-in-Publication Data has been applied for.

2 4 6 8 10 9 7 5 3 1

Typeset by Newgen Knowledge Works (P) Ltd., Chennai, India
Printed and bound in USA by Berryville Graphics, Inc., Berryville, Virginia

To the first graduating cohort of NCH: *anima cultura gaudere*

History is philosophy teaching by examples
Thucydides

Non est ad astra mollis e terris via
Seneca

CONTENTS

PART IV: FROM MAGIC TO SCIENCE

PART V: THE SOCIAL ORDER

PART VI: CONCLUSION

Holy Roman Empire
Austrian Habsburg lands
Palatinate of the Rhineland
Spanish Habsburgs
N
NORWAY
Bergen
Christiania
SCOTLAND
Edinburgh
North Sea
DENMARK
IRELAND
Dublin
Cork
UNITED KINGDOM
Bristol
London
UNITED PROVINCES
Amsterdam
Hamburg
Atlantic Ocean
SPANISH NETHERLANDS
Brussels
Cologne
Frankfurt
Rouen
Paris
Rheims
Nurenberg
BAVARIA
Munich
Nantes
Orléans
Tours
FRANCE
Bay of Biscay
Limoges
Bordeaux
Lyons
Geneva
Berne
Milan
Corunna
Bilbao
Toulouse
Oporto
PORTUGAL
Nice
Marseille
Florence
Saragossa
Madrid
Lisbon
SPAIN
Barcelona
Rome
Valencia
SARDINIA
Cordova
Cadiz
Malaga
Cartegena
Cagliari
Mediterranean Sea
Tangier
Algiers
Tunis

Europe in the Early Seventeenth Century
SWEDEN
Helsingfors
Stockholm
Reval
Novgorod
Pskov
thenburg
Moscow
Riga
RUSSIA
Baltic Sea
penhagen
Smolensk
Vilno
Königsberg
Minsk
Gdańsk
MERANIA
Stettin
Kursk
POLAND
Berlin
Warsaw
Kharkov
Kiev
Prague
Cracow
Lwów
HEMIA
Vienna
Buda
Kolozsvár
Trieste
Belgrade
Bucharest
Black Sea
OTTOMAN EMPIRE
Varna
Spalato
Mostar
Sofia
Burgas
Adriatic Sea
Adrianople
Constantinople
Angora
Salonica
Naples
Bari
Janina
Smyrna
Athens
Messina
SICILY

PART I

INTRODUCTION

1

Seeing the Universe

If you step outside on a warm clear night and look up, what do you see? Imagine answering this question 400 years ago. What did people see then, gazing at the stars? It is remarkable that in seeing the same thing we see today, they nevertheless saw a different universe with a completely different set of meanings both in itself and for their own personal lives. This marks a highly significant fact: that at the beginning of the seventeenth century the mind – the mentality, the world-view – of our best-educated and most thoughtful forebears was still fundamentally continuous with that of their own antique and medieval predecessors; but by the end of that century it had become modern. This striking fact means that the seventeenth century is a very special period in human history. It is in fact *the* epoch in the history of the human mind. In the pages to follow I support this large claim.

The seventeenth century is among the most extensively explored in the study of history. I enter this field with appropriate disclaimers therefore: my interest here is how – to speak in the most general way – the mind-set of the best-informed people in that century changed from being medieval to being modern in so short and tumultuous a time. To do this in a single book means selecting, sampling and surveying; there is no possibility of comprehensiveness. But seeing the pattern in a major movement of thought is like taking an aerial view of a landscape: one seeks out the larger contours, and because in explaining the seventeenth century the principal themes are science, philosophy and ideas, it is an arena where the philosopher and historian of ideas venture with propriety.

There is a polemical point to be made. The industry of historical scholarship requires periodic revisionism for its continuation, a good thing on the whole because it keeps debates alive and sends out fresh challenges to our understanding of the past and therefore the present too. One of the revisions offered to the thesis that the seventeenth century was the crucible of the modern is that it was *not* the crucible of the modern: 'the scientific revolution and the Enlightenment are no longer considered pivotal stages in the triumphant progress of scientific reason, and such developments are no longer seen as marking the decline of belief in the supernatural and the origin of the "disenchantment" of the world', writes a reviewer of a book about how belief in occultism persisted into the eighteenth century.[1] Both reviewer and reviewed, and whoever no longer regards the period in question as being pivotal, fail to grasp a fundamental point: that yes of course superstition and the old beliefs persisted – they still persist in many quarters – but the revolution in world-view that occurred in the seventeenth century made them *functionally* marginal; where they had once been the central and dominating outlook of all minds, they began to move towards the sidelines of metaphysics and morals, and politics and international relations, as they moved also into the more private spaces of individual lives.

My interest in the intellectual history of the seventeenth century has been a long-standing one. Over the last twenty-five years, in a scholarly examination of the thought of George Berkeley (1685–1753), a biography of René Descartes (1598–1650), a book about concepts of freedom as they grew out of debates over liberty of conscience and enquiry in the sixteenth and seventeenth centuries, and in a number of essays about Locke, the scientific revolution and the following Enlightenment, I have come to think of the seventeenth century as especially significant. I claim that it is *the* epoch in the story of the human mind:[2] there have of course been other epochs – indeed, many – but none of them changed the outlook of humanity on the universe so dramatically. Because this change occurred as Europe tore itself apart in continuous warfare, amid insecurities and oppressions, with vertiginous new systems of thought challenging old certainties, it makes for a deeply absorbing as well as intriguing spectacle. And as always with important history, one learns much from it about one's own time and circumstances.

The puzzle of the seventeenth century is how the greatest ever change in the mental outlook of humanity could occur in the confusions of the time. Or is the answer to the puzzle in the puzzle itself? One aim, in this survey of that age of strife and genius, is to suggest an answer.

The mind of a time is the joint output of leading minds of the time, in the form of their debates, ideas and discoveries. The story of the seventeenth-century mind is accordingly the story of its leading minds and their interactions.

It is also the study of what made those interactions possible and often urgent. In hindsight we pigeonhole for our own convenience, and we overlook important details. We now talk of the scientific revolution, and differently we talk of philosophy in that period as shaping subsequent debate in epistemology, metaphysics and political theory, and thus we proceed as if the scientific and philosophical revolutions were not the same thing – or rather, constituent parts of one larger thing. But they were indeed parts of each other and jointly of the greater mental revolution of the age.

Moreover, the revolution in question would not have been possible if it had not been possible for ideas to circulate, at least more freely than people could. So to understand how thought progressed in this period, we need to know about something seemingly so mundane as the postal services of the day. Significantly, there were several individuals who acted as – so to speak – internet servers connecting the savants of Europe to each other and facilitating the flow of information and exchange of ideas among them. One such was Marin Mersenne. His own varied work represents one of the signal features of the age's mental revolution, which was the effort to detach genuinely productive enquiry from the entanglements of mysticism, the occult, magic, Rosicrucianism – and of course from the proscriptions of religion, which was threatened by sceptical questioning of its authority, and therefore hostile to the growth of secular knowledge and literacy.

Other commentators on the seventeenth century have picked out the growth of publications in vernacular languages, and the proliferation of Protestant sects – some with their this-worldly focus on the blessings of material success ('Protestantism and the rise of capitalism' combines two well-known theses on this score) – as among its transformative features, and the points are good. But it matters that they are put into yet broader context. Attitudes towards material conditions of life are effects of a change of mind about what is important; increased literacy and the proliferation of vernacular publications – especially of pamphlets, satires, political tracts and news – are among the causes. They, in turn, are among the vehicles by which ideas are transported from mind to mind: and ideas are the drivers of change.

It would take encyclopaedic proportions to examine all those minds, their works and their interconnections in anything like satisfactory detail. But I hope the sketches offered here will illustrate the claim that the seventeenth century is truly the moment that history changed course, so profoundly that everything before it is another world, and that it and the times since are our world.[3]

In Part II I give a survey of the Thirty Years' War and, more briefly, the Anglo-Dutch maritime wars. Later sections of the account of the Thirty Years' War are – because of the nature of the war itself – iterative and inconclusive; but this I think captures the senselessness of the prolongation of that destructive conflict. Following it to its exhausted end matters, though: it underlay the change in history. In Part III I describe the intellectual background to the century's revolution in thought, not least in the occultist ambitions of those seeking magical routes to knowledge. Part IV tells of the rise of more responsible ways of thinking and enquiry; Part V describes the application of these to society; and in the short concluding Part VI I offer my explanation of how and why the seventeenth century produced the modern world.

2

The Epoch in Human History

For scores of thousands of years most humans thought of the world as the centre of the universe, and themselves as the centre of that centre, rather as an infant does. But given that in Europe on either side of a point just 400 years ago this view spectacularly changed, it becomes of moment to consider the question of why and how that happened. One answer – the right but unhelpful one – is of course: all history leading to that point. But the key part of this right answer is that the change was essentially one of theory, involving a ninety-degree shift in perspective that brought an entirely new picture of the world – our picture, today's picture – into view; and it was a change that happened with remarkable swiftness. There was a tipping point, and a following cascade effect, in a way that is familiar in many human affairs. But this was no ordinary tipping point.

Some speak and write now about this revolution in thought as if it were an inevitable event, one whose central features have become commonplaces of our own way of thinking. But that is to miss the significance of what was at stake for those who made the change and for those many more who were presented with it, sometimes alarmingly and uncomfortably. Other moments of change have been claimed by other traditions of thought, usually religious ones – an exodus of a people from slavery, a revelation on a mountain top, the birth of a saviour, the recitation of a prophet – but these events or supposed events are all of a piece with the infancy of the human mind. Better candidates might be the genius of the classical era and the grown-up state of parts of the world under the Romans or, in China, the Tang dynasty. But the history of the way the world has come to look to ordinarily educated and thoughtful people, and why it looks that way, was one thing before the seventeenth century, and utterly different after it.

And this change carried dramatic implications for a great deal else, given that the arrangements of society, morality, education, indeed the daily lives of millions, were controlled by the pre-modern mind-set in ways that for thousands of years kept the fundamentals of human existence and outlook the same. In the 400 years since the revolution occurred, the world has altered more than in all its history beforehand. That is the measure of the thing: that is why the period under consideration is *the* epoch in human affairs.

If this seems an exaggerated claim, consider the following two examples. In 1606 *Macbeth* was staged for the first time. Shakespeare was able to rely on the beliefs of his audience in the Banqueting Hall in Whitehall, where the premiere took place, to portray the killing of a king as subversive of nature's order, to such an extent that horses ate each other and owls fell upon falcons in mid-air and killed them. In 1649, a single generation later, a king was publicly killed, executed in Whitehall in London before a great crowd. Perhaps some of the same audience at the first staging of *Macbeth* were present at the beheading of Charles I. The idea of the sacred nature of kingship as premised in *Macbeth* had been rejected, by the time of the Civil War, in favour of new ideas about the nature and exercise of political authority, and although it was a further generation before those ideas were fully translated into the practicalities of a permanent settlement (in England at least – at the 'Glorious Revolution' of 1688 when Parliament deposed a king and installed a replacement of its own choice), the difference was already palpable.

That is an example of one kind of change of outlook in one country, though it was a consequential one for much of the world, given the globalising spread of the emerging political ideology thus represented. An even more far-reaching change is illustrated by the following example, drawn from sunnier climes.

In 1615 Paolo Antonio Foscarini, a Carmelite friar, sent the Vatican's Cardinal Bellarmino a memorandum arguing that Copernicus' heliocentric model of the universe was consistent with scripture. Bellarmino, with chilling irony, replied that 'If there were a real proof that the Sun is in the centre of the universe, that the Earth is in the third heaven, and that the Sun does not go round the Earth but the Earth round the Sun, then we should have to proceed with great circumspection in explaining passages of Scripture which appear to teach the contrary.' Earlier in his letter Bellarmino had reminded Foscarini:

> As you are aware, the Council of Trent forbids the interpretation of the Scriptures in a way contrary to the common opinion of the holy Fathers. Now if your Reverence will read, not merely the Fathers, but modern commentators on Genesis, the Psalms, Ecclesiastes, and Joshua, you will discover that all agree in interpreting them literally as teaching that the Sun is in the heavens and revolves round the Earth with immense speed, and that the Earth is very distant from the heavens, at the centre of the universe, and motionless. Consider, then in your prudence, whether the Church can tolerate that the Scriptures should be interpreted in a manner contrary to that of the holy Fathers and of all modern commentators, both Latin and Greek.

Bellarmino's warning – 'in your prudence' – could not have been much more explicit. Sixteen years before this exchange of letters, Giordano Bruno had been burned at the stake in the Campo dei Fiori in Rome for – among other things – advocating the Copernican view; sixteen years after this exchange of letters Galileo was arrested and put on trial for the same reason. If he had not recanted he would have been put to death. In the interim, in 1619, Giulio Vanini was burned at the stake in Toulouse for asserting a naturalistic conception of the world. It was mortally dangerous to espouse such views openly.

But now consider the publication in 1686 – just over fifty years after the trial of Galileo – of the delightful and impressive *Conversations on the Plurality of Worlds* by Bernard le Bovier de Fontenelle, Cartesian philosopher and author of genius. Under the guise of conversations enjoyed during a series of evening walks with an aristocratic lady who remains anonymous, Fontenelle introduces and explains the nature of the universe as conceived by the seventeenth century's 'new philosophy', contrasting it to the geocentric view it displaced and drawing out the implications for humankind's self-understanding. The account he gives of the Copernican view was intended as a preface to his argument that because all stars are suns, it is likely that there are many planets revolving about them, bearing life – a view which in recent years has been given the support not just of statistics but of actual observation of planetary systems other than our own and planets like our own.

'The universe', Fontenelle wrote,

> is but a watch on a larger scale; all its motions depend on determined laws and the mutual relations of its parts . . . It is now known with certainty . . . that Venus and Mercury turn round the sun, and not round the earth; on this subject the ancient system is absolutely exploded . . . At the appearance of a certain German named Copernicus, astronomy became simplified; he destroyed all the unnecessary circles, and crushed to pieces the crystalline firmaments. Animated with philosophic enthusiasm, he dislodged the earth from the central situation which had been assigned it and in its room placed the sun, who is more worthy of such a mark of distinction. The planets were no longer supposed to perform their revolutions round the earth, and enclose it in the centre of their orbits . . . They all turn around the sun; the earth itself not excepted.

Had Fontenelle lived seventy years earlier, at the date of Bellarmino's letter to Foscarini, or fifty years earlier at the time of Galileo's arrest, he could not have published these views freely, without a thought of punishment or proscription. Fifty years is a short time in human history, but not always in human affairs. In those fifty years the world had moved far forward indeed.

One could multiply examples of the contrast between the world-view held by almost everyone at the beginning of the seventeenth century – and the risks attached to thinking differently – and the world-view that was generally accepted at least among educated people by the end of the century – together with the complete disappearance of those risks. A case might be made for saying that almost every century in recorded history is interesting for the ideas it produced, but as regards the seventeenth century in Europe – without question an age of genius – this is therefore particularly so.

It is or should be a puzzle that this explosion of genius occurred in a century so tumultuous – a time of wars, civil strife and the continuation of post-Reformation religious agonies disruptive and destructive to an unparalleled degree in Europe's history to that point. How does one account for the flowering of genius in the midst of such conflict? Does the tumult of the century in some way explain its genius and those changes, or cause them, or might there have been even greater innovation if it had been a time of peace? Is it merely a mystery that *the* epoch in human history occurred in such circumstances, or might it be – depressingly alas, when one considers the implications – that it takes disaster to move humanity on that far that fast?

It is not just from our perspective that the seventeenth century appears as a revolutionary time. As the example of Fontenelle shows, it presented itself as such to its own inhabitants. Consider the excitement of Jeremiah Horrocks and his friend William Crabtree on 24 November 1639 when, shut in the latter's attic, they made a spectacular scientific observation: a transit of Venus – that is, the visible passage of the planet Venus across the face of the sun. Horrocks had worked out the date of the transit by studying Kepler's Rudolphine Tables of planetary motion, published twelve years earlier. It was a classic case of testing a theory by observation. Imagine the feelings of the two amateurs as they waited for iterated proof of Copernicus' system – and by significant implication, of a universe far different from its portrayal in traditional belief. They saw what they expected to see, and yet could hardly credit that they were seeing it: the black dot of Venus inching its way across the brilliant image of the sun projected onto a card in Crabtree's attic. Horrocks described his friend as standing 'rapt in contemplation' for a long time, unable to move, 'scarcely trusting his senses, through excess of joy'. The emotion he and Crabtree felt is one well known to science: the exhilaration of seeing empirical confirmation of theory.[1]

Horrocks and Crabtree knew of course that they were not making a discovery. Copernicus' work and Galileo's telescopes had between them already refuted the claim in Psalm 104 verse 5, cited by Bellarmino to Foscarini, that the earth had been 'set on its foundations, so that it should never be moved'. What was new was that Horrocks and Crabtree were interpreting what they witnessed – a planet travelling on an inner orbit between the earth and the sun – according to an account of the universe's structure radically different from predecessor accounts; and with it a completely different set of implications for everything else humanity thought, hoped and wished to believe.

Just how radical this difference is becomes clear only when we remember in more detail the view thus being upended. Humankind's admiration for the stars and the heavenly 'wanderers' (their Greek name is the source of the word 'planets')[2] which then numbered seven – sun, moon, Mercury, Venus, Mars, Jupiter and Saturn – is of great antiquity. The earliest evidence for systematic astronomy is the 25,000-year-old Ishango bone found at the source of the Nile, incised with markings corresponding to the phases of the moon. Babylonian star charts 22,000 years later were copiously detailed, recording the efforts of many centuries of sky-gazing and meticulous annotation. The Mesopotamian charts were detailed because they formed the basis of astrological divination, but when Thales in the sixth century BCE, and half a millennium after him the astronomer Claudius Ptolemy of Alexandria, used the information contained in those charts, it was for purposes of nascently genuine science rather than prophecy. Like Horrocks so many centuries later, Thales used the data to make a prediction, in his case of a solar eclipse which occurred on 28 May 585 BCE, visible in Asia Minor.[3] It was an event that so terrified the opposed Median and Lydian armies, on that day engaged in the Battle of the River Halys, that they put down their weapons – so Herodotus tells us – and agreed a truce.[4] They thought the gods were sending them a minatory message. Thales thought that the moon was passing between the sun and that bit of the world, casting a shadow. Thales' way of thinking has (almost) come to prevail.

A further 2,500 years later the work of Copernicus and Kepler began the truly great modern revolution in human self-understanding by definitively removing the earth from the centre of the universe, and arranging the planets correctly – first in their proper order round the sun, then in the elliptical pattern of their orbits. Darwin three centuries after them completed the adjustment in man's ego-geography by displacing him from the summit of creation. What a change, therefore, took place in the period between Copernicus and Darwin! – moving humankind both from *the centre of the universe* AND from *the summit of creation* to a little rock in the outer suburbs of an ordinary galaxy among billions of galaxies, and to a place at the back of the queue in the biological crowd on that rock. This is a stupendous reorientation. It is true that even today some hundreds of millions have not yet quite grasped this shift of view, still less its implications; but what is now restricted to religious fundamentalists and ignorance was once official orthodoxy, and that is the measure of the difference.

When Horrocks and Crabtree watched the dot of Venus crawl across the sun's face, the telescope had already been invented, but it was not, as noted, a telescope they relied on. In using Kepler's calculations they were relying on the only two instruments that human beings possessed from the very beginnings of evolution: the naked eye, humanity's first astronomical instrument, and reason, humanity's first and still greatest scientific tool – and the tool which, in the seventeenth century, people were once again able to use free from the limiting and too often dangerous imposition of religious orthodoxy. 'Orthodoxy' means 'correct belief': humanity's problem was then, as among some it still is now, its tendency to think that the more antique a belief, the more true it is.[5]

To emphasise how dramatic this change of perspective is, think of the far-reaching effects of what the seventeenth century thought-revolution made possible in the way of our contemporary scientific world-view. This is best appreciated by noting two examples of what would have been impossible to think – impossible even to begin to imagine – in the limited anthropocentric picture inherited from the remote history of humanity's ignorances – ignorances which had produced creation stories and legendary belief systems in large numbers.

The first example is an event in our solar system known as the 'Late Heavy Bombardment'. Nearly 4 billion years ago the inner solar system was subjected to an immense hailstorm of meteors and asteroids. So many collided with the moon that they melted its surface. Mercury was especially badly hit; vast craters like the Caloris Basin were ringed by volcanoes after the impact, and shock waves raised strangely shaped hills on the planet's far side. Given that the earth also lay in the path of this cataclysmic shower of debris falling into the sun, it too suffered. More than 1,700 craters of diameter greater than twenty kilometres were formed on the moon by the Late Heavy Bombardment, so it is calculated that, given the earth's larger size, more than ten times as many giant craters were formed here. Deep sediments in Canada and Greenland contain an abundance of extraterrestrial isotopes, which give empirical support to the Bombardment hypothesis; and moreover the fact that, according to the fossil record, life began soon after the Bombardment suggests either that an earlier emergence of life was obliterated by it and had to start over, or that life was brought to our planet by the huge rocks that collided with it.

This fascinating hypothesis is wholly unreachable from a world-view predicated on a recent – according to orthodoxy, 6,000 years ago – magical creation event which makes the universe a tiny human-being-centred place. That was the world-view not merely believed but obligatorily believed (on pain of death, at the extreme) at the beginning of the seventeenth century.

The second example is even more dramatic in its implications. It is the discovery of exoplanets – planets orbiting stars other than our own. Fontenelle was able to hypothesise their existence on rational grounds, reviving ideas held speculatively in antiquity by Epicurus, Metrodorus, Zeno of Eleusis, Anaximenes, Anaximander, Democritus, the Pythagoreans and a number of others. But the actual discovery of the first exoplanet was made in 1992 by the Polish-American astronomer Aleksander Wolszczan while measuring the rotation of a pulsar. Slight but regular variations in the timing of its pulses led him to deduce that it was being pulled backwards and forwards by the presence of three planets in orbit round it.

Exoplanets in a system more like our own were then discovered by astronomers at the Geneva Observatory, again by measurement of perturbations to a star caused by the gravitational pull of a large Jupiter-sized body orbiting it. To understand how such perturbations are detected, one must note that it is not quite accurate to say that our solar system's planets orbit the sun, but that all the denizens of our solar system, including the sun itself, orbit the system's centre of mass – which happens to lie within the sun because it is so much more massive than anything near it. This helps astronomers to know what to look for in other stars, namely, a quivering motion or oscillation detectable by spectrographic analysis. These perturbations have to be such that they are not likely to be caused by the presence of another star forming a binary system (in which planets are rather unlikely to be found because a figure-of-eight orbit would have a tendency to be unstable, leading to the planet's eventual ejection from the system; but some observations suggest that there could indeed be such systems if the planet's orbit lay outside the mutual orbit of the two stars).[6]

Using this technique the Geneva astronomers discovered, within eighteen months of Wolszczan's observations, a massive planet whirling round the star 51 Pegasi at the dizzying rate of once every four days. The star 51 Pegasi is a neighbour of ours, lying only forty-five light years from earth. To find earth-size planets, very much smaller than Jupiter with perhaps undetectably lesser gravitational effects on their stars, the search is on for 'winking' stars, slightly dimmed by the passage of the planet before its face – a transit, such as Crabtree and Horrocks observed. The most earth-like planet that had been detected when the first draft of these pages was written was COROT-Exo-7b (so named because seen by the French space satellite Corot), a bit bigger than earth, orbiting its sun every twenty hours and therefore very close to it – so close that its surface almost certainly consists of molten lava boiling at over 1,000 degrees centigrade. But as these pages were being readied for press there came news of Kepler 452b, a planet very like our own orbiting a sun very like our own at about the same distance, with an orbital period of 385 days. This 'Earth 2.0' is 1,400 light years distant, and joins other planets observed by NASA's Kepler space telescope to suggest that we can expect to detect many planets in 'Goldilocks Zones' – circumstellar habitable zones: zones 'just right' for life – around the statistically many other stars likely to have them.

The realisation that there are other worlds, that the universe is stupendously larger and more complex than pre-modern pictures of it were capable of suggesting, required a major intellectual revolution. The word 'revolution' scarcely does the point justice. It was a revolution in thought across the whole range of enquiries – and it required a liberation of the mind, a giving of permission by the mind to itself to think differently without fear and preconception.

This revolution occurred in the longer period encompassing the seventeenth century – that is, between the sixteenth and eighteenth centuries; between the Reformation and Copernicus in the former period and the French Revolution's Declaration of the Rights of Man at the end of the latter period. And here we repeat the puzzle about how it was able to happen. The question of what made that revolution possible, and then what made it actual, is all the more intriguing because of the circumstances in which it occurred. The Europe of the first half of the seventeenth century, when the intellectual revolution was getting fully under way, experienced the bloodiest period in its history before the twentieth century. The German-speaking states of central Europe were in as devastated a condition in 1648, the year of the official end of the Thirty Years War, as Germany was at the end of the Second World War in 1945. The impact and expense of this huge war, together with the century-long rumbling of civil wars and of bilateral wars between Spain and France, England and the Netherlands, France and the Netherlands – to name just a few – was enormous. One can ask again: how can it be that the flowering of genius that produced the modern world should occur not just during but – perhaps – in part *because* of that?

As this question shows, it is very apt to describe the seventeenth century as a period of 'world-changing instability'.[7] The reference is not just to the political and military upheavals of the continent and its western islands, but even more significantly to the period's mental – not just intellectual – turmoil, in the sense that the mind-set resulting from the changes wrought by enquiry turned the world-view of the period's inhabitants upside down. This is the point made by the astronomical examples cited above. But the change of mind-set was not reserved to intellectuals. One can ask again about the audience in 1606 when *Macbeth* was first staged, and the crowd in Whitehall witnessing the execution of Charles I in 1649: what change of unconscious metaphysical outlook during those forty-three years made the Whitehall crowd not believe, as the *Macbeth*-viewing audience were expected by Shakespeare to believe or half believe at least – that the killing of a king would upset a divinely instituted order of things?

Given that the key to these changes lies in the minds of its leading figures, the focus of attention has to be the nature of the seventeenth-century intellectual milieu. The educated part of the Europe of the day is often and tellingly described as a republic of letters, implying a supranational, non-denominational, informally collegial structure, made possible by the exchanges – mainly by means of letters – among learned and inquisitive men and women (yes: *and women*; it was a moment of opportunity for some women) with common interests and a similarity of outlook. Ideas and techniques were freely passed around, rendered intelligible by a shared background in such matters as knowledge of the classical languages, philosophy and theology. It was by no means an idyllic arrangement, buoyed aloft on fraternal affection and co-operation; the difference in faith outlooks and opinion often resulted in disputes, sometimes serious enough to cause riots and even murder; the republic was constantly embroiled in controversy.[8] But this itself was a source of new ideas, as well as of lively exchanges of information and influence.

In the pages that follow I sample this intellectual world, not comprehensively but selectively, to illustrate how it was that a time of genius and a time of tumult could be the same time after all.

The hunger to extract insight from history, and in particular from the story of ideas in history, explains why we are so ready – perhaps too ready – to apply labels to epochs or the movements in them: 'Renaissance', 'Reformation', 'Enlightenment'. We do it as a convenient summary of the major trends which characterise them and which influenced subsequent periods, and in this respect they are helpful. But it is also helpful to remember the obvious point that such labellings are a *post facto* matter. Not everyone living in a given period might have noticed, or valued, those features of their time which turn out to shape and direct following times in ways that we emphasise in hindsight. Did the thinkers and artists of sixteenth-century Florence know that they lived in what later generations came to signify by that large, multiple, over-inclusive term 'the Renaissance'? The answer is both Yes (in a sense) and No – and it is in the self-consciousness and unselfconsciousness of experience in the time itself that we find what explains it.

For of course – and this really is the interesting thing – some contemporaries of these events indeed recognised their significance. Examples are Petrarch and Kant, each of whom coined labels for his own era and in Petrarch's case its predecessor. To the time preceding his own Petrarch gave the name 'the Middle Ages' to mark it as an intermission between classical antiquity and his own time's rediscovery of classical civilisation's interests and values. Kant in the eighteenth century used the term 'Enlightenment' –*Aufklärung*– to convey his time's distinctive aspirations. He did not regard his age as an enlightened one but as one in which, as he put it, enlightenment was beginning to dawn – and which would see the full arrival of morning if only people would *dare to know* by casting off historically imposed constraints on their beliefs and personal autonomy.[9]

But of course we also know that labels and neat periodisations are as distorting as they are informative, that they can and too often do give rise to caricature, that history is a messier business than we are apt to think. Yet still we allow ourselves the labels: and we do so because we are looking for themes, for threads, for movements and currents, that have explanatory utility, and which themselves provide the several kinds of enlightenment that enquiry promises.

If we permit ourselves the use of some of these familiar labels for the moment, to give a rough positioning to what follows, we notice that in the extraordinary century between the Reformation of the sixteenth century and the Enlightenment of the eighteenth century, the only label that sticks with some generality is 'the late northern Renaissance' – and this as applied mainly to the century's first half. This description does some work, as capturing the efflorescence of art, literature and science in northern Europe that we associate with the age of Shakespeare and Molière, Galileo and Newton. But the 'northern Renaissance' was also just then maturing into something else, something more equivocal and complex, in which north and west Europe were to take the lead. For that reason the period surely requires its own distinguishing label, for when one looks at the conjunction of genius and turmoil that characterise it, and the distance travelled by the European mind (as much literally as figuratively) during the course of it, one is amazed that it is not more vividly recognised as the stand-out epoch of the 2,000 years before the twentieth century, this latter being the only century that compares with it.

The seventeenth century's physical, as opposed to intellectual, conflicts were world-changing in their own right. It is estimated that one in every three German-speaking people died prematurely as a consequence of the Thirty Years War alone. Its destructive effect weakened the central and southern states of Europe so much that it was in some cases the next – even the next but one – century before they recovered fully.

In England the Civil War prepared the way for dramatic changes that influenced not just that country but large swathes of the world in the centuries to follow, because key aspects of the eventual settlement of institutions in England were exported with its globalising empire.

It is a too-little-regarded fact that the hitherto incessant effort of the Ottoman Empire to extend its dominion further into Europe was at last definitively halted at the raising of the siege of Vienna in 1686 and the defeat of the Ottoman armies at the Battle of Zenta in 1697. But for most of the seventeenth century beforehand it was a threat, exerting pressure on an overstretched and complicated Holy Roman Empire equally pressed on all borders and racked with internal problems.

In fact the century had scarcely a year without war somewhere from Scandinavia to Poland, from Russia to Turkey, from Crete to Italy, from Spain to the Netherlands, from England to Ireland – and even to the eastern margins of North America where native Americans resisted the English invasion of their land (the Powhatan Wars). And all this was in addition to the century's devastation of German lands from the Rhine to regions beyond the Elbe and Danube. France, Spain, Sweden, the Netherlands, Russia, England, Turkey, the Holy Roman Empire and most of the German principalities were in an almost constant state of arms, and periodically fighting by land or sea, throughout the century.

Looking back now one might be surprised to see which countries were the big players then, and the nature of their influence. They were the United Provinces of the Netherlands, Sweden, and the entity known as the Holy Roman Empire. The Thirty Years War ended with the Treaty of Westphalia in 1648, a bad compromise that disposed Europe to a new and sometimes terrible history of problems which continue to this day; but that treaty did not stop the fighting. How can the politics and conflicts of this period not be of vital interest to understanding ourselves now?

Yet against this background of destruction and upheaval, there was a luxuriance of genius of a kind that would make any stretch of history boast. Consider – and here we are just mentioning some of many – in literature there were Cervantes, Shakespeare, Jonson, Donne, Milton, Dryden, Pepys, Racine, Molière, Corneille, Cyrano de Bergerac, Scarron, Malherbe, La Fontaine, Alcoforado, Grimmelshausen, Gryphius, von Lohenstein; in philosophy Descartes, Bacon, Grotius, Hobbes, Spinoza, Locke, Leibniz, Malebranche, Bayle; in science Mersenne, Pascal, Galileo, Gassendi, Huygens, Kepler, van Leeuwenhoek, Hooke, Wren, Boyle, Roche, Newton, Tradescant, Lyte; in art – but here space fails: I began with Poussin, Caravaggio, Rubens, El Greco, Rembrandt, Hals, Terbrugghen, Ruysdael, Avercamp, Lievens, Cuyp, Jan Steen, Vermeer, Hobbema, but then realised while typing these names that the list of superb artists in just one country, the Netherlands in its Golden Age, stretches too far ahead: over 700 individual artists of this place and period are represented in major gallery collections, and I had not even begun properly to list the contributions from elsewhere.

In music, it is true, the major names – Vivaldi, J. S. Bach, Handel – were still young when the seventeenth century ended, but there were Buxtehude, Monteverdi, Purcell, Wilbye and others: the century was not wholly silent.

This litany of names glorious in their contributions to art, literature, thought, politics and science by themselves tell us little about an age whose ebullience of creativity was something much more besides. The Italian cities of the high Renaissance had been theatres of great creativity too: but the difference is that seventeenth-century creativity, in both reflecting and motivating a remarkable change in the way people saw themselves and the world, thereby definitively redirected the course of world events. Think of France or England in the 1590s; compare them to how they were in the first decade of the eighteenth century. The contrast is far greater than for all periods before or afterwards. The claim that I think might be made about the audience at *Macbeth* in 1606 and the crowds at the execution of Charles I in 1649 is that the former consisted of pre-moderns, the latter of moderns or at any rate those who were fast inventing the modern: and this is a change discernible even by the middle of the seventeenth century.

PART II

A TIME OF WARS

3

The Origins of the Wars

To get a general sense of an historical period one learns much by looking at what generated its legacy, which in the case of the seventeenth century is nothing less than the world – apart from China and Japan – that we know today.

In the seventeenth century Galileo, Newton and others laid the basis of modern science, Descartes and Spinoza altered the history of philosophy, Hugo Grotius founded international law, and Hobbes and Locke set the terms of modern political theory. A reorganisation of independent and centralised European states competed for empire abroad and fought each in their home continent, in almost continual and ever more costly and complicated ways that required rapid advances in military technology – advances which at the same time gave the European powers superiority over the peoples they colonised in America, Asia and Africa.

The seventeenth century saw the decline of Spain and the rise of France as great powers. Spain had based its might in the previous century on the flood of bullion from its transatlantic possessions; by the end of the seventeenth century France was the new superpower, its language the international language and its culture dominant to such an extent that two centuries later the aristocratic elites of Europe were still speaking French as the language of diplomacy and polite life.

But France's power, based partly on the devastation of the German-speaking regions of Europe in the Thirty Years War and partly on the personal rule and influence of Louis XIV in the century's second half, united others in Europe against it. France dragged Europe's economic and political centre of gravity westward, but the major beneficiaries of the shift were the United Provinces of the Netherlands and England. The accumulation of wealth in the latter led the way in the following centuries to the agricultural and industrial revolutions that made Britain a greater superpower than the France of Louis XIV.

Among the central facts explaining many of the seventeenth century's transformations and innovations are its wars, principally the Thirty Years War in the heart of the continent, and afterwards the conflicts which might variously be denominated the Dutch Wars. The Anglo-Dutch aspect of these latter wars was fought almost exclusively on the high seas as befitted two powers with colonial interests; they ended with an alliance between the two countries which by far benefited England more, though England cannot be characterised as the clear military victor in the actual fighting that went before.

All these conflicts were messy and complicated affairs. But it is important to have an overview of them to hand, particularly of the Thirty Years War, giving a sense of the roots, the course and the outcome of what was a devastating and horrific series of struggles, back and forth across an increasingly ravaged Europe in which millions died from fighting, famine, disease and rapine. The various opposed parties alternated success with failure, the fortunes of the struggle going back and forth without definitive result, their armies swarming up, down and across Europe, trampling on crops, burning towns, raping and murdering civilians, stealing and looting – and for thirty long, exhausting, appalling years.[1]

The Thirty Years War was the last fully international religion-inspired conflict in Europe (to date at any rate), and was made all but inevitable by the Reformation in the preceding century. By contrast, the wars later in the century were, though frequent, more limited in objective and duration. This was the case with the Anglo-Dutch Wars fought to achieve the maritime mastery necessary for control of overseas trade and possessions, the prelude to increased imperial expansion by both parties, and especially by England. All these conflicts, with the continual bicker of fighting elsewhere in all corners of Europe and the Civil War in England, achieved a reconfiguration of Europe's mind and character in sometimes inadvertent ways, as so often happens in unsettled times.

The claim that the Thirty Years War was the last major religious conflict in Europe is elegantly expressed by C. V. Wedgwood in her remark that when the war ended with the Treaty of Westphalia in 1648, people at last 'grasped the essential futility of putting their beliefs of the mind to the judgment of the sword. Instead, they rejected religion as an object to fight for, and found others.'[2] This applies to Europe and the world it influenced; alas it is not true for the more zealous among today's devotees of Islam, and perhaps never has been. Of course the Thirty Years War was not exclusively about religion – there were dynastic and economic considerations in play too, to say nothing of demographic and climatic factors; but it was so closely annexed to the desire of the Holy Roman Emperor, Ferdinand II, egged on by his Jesuit confessor Wilhelm Lamormaini, to reclaim for Catholicism what had been lost to Protestantism, that all but one of the major alignments in the war ran on religious lines. The exception was France, a Catholic country reluctant to see Habsburg influence grow, which is why it sided with the Protestant side of the argument, though not for the Protestants' reasons.

This view is contrary to that of the major Thirty Years War historian Peter H. Wilson, whose huge and magisterial account of the war has as one of its interpretative bases the claim that the war was not *primarily* religious.[3] With due deference to his expertise, and while accepting that there were other important factors involved, his claim is difficult to accept. Take just three from very many examples substantiating the reason why (the first two shortly to be discussed, the third pervasive throughout this book): the causes of the Defenestration of Prague, which was the proximate trigger for the war; the Edict of Restitution, which prolonged the war; and the general background evidenced in the struggle by Europe's intellect to free itself from the demands of religious orthodoxy. It is impossible to make sense of the conflict without appealing to the framework of confessional divisions which, by their nature, explain it. All the war's contemporaries, and almost all of its historians since, have seen matters this way. In the case of the former especially, perception is reality.

The Thirty Years War falls into two distinct chapters. It was triggered in 1618 by the Bohemian revolt, in which the famous Defenestration of Prague was a salient moment; and for a decade thereafter it ran so much the Habsburg way that it prompted Emperor Ferdinand II and Lamormaini to make a major mistake of policy. This was the issuing of the Edict of Restitution on 6 March 1629. The Edict required that property originally belonging to the Catholic Church, but sequestered by Protestants since the Peace of Augsburg in 1555, should be restored to Catholic ownership. This retroactive effort to enforce the Augsburg provisions implied a change of control of Bremen, Magdeburg, a dozen bishoprics and more than a hundred religious houses scattered over the various German states. Even though it was not in the event fully implemented, its immediate effect was the uprooting of many thousands of Protestants who fled to Protestant states from their new masters, who were keen to enforce Catholic orthodoxy among any who stayed. The Edict upset the two most powerful Protestant electors, Georg-Wilhelm of Brandenburg and Johann-Georg of Saxony, who therefore refused to attend an Imperial meeting in 1630 called by Ferdinand to have his son recognised as King of the Romans (and thus by tradition as heir to the throne of the Holy Roman Empire).

The tensions induced by the Edict of Restitution encouraged King Gustavus Adolphus of Sweden to see an opportunity in a duty. The duty was to come to the aid of the Protestant cause, but it simultaneously offered the opportunity to enlarge his possessions and therefore his (then compromised) revenues. He invaded Pomerania in northern Europe in 1630, and by doing so turned the course of the war – not by giving the Protestant cause the edge, but by blunting the edge of the better-organised Catholic cause. In one sense his intervention might be regarded as prolonging the war by another eighteen years, but the eventual failure of the Habsburg–Jesuit project to recover all Europe for Catholicism might be said to have made his intervention worthwhile.

As these events show, the origins of the war lie – as too often with wars – in a peace treaty: that selfsame Peace of Augsburg, concluded long before in September 1555. This was a jerry-built affair, viewed by the then Emperor, Ferdinand I (who had just succeeded his abdicated brother Charles V), as a temporary measure to end disputes engendered by the Reformation's great sectarian split. It was not so viewed by the Lutherans under the leadership of the then Elector of Saxony, who regarded it as a permanent settlement of the Lutherans' right to exist in the Empire. It was the outcome of mounting tensions over many years, typical of the effects of the Reformation everywhere.

In an effort to mute the tensions between his Catholic and Lutheran subjects, Charles V had earlier – in 1548 – instituted an even more temporary settlement known as the Augsburg Interim, which he hoped would give time for the opposed religious parties to resolve their differences and reunite. But in allowing that priests could marry and that communion could be taken in both kinds (bread and wine), the Interim in effect entrenched differences rather than paved the way to overcoming them. This was because the Interim was seen by Lutherans as too Catholic in its emphases, despite the liberalising compromises about priestly marriage and communion.

Seventeen years earlier the Protestant princes of the Empire had formed a defensive alliance, under the leadership of the electors of Hesse and Saxony, to protect the interests of their Reformed religion. It was known as the Schmalkaldic League. In the following years members of the League confiscated much Catholic property and expelled many Catholic clergy, by these means successfully promoting Lutheranism in northern Germany. While Charles was distracted by long-drawn-out hostilities with France and the Ottoman Empire, the Schmalkaldic League spread Lutheranism unimpededly. But as soon as Charles concluded treaties with both his major enemies, he was able to turn his attention to the League, defeating it in battle and obliging its members to accept the Augsburg Interim.

The pacifying effects of the Interim were short lived. Within a very few years dissatisfaction prompted the Schmalkaldic League to revolt openly against Charles, and this time he was obliged to make terms less congenial to himself, first in the Peace of Passau of 1552 – in more ways than one a capitulation, a result of the fact that he had spent three exhausting decades fighting on too many fronts – and then in 1555 in the Peace of Augsburg itself.

This latter settlement was of immense historic significance, in that it granted official recognition to Lutheranism in the Empire, and established the principle of *cuius regio, eius religio* – the religion of the ruler is the religion of the state. Note the words 'to Lutheranism'; at that time there were no Calvinist princes, as there were soon to be, and tensions between Calvinists and Lutherans were to prove at times as great as those between Protestants and Catholics.

The sharpest stone left in the shoe, however, was the part of the Peace of Augsburg known as the 'Ecclesiastical Reservation'. It provided that no more Catholic lands would pass to Protestant control after the date of the treaty's acceptance by the Imperial Diet then being held at Augsburg. It was a clause that quickly came to be honoured more in the breach than the observance, for when heads of states converted to Lutheranism they applied the *cuius regio* principle in making their possessions conform to their own confessional preference, so that by the beginning of the Thirty Years War the Reservation was a dead letter. The danger it represented was plain to all – at the Diet of Regensburg in 1608 the Protestant princes demanded a reaffirmation of the Augsburg principles in the face of an Imperial demand that formerly Catholic property be returned, and when the assurance was refused they walked out. They did so again at the Diet in 1613, the last time an Imperial Diet was held until 1630. Habsburg successes in the first ten years of the war gave Ferdinand II and Lamormaini enough misplaced confidence to enforce the Reservation unilaterally and retroactively, which they did by issuing the aforementioned Edict of Restitution.

The effect of the Edict was, in the long run, disastrous for the Habsburgs' cause and therefore the cause of Catholicism. The transfer of wealth and property back into Catholic hands, the appointment of Imperial supervisors in areas of the Empire which had been free of direct Imperial control for a century, the enforcement of Catholic requirements on Protestants who therefore fled to Protestant states taking their grievances with them, the alignment of previously neutral princes with the Protestant cause, the decision by France to become more active in opposing any increase of Habsburg power, and most of all the encouragement to Sweden's Gustavus Adolphus to invade Pomerania, combined to make the Habsburg cause at length and at last unwinnable. Thus was the tide of affairs turned, though much suffering lay in the twenty years that had yet to elapse before the war ended.

But though the Edict was the occasion for a change in the course of the war, there was another and more germane way that the previous century's Peace of Augsburg served as a major factor in causing the war in the first place.

In 1606 an incident occurred in the little Lutheran city of Donauwörth on the banks of the Rhine. The city council issued a decree prohibiting members of the city's Catholic minority from making public manifestations of their faith. The Catholics held a demonstration, which turned into a riot. The then Emperor, Rudolf II, took punitive action; he revoked the city's privileges and purged the council of its Lutheran members, putting Catholics in their place. This was in direct contravention of the *cuius regio* terms of the Peace of Augsburg.

Rudolf II then removed Donauwörth from the 'Swabian Circle' – one of the ten 'circles' or administrative districts of the Empire – and placed it in the 'Bavarian Circle' instead. The Swabian Circle's director was a Lutheran, the Bavarian Circle's director was a champion of the Emperor and the Catholic cause, Duke Maximilian of Bavaria.

Rudolf's measures alarmed and enraged not only the citizens of Donauwörth but all of the Empire's Protestant princes and peoples. Whatever their other differences on matters of opinion, doctrine or politics, the princes were united in opposing the breach of those Augsburg principles that suited them, and they therefore decided to form a new protective league – the 'Evangelical Union'. It came formally into existence in 1608, with Frederick V, Elector of the Palatinate, as its leader.

To all outward appearances Frederick V was the natural choice for the role, because he was both an Imperial elector and a Calvinist determined to resist Catholic encroachments. But in fact Frederick was not a good choice. He was hesitant, timid, not very intelligent, and heavily dependent on the opinions of others, not least on his chief counsellor, Christian of Anhalt. Generally speaking, an insufficient ruler lucky enough to have a wise counsellor can leave matters to the latter, and the arrangement works well because the counsellor can, like Teucer behind the shield of Ajax, act all the more effectively for being partly invisible. But alas, Christian was not much more astute than Frederick, and although he had great charm and a large amount of self-confidence, he was not a match for the complexities of the time, which in fact he made worse by his over-ambition.

The electors either of Saxony or of Brandenburg would have been better leaders of the Evangelical Union, but the problem was that the first was a Lutheran and the second a Calvinist, and their dislike of each other was as great as their dislike of Catholics – this was particularly so in the case of Johann-Georg of Saxony's dislike of Calvinists. Moreover neither of them thought that the threat of a Catholic attempt on Protestant lands and privileges was as serious as Frederick V and others represented it to be.

In 1608 Henri IV of France agreed to serve as the Evangelical Union's patron, not because he was reverting to his former Protestant allegiance (he was by then, having originally been a Huguenot, in his second and final phase as a Catholic on grounds of pure expediency: 'Paris is worth a Mass' he had said when securing the French crown) but because he saw the utility to France of using the Union as a balance to Habsburg power. Naturally, this increased the stakes, so by way of reaction the Empire's Catholic princes set up their own organisation, the 'Catholic League', choosing the most obvious person to serve as their leader, Duke Maximilian of Bavaria. It had as its official sponsor Rudolf II's cousin Philip III of Spain. Until his actions over Donauwörth upset his Protestant subjects, Rudolf had appeared to be neutral between all sides of the religious divisions in his Empire, eager not to polarise his subjects' sentiments further. The change of tack posed a threat to the unstable equilibrium. But it did not trigger general war at that point because, having grown increasingly mad and out of control, Rudolf was no longer fully in the Empire's driving seat. He was bit by bit being moved aside by his brother Matthias, who eventually, in 1612, replaced him as emperor.

But deeper polarisation was the unavoidable result of there being two opposed Leagues founded on religious differences. An immediate illustration of the danger occurred in 1609 when the Duke of Jülich and Cleves died. The two Leagues disagreed not about which prince but which religion should inherit the territory. The late Duke had been a Catholic, but his closest blood-heirs were both Protestants – the Elector of Brandenburg and Philip Ludwig of Neuberg. To make matters worse, the duchy of Jülich and Cleves straddled the tenuous land route connecting Spain's Italian possessions with its Low Country possessions, a route known as the 'Spanish Road'. It was a vital asset for the Habsburg cause, for along it passed troops and supplies for the Spanish Netherlands. The Habsburgs were accordingly anxious not to see the duchy fall into Protestant hands.

In this flammable situation the Catholic League looked to Philip III of Spain for support, while the Evangelical Union looked to Henri IV of France, and war threatened. At this crucial moment Henri IV was assassinated by a lunatic Jesuit – a terrible irony, given that he had allowed the Jesuits back into France after his predecessor had expelled them, and had even given them the palace in which he was born – La Flèche – to serve as a school where they could breed up more of their kind. (René Descartes was a pupil of that famous institution, and was indeed present when Henri's heart was taken there to be buried. Marin Mersenne was also a pupil there.)

Henri's widow Marie de' Medici became regent because their son Louis XIII was still an infant. Marie immediately effected a rapprochement with Spain, thus removing at a stroke the Evangelical Union's chief support. Without France the Union had little appetite for continuing to confront the Catholic League militarily, and perhaps not much of a realistic chance of winning if it had done so.

But there was soon enough another twist: Philip Ludwig of Neuberg, following Henri IV's example, himself decided to convert to Catholicism, and capped the move by offering to marry the daughter of

Duke Maximilian. This neatly created the possibility of a compromise: in the Treaty of Xanten signed in 1614, the duchy of Jülich and Cleves was divided between the newly Catholic Philip Ludwig and the still Protestant Elector of Brandenburg, the former receiving Jülich for his son, while Cleves passed to Brandenburg.

The outcome of this perilous sequence of events did not prevent war, only delayed it. All that was lacking for a more general conflict to begin was a triggering set of events. One aspect of this was waiting in the Palatinate where the Elector Frederick V and Christian of Anhalt were reading Rosicrucian prognostications of a Protestant saviour for Europe, and astrological prognostications of Frederick's own impending greatness. Together these indicators, as they saw them, made them all the more disposed to believe reports by Christian's intelligence agents that the Holy Roman Empire would collapse when the Emperor Matthias died. Christian believed this because it seemed that the divisions and tensions within the Empire had not been overcome – indeed had not even been properly managed – by Matthias' efforts since 1612. A cursory look at a map of the Empire at that time seemed to show why: the Imperial possessions sprawled as widely over differences of faith, culture and language as they did over geography, for they comprised not only the German electorates and duchies but Austria itself, and alongside it Carinthia, Carniola, the Tyrol, Styria, Bohemia, Hungary and part of Transylvania. At that period much of Hungary was in Ottoman hands, and the remainder formed an almost completely independent fiefdom under the Magyar nobility.

But the most complicated problem of all was Bohemia. Bohemia and its three dependent provinces of Moravia, Lusatia and Silesia each had its own capital city, so there were four capitals each with its own independent Diet. The population of all four regions was mainly Slav and Protestant, with some admixture of Protestant and Catholic Germans. What perennially irritated the Habsburgs was the fact that the Bohemian monarchy was elective. This meant that the Habsburgs had to pay careful attention to local traditions in order to keep hold of the Bohemian crown. Until then the Habsburgs had generally succeeded; now the stresses in the Empire were making Bohemians and everyone else less certain that the Habsburgs could count on precedent and custom as usual.

None of the emperors in the decades before 1618 had managed to establish unitary control over all of their diverse Empire, nor genuine authority in any of its more autonomous parts. They alternated between strong-arm and concessive tactics, each bringing its own set of usually unwanted consequences. Repression was Rudolf II's choice in Donauwörth, concession was his choice in dealing with the Bohemian Diets, to whom he gave a 'Letter of Majesty' reinforcing their independence. Both choices merely weakened the Empire. When Matthias was ousted from the throne, therefore, Christian of Anhalt and Frederick thought their hour of advantage had come. They were wrong; they had completely misjudged the nature of the man who replaced Matthias in 1617. This was Archduke Ferdinand of Styria, soon to be officially crowned Emperor Ferdinand II. He was a far more single-minded character, not interested in concessions, and he was under the influence of his ambitious Jesuit confessor, the aforementioned Wilhelm Lamormaini.

Ferdinand took power just as the situation in Bohemia ran out of control from the Imperial point of view, thus offering the trigger for war. Matthias had angered his Bohemian subjects by appointing Catholics to leadership positions on the Council of Regents in Prague. The regents' first act – prefiguring the Edict of Restitution ten years later, and with no more pacific an outcome – was to press on the perennial sore point: they ordered that all religious bodies must revert to the terms of their original foundation. This meant that all Protestant churches, complete with their endowments and properties, had to return to Catholic control. The Bohemians immediately rebelled. On 22 May 1618 a crowd of them marched to Prague Castle, led by the 'defensors' under the command of Count Matthias Thurn. They seized two of the leading regents and threw them out of a window. This was the famous 'Defenestration of Prague'. The terrified regents fell into a rubbish dump twenty metres below the window, suffering injuries more to their dignity than to their limbs. (Subsequent Catholic propaganda said that they had been caught in mid-air by angels or the Virgin Mary, and gently lowered into the rubbish dump. This detail – why lower them into a rubbish dump? – did not receive an explanation in the propaganda.)

The resulting damage suffered by Bohemia was immensely greater than that suffered by the regents. The sacred laws of diplomacy and Imperial representation had been impugned, and this was a direct insult to the Imperial authority itself. The Bohemians realised that they had cast a die, and had no option but to follow through. They set up a board of deputies to administer the kingdom, called on the other three provinces to join them, and raised an army. They sent the Emperor a letter demanding that the four provinces should henceforth be autonomous, and that only Protestants should occupy official posts. These were not demands likely to be met by an emperor, still less the soon to be crowned Ferdinand.

Matthias died in March 1619, and the process of Ferdinand's election began. He believed himself to have in his pocket all seven votes required for gaining the Imperial throne, as had almost always been the case in what was a formulaic and notional exercise. He certainly had the three archbishop-electors in his pocket, he had been elected King of Bohemia in 1617 and therefore had that vote in his own gift already, and as usual the three Protestant electors of Saxony, Brandenburg and the Palatinate were at odds with one another, and in no position to seek an alternative to Ferdinand. There was no obvious alternative to him anyway.

But Ferdinand's confident expectations were in process of being upset by the Bohemian Estates, who were reconsidering their relationship with Ferdinand. The new circumstances created by the Defenestration offered them the opportunity to take an independent path and get themselves a Protestant for king. This they did: they voted to depose Ferdinand and chose Frederick V of the Palatinate in his place.

Frederick asked his father-in-law, James I of England, whether he should accept the crown. He asked his fellow members of the Evangelical Union for their advice also; and he asked his own council. They were all of one unequivocal and emphatic mind: they discouraged him. Frederick should have had the wit to heed such unity of opinion. But he was far more swayed by the views of two people closer to him in every way: his wife, Elizabeth Stuart, daughter of James I of England, and his chancellor Christian of Anhalt. Invoking the sincerity of his commitment to Protestantism, and citing the prophecies and prognostications of greatness they had come across in their study of arcana, Elizabeth and Christian urged Frederick to accept the Bohemians' invitation. He therefore did so, grandiloquently announcing that he felt a divine call to lead the Protestant cause, and was obliged to obey it.

Bohemia's revolt from Imperial authority was thereby complete, and the Thirty Years War had begun. Ferdinand II announced that Frederick's electorship and his Palatine territories were forfeit because of his treason. He offered the electorship and Upper Palatinate to Duke Maximilian of Bavaria. He pledged the Lower Palatinate, the area lying to the west of the Rhine, conveniently for the Spanish Road, to his Spanish Habsburg relatives. He offered Lusatia to its next-door prince, Johann-Georg of Saxony, thus dividing the Protestant cause. The armies of Maximilian, Spain and Saxony thereby became available to him.

Frederick V arrived in Prague while these armies were gathering. With him came his entourage of German Calvinists. Bohemia's Lutherans immediately took a powerful dislike to them; the doctrinal differences between Lutherans and Calvinists were sharp. As a way of manifesting opposition to Ferdinand II, several states – Sweden, Venice, Denmark and the United Provinces of the Netherlands – had recognised Frederick's elevation to the Bohemian throne, but none of them had any intention of sending armies to keep him in it. His father-in-law James I of England abandoned him. Frederick's timid and hesitant manner, his Calvinist principles, his uncongenial German courtiers and his lack of international support quickly showed the Bohemians that they had made a grievous error in choosing him for their king.

Frederick is known as 'the Winter King' because he occupied his throne for a very brief time, from the winter of 1619 to the autumn of 1620, which is when the campaign to oust him began. His possessions in the Palatinate succumbed without a fight to the plundering troops of Spain and Duke Maximilian. Johann-Georg of Saxony enjoyably and without effort helped himself to Lusatia. On 8 November 1620, in a single morning on the White Mountain on the outskirts of Prague, Maximilian's 20,000-strong army under the astute command of Count Tilly overwhelmed Christian of Anhalt's 15,000 soldiers. It took just two ignominious hours for Frederick and Christian to be defeated, and those two hours represented the last vestige of Bohemian resistance.

Frederick fled into exile in the United Provinces, there to try to win back the Palatinate with Dutch help. He left behind him a Bohemia and Moravia at the mercy of Maximilian's savage repression of Protestantism combined with punishment for the *lèse-majesté* of their revolt. The Bohemian rebel leaders were put to death in the main square of Prague, those who had blasphemed as well as revolted having their tongues nailed to the scaffold before they were killed. Protestant clergy were outlawed and their chapels destroyed. The Jesuits swarmed in behind the army, taking control of schools and universities. The entire country was returned to Catholicism at sword-point. The philosopher Descartes was with the Imperial troops under the comte de Bucquoy when they captured and destroyed the Moravian town of Hradisch which, like other towns on Bucquoy's destructive progress, was subjected to horrors: rape and massacre were commonplace as a technique of terrorisation and subjugation, breaking any resistance to the Habsburgs' aim of seeing Catholicism flourish again.

Although these events appeared to be a victory for Ferdinand II and Catholicism, in fact it was a pyrrhic one. Neither France to the west, nor in the far north of Europe the burgeoning power of Sweden, would be able to stand aside permanently while Habsburg strength grew. Sweden's ambitious king was uneasy at the danger represented by Ferdinand to his Protestant co-religionists – and, as mentioned, he saw at the same time opportunity for himself and his kingdom in that danger. Ferdinand II had stirred the hornets against himself by his too easy early victories; instead of setting course for the recovery of Europe for Catholic dominion, he had set going events that, over the next thirty years, would permanently result in its loss.

As these events unfolded in the heart of Europe in the years 1618–20, equally consequential events were happening far across the world, on the margins of European consciousness. In May 1619 troops of the Dutch East India Company captured the city of Jayakarta, burned it to the ground, expelled its residents, and thereby asserted the beginnings of control over the entire region of what became the Dutch East Indies.

The Dutch had arrived in the East Indies twenty-five years before, intent on getting a foothold in the spice trade. Tensions with English traders in the region, and with the ruler of the port of Jayakarta on the Ciliwung River, led to the military action in question. The new town and trading post that rose on the ruins of Jayakarta was named Batavia by the Dutch, in honour of the ancient Germanic Batavi tribe from whom the Dutch claimed descent. The new name stuck for the next 300 years.

At the same time, in the West Indies on the other side of the world, African slaves were beginning to arrive in increasing numbers to work the sugar plantations. The original native populations, first enslaved by Spanish settlers, had been driven to extinction, and the African slaves who took their place were dying faster than they could be replaced. English and French colonies began to be founded in the Caribbean from 1612 onwards, increasing the demand for slaves as tropical agriculture rapidly spread across the islands in response to demand for their products in Europe.

Perhaps one of the most significant if then little-noticed events of this period was the first settlement of pilgrims on the east coast of North America, just south of Massachusetts Bay. The group, which called its new home Plymouth Colony, faced serious hardships and failed to flourish; it was not until better-organised settlements were established at Cape Ann and then Salem, where the 'Winthrop Fleet' arrived in 1630, that the settlers' foothold in New England was secure. But a train of events had been put in motion which neither the Algonquin 'Indians' of Massachusetts, nor the contending parties in Europe itself, could possibly then have foreseen.

Back in Europe the war of belief was continuing alongside the shooting war. In February 1619 Lucilio Vanini (known also as Giulio Cesare Vanini) was put to death as an 'atheist and blasphemer' in

Toulouse. His tongue was cut out before he was strangled and burned in the city's Place du Salin, a victim of the Church's intolerance of views that contested orthodox doctrine. His story is more fully told later in these pages.

4

The Loss of the Palatinate

When the hapless Winter King was ejected from Bohemia after the fateful Battle of the White Mountain, his choice of a place of exile was a natural one. He fled to the United Provinces of the Netherlands because they were Calvinist and were in conflict with Habsburg Spain, from whose rule they had revolted in the previous century. Spain stood to gain from the Habsburg seizure of Frederick's Rhine dominions because the Spanish Road, their route to that part of the Low Countries still under their sway, was thereby secured. This was a further reason for the Dutch to back Frederick, in the hope that he could regain his Palatine territories.

The Dutch–Spanish conflict had begun in earnest half a century earlier. In January 1579 the seven Protestant provinces of the northern Netherlands – Holland, Zeeland, Utrecht, Gelderland, Overijssel, Friesland and rural (not urban) Groningen – formed themselves into the Union of Utrecht as a response to the formation by the Catholic southern provinces of the Union of Arras. The latter represented a reaffirmation of the southern provinces' loyalty to the Spanish Crown and Catholic faith, and was itself a response to increasing tensions between the Catholic and Calvinist sections of the Netherlandish population. These tensions were a direct result of the intransigent hostility of Philip II of Spain to the Reformed sects. He wished to see Catholicism restored to the northern provinces, and was prepared to take harsh measures to succeed. The Protestants of the northern provinces were deeply mistrustful, indeed fearful, of Spanish intentions. They found the cruelty of Spanish activities in the New World, and the Spanish Inquisition's continuing persecution of Jews and Moors – even those who had converted, or whose ancestors had converted, to Christianity – a legitimate source of anxiety.

Just how legitimate was put beyond doubt by such events as the *Beeldenstorm* destruction of art and icons in Antwerp's Cathedral of Our Lady on 20 August 1566. Philip II had sent orders to the Netherlands for enforcement of Catholic observance; an angry Calvinist crowd invaded the cathedral in Antwerp in protest, and set about tearing down that beautiful building's statuary and artworks, and even the decorative stonework of the pillars and walls. The reserved host was fed to animals, the communion wine was drunk, paintings and tapestries were shredded, stained-glass windows smashed. The only part of the cathedral not wrecked on the first day of rioting was the chapel of the Habsburgs' principal order of chivalry, the Order of the Golden Fleece. But on the third day, after the iconoclasts had been at churches and chapels elsewhere in the city to destroy and burn, they returned to finish their work in the cathedral. A group of Knights of the Golden Fleece in full armour fought their way into the cathedral to defend their chapel, and killed a number of the rioters, some of whom they hanged outside the cathedral, slashing at their twisting bodies with swords and spears as they died.

Such events, and the ensuing alignment of the two religious camps, did not portend well for Spanish government of the region. Less than two years after forming the Union of Utrecht, in 1581, its members declared themselves independent of Spain by the Oath of Abjuration, and a long and difficult war began. Philip sent the Duke of Alva with an army to reduce the rebellious provinces, but their resistance, and the burden on the Spanish exchequer, saved them.

The outcome was the transformation of the Union of Utrecht into the United Provinces, a new independent state which throughout the seventeenth century flourished mightily because of its maritime successes, overseas trade and Eastern empire. The resulting access of wealth prompted a flowering of culture. It was the superlative age of Dutch painting; as Europe's most liberal and tolerant country it attracted thinkers, scientists, writers and political exiles to settle there. This part of the Netherlands' history has aptly been called 'the Dutch Golden Age', a phrase that applies both literally and metaphorically.

By contrast, most of the remaining part of the Netherlands continued under Spanish dominion as a Catholic country – and eventually became Belgium. The Low Countries had long been one of the richest parts of Spain's Empire, and the loss of half of it hastened the demise of Spain as a world power.

Philip II tried hard to recover the United Provinces, but because Spain was a dying force, though dying slowly, he soon understood that the effort was beyond his powers. He came to this view in the late 1590s, by which time the United Provinces had constructed a powerful defensive line along the Maas and Waal rivers, and had inaugurated its lucrative independent trade with the East Indies, Spanish America and the Mediterranean. Hoping at least to limit the United Provinces' progress, Philip gave the Spanish Netherlands a degree of autonomy under his daughter Isabella and her husband (who was, in the Habsburg way, also her cousin), Archduke Albert of Austria. Albert had for several years already been Governor General at Brussels. The husband-and-wife team came to be known as 'the Archdukes', and though always subject to the Spanish Crown, they gradually became more independent, though never wholly so.

The Archdukes hired Ambrogio Spinola to lead their army – an inspired and at the outset apparently eccentric choice, for Spinola was a Genoese banker without military experience. The standing joke about him at the time was that he was a general before he was a soldier. But if he had been a soldier before becoming a general he might not have displayed such military genius, giving the Calvinists of the United Provinces not a few grey hairs before, after a decade of fighting, helping the Archdukes and the United Provinces to agree a twelve-year truce. This occurred in 1609 and was *de facto* a recognition of the United Provinces' independence.

This truce infuriated Spain's Philip III (Philip II's successor), who loathed the idea of making peace with any Calvinists, and still less with the rebellious Dutch Calvinists. But he was in no position to interfere: his kingdom was bankrupt, unable to negotiate further loans, and moreover was just about to go to war with Venice: a difficult combination of affairs. It did not take long for Philip III to accept that a dozen years of peace in the Low Countries might help with the rebuilding of Spain's finances. In any case he was soothingly reassured by the Archdukes and Spinola that the Dutch could be vanquished once the truce was over and the Spanish were in better shape to fight.

By the start of the Thirty Years War in 1618, when this truce was nearing its end, the United Provinces had entered a state of some political turmoil. Several years of external peace had given opportunity for disruptions to internal peace, as so often happens. In part this was the result of the way the United Provinces administered themselves. The closest thing to a head of state was Prince Maurice of Nassau, who in that year – 1618 – had just succeeded to the princedom of Orange, having previously been Count Maurice of Nassau. His authority derived from the fact that he was the Captain General of the federal army and Stadthouder of five of the seven provinces, his cousin William-Louis being Stadthouder of the remaining two. Already some inter-provincial government institutions had come into being: a mint for the common currency, a military council of state, the admiralty, and an audit board. But each province had its own assembly, each of which in turn sent delegates to a federal assembly called the States-General. The members of this small body, usually numbering fewer than a dozen, had to refer all its decisions to their home provincial assemblies for discussion and – sometimes – ratification. This was a time-consuming and often fractious business, the more so because each provincial assembly in its turn had to consult the magistrates in its more populous towns and the nobles in their country estates, before any final decision could be made.

This structure would have resulted in paralysis and division far more often had it not been that Holland, the richest province, usually got its way, because it provided two-thirds of the United Provinces' tax revenue – and power runs alongside money. Indeed it was Holland which, when the truce with the Archdukes was under discussion in 1609, forced the deal through against the intransigence of other provinces, whose hard-line Calvinist clergy were as opposed to a truce as Spain's Philip III himself.

Another reason why the Provinces' governance arrangements worked as well as they did was that for a number of years they were astutely, even cunningly, managed by the States-General's chief permanent official, Johan van Oldenbarnevelt – in effect the United Provinces' prime minister. Aided by a trusty standing committee, Oldenbarnevelt arranged the agenda for the States-General's meetings, but only after he had negotiated, wheedled, persuaded and twisted arms, in this way applying Sun Tzu's excellent advice to go into battle only when victory is already won. Oldenbarnevelt chaired the meetings too, which was a further help.

Nevertheless, with so much potential for upsets to the internal unity of the Provinces, something was sure to provide the occasion for one – and inevitably, one wearily supposes, religion provided it. In 1605 a dispute arose between two theologians at the University of Leiden concerning the question of predestination. One of the two was a strict and enthusiastic Calvinist called Francis Gomarus, the other was a liberal-minded Reformed theologian called Jacob Arminius. Gomarus held to Calvin's uncompromising line that each individual is saved or damned from the beginning of time, and that the total number of the saved is relatively small. Arminius held that human beings have free will. Faculty and students took sides; eventually so too did the clothworkers of Leiden. Neither the academics nor the clothworkers proved to be above throwing stones and cracking their opponents' skulls in defence of religious truth as they saw it.

As the unrest grew more serious, so Oldenbarnevelt became more concerned. He called a meeting of the country's leading clergymen to discuss whether, in hope of quietening matters, there should be a revision of the Reformed Church's Confession of Faith. The clergy vehemently refused to consider any such thing; they regarded the Confession as sacrosanct, and hotly told Oldenbarnevelt that there could be no question of civil authorities interfering with doctrinal matters.

These events occupied the last years of the first decade of the seventeenth century, at the close of which Arminius died. His followers were however determined to carry on the fight. They presented a 'Remonstrance' to the assembly of Holland, in their turn calling for a revision of the Confession of Faith, and iterating the demand that Church and state matters be kept strictly separate. The Gomarists fired back a 'Counter-Remonstrance', containing among other things the demand that all Arminians should be sacked from their teaching and preaching positions. The Arminians sought Oldenbarnevelt's help; they already had the backing of the great jurist Hugo Grotius, then serving as chief magistrate of Rotterdam. Grotius criticised the Gomarists for threatening the state's safety, the Church's unity, and – in his view, and rightly, worst of all – the principle of freedom of conscience.

Unless one has a little knowledge of doctrinal affairs, the reason for the bitterness of this dispute might escape notice. The hottest point at issue was the fact that the Arminian position was close to the Roman Catholic view on free will: both Catholics and Arminians believed in it, Calvinists did not. From the Gomarist perspective this put Arminians into the same vile and heretical category as Catholics. One can see the point of the Gomarists' objections: to be told that you are saved whatever you do, and have been so from the beginning of time, as Calvinists were assured they were by virtue of being Calvinists, is much less hard work than having free will and being required to live your whole life in ways that will secure entry to heaven: which is more than merely an annoying imposition, because it introduced an uncomfortable degree of uncertainty and obligation. As the Gomarists saw it, the Arminians were both insulting them and threatening them by telling them that they were not saved, and that, like Catholics, they had to work for their salvation. The Arminians, for their part, deeply disliked the imputation that the deity created most of humanity in order to destroy it no matter how nice and good it was, saving only the stiff-necked arrogant Gomarist-type Calvinists who regarded themselves as the Elect.

In any case the Calvinist line is hard to reconcile with the salvific message of the Gospels, in which the sacrifice of Christ is portrayed as reuniting the posterity of Adam – all of it; or anyway, all who would believe – with God in the atonement. Indeed St Paul gave hope even to those who had not heard the message but were still good, having God's law inscribed on their hearts. How, asked the Arminians, could this be consistent with Calvinist teaching?

In the climate of the times the outcome of this extremely deep division of opinion was inevitable. Arminian preachers and their churches were attacked by Gomarist mobs. Riots occurred, disorder increased, both became more frequent, and began to spread to other matters besides, as for example in Delft in 1616 when several days of rioting were prompted by a rise in corn taxes. These riots had troubling extra features in Oldenbarnevelt's opinion – barricades were erected in the streets, and the houses of wealthy citizens were stoned, these developments suggesting that a more general breakdown of order was imminent.

Maurice of Nassau was not on the same side of the dispute as Oldenbarnevelt and Grotius. He was a Gomarist. He began to say to friends that he did not think the dispute could be settled by anything less than civil war. He disagreed with Oldenbarnevelt not only on the issue itself, but on how its attendant growing unrest should be handled. Eventually the two men quarrelled outright; and the quarrel brought into public view the differences between them, as the two most significant men in the state. As a result the Gomarist cause, with Maurice behind it, began to get the upper hand. In towns with only an Arminian minister, crowds marched away on Sundays to places where they could hear a Gomarist preacher instead. Harassment of Arminian clergy and adherents increased, and Maurice instructed his troops not to intervene – in effect, stripping protection from Arminians.

In this worsening situation Oldenbarnevelt decided that the interests of public order obliged him to act. He persuaded Holland's assembly to allow each of the province's towns to raise a militia company of *waardgelders*, if they thought circumstances warranted it. The *waardgelders* were to swear loyalty to the town, not the province or the country or the Stadhouder. The mistake made by the Holland assembly's proclamation was that it stated that soldiers in the federal army whose pay came from Holland had, for that reason, a primary loyalty to Holland rather than to the United Provinces as a whole.

This greatly angered Maurice; he saw it as both an affront to himself personally and a challenge to his authority. He ordered the States-General to issue an order disbanding the *waardgelder* companies; they voted by five provinces to two to do so, and he instantly put the order into effect. In July 1618 he marched into Utrecht with a large force of troops, disarmed its *waardgelders* and purged the city's offices of all Arminians, installing Gomarists in their place. By August all the towns of Holland had submitted to Maurice, who repeated the substitution of Gomarists for Arminians everywhere, and at the same time arrested Oldenbarnevelt and Hugo Grotius.

The whole of Europe watched agog as these events unfolded. Nowhere else, at that moment, were matters of religion so delicately poised, or so important to the fate of Reformation and Counter-Reformation alike; for this was a quarrel within Protestantism – and not even between Calvinists and Lutherans (who, as mentioned, loathed each other anyway: no news there) but within the Calvinist camp itself.

Prince Maurice's next actions sealed the future course of Dutch history in respect of both its political and its religious character, and thereby helped shape the course of Europe's history too. He called together an assembly of Calvinist clergy and theologians, including a number from England, Switzerland and Germany, to hold a general synod at Dordrecht (then known as Dort). After six months of debates the Synod of Dort condemned Arminianism and its adherents, calling the latter heretics and 'disturbers of the peace' in Church and state alike. On the instant, 200 Dutch Arminian preachers were driven from their churches, half of them going into exile. Maurice dismissed all of Oldenbarnevelt's followers in official positions in all seven provinces, putting inexperienced men in their place. The obvious disadvantage of this was outweighed for Maurice by a major advantage, namely, that it put more direct power into his own hands. Hugo Grotius was sentenced to life imprisonment (but happily escaped two years later), while Oldenbarnevelt was condemned to death. He went with great dignity to the scaffold the very next day, 13 May 1619. He was seventy-two years old, and had been a great servant to the United Provinces for the majority of those years.

Because the rest of Europe was watching these events intently, and with mixed emotions, Maurice set his propaganda machine to work. It represented Oldenbarnevelt and the Arminians as having attempted a *coup d'état*, which is how he justified sending the elderly statesman to his death and driving Arminian clergy from their posts. Europe generally accepted his version of the matter. In one respect his version was not inaccurate, for it had truly been a struggle for power, given that Oldenbarnevelt stood in the way of Maurice's aim of tightening his personal grip on the United Provinces, and furthering his private ambitions to be named king. In the latter respect the republican instincts of the Dutch continued the job that Oldenbarnevelt had been doing; it took an invitation from the English Parliament in 1688 to turn a prince of Orange into a monarch. Nevertheless Dutch painters portrayed the surrender of the *waardgelders* as a great military victory for Maurice. Within a short few months the English playwrights Fletcher and Massinger brought their 'Sir John Van Olden Barnevelt' on to the London stage, such was the universal interest in the affair.

Maurice was not the only one to benefit from Oldenbarnevelt's fall. Merchants in England and elsewhere in Europe – even in certain other of the United Provinces themselves – were pleased that he had gone, because his canny ways had served the advantage of the merchants specifically of the province of Holland at everyone else's expense. Calvinists everywhere now saw Maurice as a new champion for their view of Christianity, and believed that Calvinism was poised to triumph. And it was to Maurice that Frederick V and his ejected family turned as they fled from Bohemia.

But with Oldenbarnevelt and all his experience of statecraft and diplomacy gone, leaving the less astute Maurice at the United Provinces' helm, any satisfaction at the old man's fall was as premature as it was misplaced. For its real significance was that Spain, and the Habsburg cause in general, had been handed a prime chance to take back the international initiative. The Thirty Years War was beginning in earnest.

5

The Mercenary Captains

AT THIS JUNCTURE it is pertinent to introduce three characters whose role in the Thirty Years War was central: Johann Tserclaes, Count of Tilly (1559–1632), Ernst Graf von Mansfeldt (1580–1626), and a man born poor but who rose to be Duke Albrecht Wenzel Eusebius von Wallenstein of Friedland and Mecklenburg (1583–1634). These were the generals – the generals-for-hire, free-lancer generals, mercenary leaders of armies – who, on commission from the princes they served, raised armies and conducted campaigns, paid for by various monarchs and states as the occasions of the latter two demanded. They were in effect what Italians called *Condottieri* – *condittiero* literally means 'contractor' but came to have its specifically military meaning as applied in the Italian Renaissance style of war to the likes of Federigo da Montefeltro and Sigismondo Malatesta. Another name for them in Italy was *capitani di venture*, 'venture captains'. The English called them 'Mercenary Captains'. Whereas Tilly and Mansfeldt began their participation in the Thirty Years War as counts ('graf' means 'count'), Wallenstein – immortalised by Friedrich Schiller in his trilogy of plays about the great general's fall and death – became a duke as a result of his achievements, raised to dizzying heights by the Holy Roman Emperor until he was second only to the Emperor himself: and thus an object of resentment and opposition among all others, even though they were putatively allies.

Mansfeldt was the general on the Protestant side. Born a Catholic, he had for a time been in the Imperial military service, but he came to resent the treatment he received at the hands of Archduke Leopold, son of Emperor Ferdinand II, during the War of Jülich Succession, and therefore defected to the Protestant cause.

Tilly was a successful servant to Ferdinand II and the Catholic League in the war. He was born in Walloon Brabant, was educated by Jesuits and learned his military trade in the effective Spanish style. This was the *tercio* system, in which infantry units consisted of one-third pikemen, one-third swordsmen and one-third musketeers. More important than the configuration of these units was the fact that experienced soldiers were encouraged to remain in service, making the resulting force a professional one. The *tercio* system, which achieved much success right up to the mid-seventeenth century, had been devised by the great Spanish general Gonzalo de Córdoba at the end of the fifteenth century, who also introduced the *colunella* or cavalry unit, from which the word 'colonel' originates, denoting the leader of such a column.

Tilly was a formidable general, and along with Wallenstein dominated the first fourteen years of the Thirty Years War. But he is also a controversial figure: did he order the massacre of Magdeburg in 1630? Did he encourage it, or even just not discourage it? The fact that it happened is a stain on his reputation.

Wallenstein was a phenomenon, by any measure. He was born into a poor Protestant family in Bohemia, but converted to Catholicism under the influence of Jesuits while studying at Olomouc University. After a spectacular rise to fame, titles and fortune, he was twice ordered by the Emperor to retire to his estates in Bohemia. Necessity forced the Emperor to recall him after the first episode, but having been prompted to suspicion of Wallenstein by the jealousy of the latter's rivals, Ferdinand II at last recognised that he had invited a cuckoo into his nest. Wallenstein took his army with him into retirement, which made Ferdinand II suspect him of treason. He was indeed meditating treason, as Schiller in his trilogy shows; he was negotiating with the Emperor's enemies, the Swedes, with a view to joining them. He was assassinated on the night of 25 February

1634 with the Emperor's knowledge and approval: reminiscently of England's King Henry II and Becket, the Emperor must at very least have said aloud, to suitable persons, something like 'Who will rid me of this turbulent general?'

Schiller completed his trilogy of plays about the great general in 1799. It is loosely based on what happened to Wallenstein in the final months of his life. The drama is one of betrayal and loyalty, and in investigating the fate of a man who rose from nothing to vertiginous heights, it offers the parallel of another man who did likewise but with more restraint, thereby keeping the gains he made: this was the rise to a princedom of the man who orchestrated Wallenstein's murder, Octavio Piccolomini.

Tilly's victory at the Battle of the White Mountain and the flight of Frederick V saw the end of the Bohemian phase of the Thirty Years War and the beginning of the Palatinate phase, in which Frederick attempted to defend his hold on his ancestral territories with the help of Dutch money and an army raised by Mansfeldt.

As Frederick fled from Prague he tried to rally the Moravians, Lusatians and Silesians to his cause, while simultaneously negotiating with Ferdinand II in an effort to fend off further hostilities and to keep his title in the Rhinelands. Both efforts failed; as he travelled westwards he stopped in Brandenburg to ask for its Elector's help. The Elector said he would give it if James I of England did likewise; but James refused, so Frederick had to resort to his Orange relatives in the United Provinces for help and sanctuary. Ferdinand II issued a ban on Frederick, making him an outlaw in the Empire. This gave the leaders of the rest of the Protestant Union – of which Frederick was the nominal head – cause for hesitation, for at the conventions held by their leaders at Worms in the autumn of 1620 and again at Heilbronn in February 1621 there was much reluctance to give Frederick the military support he requested.

While Frederick scrabbled for help, the Upper Palatinate fell to Tilly without any fighting, and only the intervention of the winter of 1621–2 prevented the Lower Palatinate falling into his hands likewise. Frederick's general, Mansfeldt, was able to avoid engagement with Tilly, instead raising the Spanish siege of Frankenthal and then moving into winter quarters in Alsace.

In 1622 Frederick gathered three armies – Mansfeldt's forces, the army of Margrave Georg of Baden-Durlach, and the army of Christian of Brunswick – and resumed his efforts. Both of these Protestant princes, Georg and Christian, felt that their fates were too entangled with Frederick's not to support him. While Christian's army was in Westphalia, looting the bishoprics of Münster and Paderborn, Mansfeldt and Georg joined forces at Wiesloch in April 1622 and there defeated a well-organised Spanish force. They then separated and marched north to join Christian's forces. Georg's army was surprised by Imperial and Spanish troops while trying to cross the River Neckar, and was cut to shreds; Christian's forces nearly met the same fate on the banks of the Main before he could combine with Mansfeldt's troops.

The defeat of Georg's army seems to have been the last straw for Frederick, even though several of his former cities had remained loyal to him – chief among them Heidelberg, Mannheim and Frankenthal – and were continuing their resistance.[1] In July 1622 he declared that he would disband his own forces and retire from the fray. This left the armies of Mansfeldt and Christian without a leader or a cause, and so they decided to offer their services directly to the United Provinces, which still had a lively interest in preventing the Rhinelands from falling into Catholic hands. Together Mansfeldt and Christian fought their way through a Spanish blockade at Fleurus, leaving many corpses and one of Christian's own limbs on the field of battle, and raised the Spanish siege of Bergen-op-Zoom. A grateful United Provinces accordingly gave them a warm welcome.

The only hope for the Protestant cause at this juncture seemed to be James I of England. But James had conceived a grand design of marrying his son Charles to the Infanta of Spain, and was keen to find a diplomatic means out of the debacle caused by Frederick's Bohemian adventure. While negotiations between London and Madrid continued through 1623 – they were held in the Spanish Netherlands – the Emperor took unilateral action: he declared that Frederick's lands in the Palatinate were forfeit, and bestowed them on Maximilian of Bavaria.

This action galvanised the Protestants again. Mansfeldt and one-armed Christian now formed an alliance with Count Thurn of Bohemia and Bethlen Gábor, Prince of Transylvania and briefly King of Hungary. Their four respective armies marched from the north, east and south of the compass towards Bohemia, between them appearing to offer a formidable challenge to Ferdinand. But they were not a match for the wiles of Tilly. He manoeuvred his forces into Christian's path before the Brunswicker could combine with his allies, and his experienced troops easily defeated Christian's recruits, chasing them to Stadtlohn and there annihilating them. This marked the bloody and decisive end of the Palatinate phase of the war.

Once again, while an anxious Europe watched the fate of Frederick unfold, sailors and the sea were busy helping to change history far away. Events that had taken place some years before were now accelerating both change and conflict in other regions. One such was the Caribbean. A band of shipwrecked English sailors had been washed up on the pleasant shores of Bermuda in 1609, and when their reports of the place reached England a decision to colonise the island was taken, and a group of settlers arrived in 1612. This was the first English post in the Caribbean, whose largest islands – Cuba, Hispaniola and San Salvador – had already been in Spanish hands for a century.

Thirty years later disputes over religious matters within the Bermudan colony prompted a number of the colonists to leave and plant themselves in the Bahamas, then uninhabited because the Spanish had long since transported all the native inhabitants (the Arawaks) into slavery in the mines of Hispaniola.

Before this, however, the fact that there were uncolonised islands in the Caribbean set off a race between the English and French to take as many of them as they could. The English occupied St Kitts in 1623, Barbados in 1627, and by 1636 they were in possession of Antigua, Nevis and Montserrat. Meanwhile the French succeeded in getting a toe on another shore of St Kitts in 1627, and they occupied Dominica in 1632 and Martinique and Guadeloupe in 1635.

The process of colonising the islands was cumulative; having a port on one island served as a base for establishing occupancy of the next on the list. More than that, it provided a means of capturing some of the existing Spanish possessions; in 1655 England took Jamaica from the Spanish, and in 1664 France wrested half of Hispaniola from them, the half now known as Haiti.

The Spanish had sought to mine gold in their Caribbean possessions, but the islands yielded relatively little of the stuff in comparison to the immense wealth extractable from Mexico and Peru, so the islands became staging posts for their galleons rather than centres of economic activity themselves. In the English and French possessions matters were different; the settlers engaged in agriculture, starting with tobacco but soon diversifying into the highly lucrative sugar business. Because the original populations had been wiped out by labouring as slaves (and by European illnesses from which they had no immunity), African slaves were required; by the mid-seventeenth century Jamaica was the largest slave market in the West Indies.

With several major powers grabbing at opportunities in the region, it is no surprise that it quickly became a theatre of almost constant war. It had been a focus of piracy for many decades already; English pirates had preyed on the big Spanish bullion galleons with the sanction of the English government since Elizabethan times. The Caribbean quarrels went on until the Napoleonic Wars a century and a half later, but they paid for themselves, as did the less frequent quarrels in the East, because both the West and East Indies offered lucrative resources for the English, Dutch and French nations whose sailors and merchants took their opportunities there.

Back in Europe the failure of Frederick and the Dutch-sponsored armies to contain Habsburg power, and the latter's consequent approach towards the northern and wholly Protestant reaches of the Empire, now brought more actors into play. It was not only Protestants who were concerned; Cardinal Richelieu had been appointed to the Royal Council of France in April 1624, and was vigorously opposed to further extensions of Habsburg influence. James I had at last given up the idea of a Spanish alliance, and had entered into treaty arrangements with the Dutch and French against Spain. James commissioned Mansfeldt to raise a new army, and invited him to London, where he was fêted as a hero. But disagreements among the new set of allies about how his army should be used – was it to recover the Lower Palatinate as the English desired? was it to relieve the siege of Breda as the Dutch desired? how was it to do anything if it was not to cross French territory, as Richelieu refused to let it do? – resulted in it dissolving away through lack of supplies and activity: the soldiers just went home.

The need to muster opposition to the Empire was however still pressing, so James I in concert with the Elector of Brandenburg resolved to bring in the Danes and Swedes, an unlikely idea at first given the bitter and long-standing hostility between these two northern states. Gustavus Adolphus of Sweden agreed to join the alliance if his terms for doing so were met: he said he would raise an army of 50,000 men, a third of whom must be paid for by England – the money to be supplied up front – plus the cession to the Crown of Sweden of a port on the Baltic coast and another on the North Sea coast.

These exorbitant terms made England and the other allies turn to Denmark, whose King, Christian IV, proposed more modest terms. Gustavus Adolphus promptly refused to take any further part, and made preparations instead for a war on Poland.

Christian IV was not only King of Denmark but also Duke of Holstein and ruler of other territories in northern Germany, so he was greatly interested in halting further northward extensions of the Emperor's writ. Denmark was a wealthy state, mainly because of revenues from the tolls imposed on shipping in the Baltic. Christian accordingly had means as well as motive. The rulers of the Lower Saxon Circle states, which was his sphere of interest, rallied to him – only two dukes and the Hanseatic towns were persuaded by Ferdinand II to remain neutral.

In response to the gathering of forces under Christian, Maximilian of Bavaria commissioned Wallenstein to raise an army, and asked Tilly to join his forces with Wallenstein's. As Tilly's troops marched north-west towards the Lower Saxon Circle they left a swathe of destruction and terror behind them, presaging the horrors of the Sack of Magdeburg a few years later.

While Wallenstein and Tilly arranged themselves in winter quarters as 1625 passed into 1626, the English, Dutch and Danes signed a treaty at The Hague. Its terms were that Christian IV was to maintain an army of 30,000 infantry and 8,000 cavalry, and the English and Dutch were to pay him monthly subsidies of 300,000 and 50,000 florins respectively. (In the event Charles I of England, newly crowned but already at odds with his Parliament, never sent Christian the promised sums.) As a final touch, Christian IV agreed with Bethlen Gábor that his Transylvanian troops would make a diversionary attack into Silesia and Moravia.

Whatever hopes these dispositions raised in the breasts of the anti-Habsburg allies, they were not realised; the campaigning season of 1626 went badly. Mansfeldt was heavily defeated by Wallenstein at the Bridge of Dessau, Christian IV was even more decisively beaten by Tilly at Lutter-am-Bamberg. Temporary relief came from Gábor's diversionary activities; Mansfeldt managed to muster a remnant force and to join Gábor, and their combined forces captured Silesia. But their victory was short lived. Gábor's paymasters were the Ottomans, who just at that point were defeated by Persia at a battle outside Baghdad and ceased to be able to send him money. Mansfeldt, en route to seek new financial support from Venice, fell ill and died at Sarajevo.

As a result the Protestant alliance was in disarray. Wallenstein had been pursuing the combined forces of Gábor and Mansfeldt, but because they were now leaderless in one case and moneyless in both cases, the soldiers melted away, and there was no one for him to fight. In France Richelieu was dealing with the Huguenots, England was distracted by its internal troubles, and the Dutch were not prepared to throw good money after bad, so Christian IV was in a parlous state. Wallenstein and Tilly joined forces and inflicted a massive defeat on his army at the Battle of Grossenbrode in September 1627. Christian fled, taking refuge in his Danish islands, knowing that because Ferdinand II had no naval forces he would not be pursued there. But neither was there anything further that Christian IV could offer the Protestant cause against the Emperor and the Catholic League.

The Protestant cause now seemed hopeless. Wallenstein had reached the zenith of his power and fame; he had a huge army – he claimed it was 100,000 strong, and he and his soldiery could help themselves to whatever they liked wherever they went. He had now reached the point at which he was second only to the Emperor in standing. The Emperor showered titles of high nobility on him: he was invested with the dignities of Prince of Golgau and (what was in fact more substantial in terms of wealth and influence) Duke of Mecklenburg.

With the predictable elements of any tragic fiction, Wallenstein's dizzy ascent and consequent behaviour turned people against him. Rulers of other imperial states complained to the Emperor about him. They began to ask for a share of the spoils of his victories. They also began to demand that the lands he had wrested from Protestant rulers should be returned to the Catholic faith.

Wallenstein was meanwhile meditating the construction of a navy so that he could pursue Christian IV to the Danish islands. In this he was supported by the Spanish Habsburgs, who persuaded Ferdinand II to declare Wallenstein 'Admiral of the Baltic'. The aim of course was to make the Baltic a Spanish pond for Habsburg trade. Overtures to the Hanseatic cities, and what proved to be half-hearted attempts to build an Imperial fleet, at last persuaded the Danes and Swedes that they had a common interest; they might be at odds over which of them controlled the Baltic, but they were united in not wanting anyone else to be party to that quarrel.

This at last gave Sweden's Gustavus Adolphus the opportunity he was waiting for. In August 1628 a combined Danish–Swedish force defeated Wallenstein's forces besieging Stralsund and forced them to retreat. By raising this siege Gustavus Adolphus achieved his first foothold on the southern shore of the Baltic. His victory over Wallenstein meant that the latter had to abandon efforts to conquer the Baltic Sea. But Wallenstein's formidable land power remained. When Christian IV, emboldened by the success at Stralsund, quitted his islands, gathered fresh forces and marched them south from the mouth of the Oder, he thought that he was in pursuit of a beaten enemy. He was soon disabused; on encountering Wallenstein's well-prepared dispositions he was again soundly beaten.

That was the last straw for Christian. He initiated peace negotiations with Ferdinand II, and in the event escaped relatively lightly, though losing all his north German possessions. The English and Dutch, now keen for the Swedes to take the lead in the struggle, set to work to help Gustavus Adolphus make peace with his cousin King Sigismund of Poland so that he could devote all his attention to Wallenstein. It was at this juncture, the high point of Catholic successes in the war to date, that Ferdinand II fatefully allowed himself to be persuaded into his greatest mistake: the issuing of the Edict of Restitution on 6 March 1629.

6

The Edict of Restitution, 1629

THE EDICT OF Restitution was a significant moment in the war, but it was of course not the only significant moment in the century. Three years before the Edict was promulgated, the Dutch bought themselves another island. In exchange for a pile of fish hooks and trinkets they were given the island of Manhattan off America's east coast by the Lepane tribe of the Wappinger Confederacy. A year before the Edict of Restitution, William Harvey announced the results of his researches into the circulation of blood. In the same years as the Edict, hundreds of witches were burned to death in various parts of Ferdinand's Empire. In their different ways these occurrences are as emblematic of the century as the Thirty Years War itself.

Manhattan Island had been visited by Europeans long before. In 1524 Giovanni di Verrazzano, in command of a French ship called *La Dauphine*, had explored the narrows leading to the island's south-eastern coast, and the coast itself, and in that same year the Portuguese navigator Estêvão Gomes sailed up the island's west coast. But serious interest in its possibilities only began in 1609 when an English navigator in Dutch employ, Henry Hudson, sailed his ship the *Half Moon* up what therefore came to be called the Hudson River, and anchored on the northern tip of the island. This event took place on the now resonant date of 11 September in that year.

The Dutch who secured the island from the natives with their trinkets – allegedly worth $24 in total – called it New Amsterdam.

In 1626 they began to build a fort overlooking the harbour; in the succeeding decades it proved useful in the wars with the Algonquin Indians who soon began trying to expel them. However it proved unavailing against the English, who captured the fort in 1664 and renamed it New York after the Duke of York, later James II. Despite New York's propensity for uncomfortable extremes of weather – horribly hot and humid in summer, very cold in winter – the settlement became an important trading port because of its large natural harbour and its central position on the continent's eastern seaboard. By the end of the following century it was America's largest city, and remains so to this day.

Blood was spilled repeatedly in and because of New York, but the circulation of unspilled blood was not understood until the empirical work of scientist and physician William Harvey. Harvey was born in Kent in 1578, and studied at the universities of Cambridge and Padua, which latter had a famous medical school. After qualifying as a physician he practised at St Bartholomew's Hospital in London. While at Padua he was taught by Hieronymus Fabricius, a physician and anatomist who had noticed that veins have one-way valves in them, but could not work out their purpose. Harvey became interested in this puzzle and dissected animals in pursuit of solving it, which he soon enough did; he announced his findings in the course of delivering the Lumleian Lectures on anatomy at London's College of Physicians in 1616. But it was not until 1628 that he published his book *Exercitatio Anatomica de Motu Cordis et Sanguinis in Animalibus* (*An Anatomical Study of the Motion of the Heart and of the Blood in Animals*), bringing it out at the Frankfurt Book Fair to ensure its widest possible dissemination in the world of learning.

It is not surprising that his findings were first regarded as controversial. Other physicians simply disbelieved him, having been brought up on Galen's theories which they were reluctant to abandon. Galen thought that the liver produced venous blood, that venous and arterial blood were separate systems, that the function of the heart was to produce heat while that of the lungs was to cool the heart, and that the arteries sucked in air and then expelled it as vapours through the pores of the skin. The medical practice of bloodletting was premised on this view; Harvey's account of blood circulation called that practice into question.

Despite the meticulous care of the empirical work reported in his *De Motu Cordis* and the logic of its arguments – for example, on the impossible quantity of blood that the liver would have to produce each day on Galen's view – the negative view prevailed for a time, resulting in a diminution of Harvey's medical practice. His reputation recovered; he became physician to Charles I, and as microscopes grew more powerful Harvey's conjectures about capillaries (he was not able to see them, having lenses too weak) were shown to be correct.

Harvey dissected an extraordinary range of animals, fishes and birds and conducted an extraordinarily clever range of experiments in his effort to understand the cardiovascular system. It was no mean feat to work out the different contributions of the ventricles of the heart given that they had to be observed in operation – hence, through vivisection – and in small creatures the rapidity of the heart's motions made it nigh impossible to distinguish the different functions of the heart's four chambers, their interconnections, and their respective connections with the lungs and venous and arterial systems. But he did it; and all Europe wondered. In a letter written in the 1640s Princess Elizabeth of Bohemia mentions that she had spent the previous evening discussing Harvey's theories with friends – one small mark of how scientific developments were as striking to contemporaries and near-contemporaries as the events of the war.

The third matter mentioned, the witch burnings, also involved Harvey in a not insignificant way. He did not believe in witchcraft, and was a sceptical participant in the examination of witches in trials held in Lancashire in 1634. The four women involved were acquitted as a result of his assessment of them. On another occasion he visited a woman alleged to be a witch, and, pretending to be a wizard to gain her confidence, asked her if she had a familiar. She put down a saucer of milk and a toad came and drank it. While the woman was engaged elsewhere Harvey dissected the toad – he appears to have been an incontinent dissector – but found nothing unusual about it. The woman was very annoyed to find that he had killed her toad.

The many unfortunates involved in the witch trials of the years 1626–31 in the Empire, at the climactic peak of the witch scares of the period between 1580 and 1630, could have done with Harvey's help. The worst excesses were at Würzburg and Bamberg. The Würzburg trials resulted in the deaths of some 900 people, those at Bamberg nearly 600. Witch scares followed the Catholic reconquests of Protestant territory, and were often instigated by Jesuits or by the 'prince-bishops' who ruled small states of the Empire, such as Prince-Bishop Philipp Adolf von Ehrenberg of Würzburg, and the Archbishop-Elector of Mainz. When Baden was reconquered for Catholicism by Tilly in 1627 a persecution of alleged witches followed, lasting until 1629; scores were killed. Eichstätt, Reichertshofen, Coblenz, Mainz, Cologne, Bonn – all were visited by the same madness as had killed the hundreds at Würzburg and Bamberg.

Such was the mass hysteria that prompted the trials that accusation or suspicion could fall on anyone – children as young as seven were executed, along with people from all ranks and walks of life, and of both sexes. The superstition was thoughtless beyond belief: Ehrenberg of Würzburg credulously wrote that there had been a satanic mass outside the city at which 8,000 followers of the devil had committed blasphemies and obscenities, and had 'vowed not to be enrolled in the Book of Life'.

A Jesuit who witnessed the trials and executions at Würzburg came to the horrified conclusion that accusations of witchcraft were spurious, and that none of the victims was guilty. He was Friedrich Spee von Langenfeld, and his book questioning the conduct and content of the trials in which he participated, the *Cautio Criminalis*, helped to bring the witch-hunting craze to an end. Persecution of alleged witches did not stop until the eighteenth century, but by then executions were rare (the Salem witch-hunts resulted in the executions of six women and two men in September 1692; the last person executed in Britain for witchcraft was the Scottish victim Janet Horne, in 1727).

Tragic and foolish as the witch executions were, the numbers involved were insignificant in comparison to the deaths both in battle and resulting from famine and plague that followed the footsteps of war. Travelling in Europe during this period Harvey wrote,

> I can complain that by the way we could scarce see a dog, crow, kite, raven or any other bird, or anything to anatomize, only some few miserable people, the relics of the war and the plague where famine had made anatomies before I came. It is scarce credible in so rich, populous, and plentiful countries as these were that so much misery and desolation, poverty and famine should in so short a time be, as we have seen. I interpret it well that it will be a great motive for all here to have and procure assurance of settled peace. It is time to leave fighting when there is nothing to eat, nothing to keep, and nothing to be gotten.[1]

One result of the military successes of the Imperial and Catholic cause, and the consequent Edict of Restitution's promulgation, was the 'Leipzig Colloquy', a meeting of the Protestant Electors of Saxony and Brandenburg. Realising the dangers they faced in the impending clash between the Swedish and Catholic armies approaching their territories from north and south respectively, the two princes – one Lutheran, the other Calvinist – wished to overcome their differences and make an alliance, constituting a neutral 'third force'. They brought their university professors and theologians with them to work out the doctrinal differences between their respective Protestant confessions so that these would not prevent an agreement.

A leading figure in these discussions was Johannes Bergius, an 'irenicist' ('peace-maker') who argued that the doctrines of the two confessions were not in fact so far apart. His arguments were accepted by the theological representatives of both sides in the case of twenty-six out of the twenty-eight articles proposed for discussion. The two remaining articles, relating to the Eucharist and the very thorny matter of predestination, were postponed for later debate. Historians of the religious debate in the seventeenth century regard the Leipzig Colloquy as the period's 'greatest moment for any irenical attempt'.[2]

Two years earlier, in July 1630, some of the Empire's Catholic electors had also engaged in conversation – but with a much less irenic tendency – at the Diet of Regensburg. The Archbishop-Elector of Mainz, witch-hunter and Wallenstein's most vociferous critic, had requested that the Diet be called. Because of the Edict of Restitution neither of the Protestant electors agreed to go, but the importance of the Diet was such that it was attended by ambassadors from France and Spain. Their interest was in one of the side-theatres of the Thirty Years War, the War of Mantuan Succession, then being fought in northern Italy.[3] France did not want to see Imperial forces combining with Spanish forces in the dispute over who should hold Mantua, so their desideratum was a reduction in the size of the armies at the disposal of Ferdinand II and the Catholic League.

The quarrels between the Catholic electors about the division of the war's spoils, and their complaints about the egregious power that Wallenstein now wielded, played into French hands. In their dislike of Wallenstein the Catholic princes were motivated not just by jealousy but by fear. Ferdinand II found himself opposed by the electors in his desire to have his son, the Archduke Ferdinand, named King of the Romans, the titular position of the heir to the Imperial crown. He was forced to do three things: to drop the Dutch war plan on which his Spanish cousins were so keen, to agree to dismiss Wallenstein, and to reduce the size of the Imperial army.

Dropping the Dutch war project was a difficult choice because Spain, which was keen to recover the United Provinces, was a major source of income for the Empire through its subsidies, and the Spanish wished for a vigorous prosecution of war against the Dutch. Dismissing Wallenstein to placate the Catholic electors was more easily done. It carried risks in view of the huge army he commanded, but this army was a major drain on Ferdinand's resources, and the Spanish subsidies played a role there too: they were vital to keeping the army in the field, and because Madrid was at one with the Catholic electors in disliking and mistrusting Wallenstein, the argument of money won.

So Ferdinand reduced the Imperial army to 39,000 men, the Catholic League army to 20,000, and put both under the command of Tilly. The Habsburgs had just captured and sacked Mantua, which made Ferdinand think he did not need a Wallenstein-sized army after all. Moreover Ferdinand, despite this victory, gave the French good terms over Mantua in the Peace of Regensburg which he concluded with them even as the Diet was being held. His reason was that it enabled him to extract a promise from France not to meddle in the Empire's affairs, which to him was worth more than the question of succession to the now devastated duchy. Mantua accordingly went to France's choice, the duc de Nevers.

While the Catholic electors were quarrelling in Regensburg, and while Ferdinand was signing the Mantuan peace treaty with the ambassadors of France and Spain, something happened that rudely disrupted all their calculations: the Swedes invaded Pomerania. The aged Duke Bogislav XIV of Pomerania capitulated, and accepted a Swedish occupation and even (with great unwillingness) alliance. By the end of the year Gustavus Adolphus had gained control of a considerable part of the Oder valley and the southern Baltic coast. He hoped that the people of Mecklenburg would rise to join him, but they liked the good government of the usurper Wallenstein too much and did not want their old rulers back, which is what Gustavus promised them. This was a setback, but in other respects Swedish arms were successful, forcing the Imperial troops to retreat to Frankfurt an der Oder and Landsberg.

On the fateful day of 1 August 1630 the rich and beautiful city of Magdeburg, which by the Edict of Restitution had been forced to re-Catholicise, revoked its allegiance to Ferdinand II and entered an alliance with Gustavus. The Magdeburgers rallied their neighbours and gathered troops to fight alongside the Swedes, but before they could properly organise themselves they were attacked and routed by the cavalry of Tilly under the command of Gottfried Graf zu Pappenheim, who then laid siege to their city. This was the prelude to the Sack of Magdeburg and the terrible atrocity accompanying it. Gustavus sent a small garrison to help with Magdeburg's defence, telling its commander that the Swedish army would arrive within three months to raise the siege. In the event, no Swedish army came.[4]

Impressed by Gustavus' successes, Richelieu sent an ambassador to negotiate a Franco-Swedish alliance: so much for the terms of the

Peace of Regensburg in which he had promised the Emperor to do no such thing. The ensuing Treaty of Bärwalde, signed on 13 January 1631, provided substantial French subsidies in return for Gustavus' undertaking to maintain an army in northern Germany. Part of the deal was that Gustavus would concentrate on fighting the forces of Ferdinand II but not, if it remained neutral, the army of the Catholic League, and that the Swedes would not impose their Protestant ways on any Catholic territory they occupied.

In his characteristically duplicitous way, while Richelieu was concluding this deal with Gustavus he was simultaneously negotiating another treaty with Maximilian I of Bavaria, head of the Catholic League. The resulting Treaty of Fontainebleau, signed on 30 May 1631, was a paradigmatic piece of Thirty Years War conceptual architecture: even as France – a Catholic power – supported a Protestant army resisting the expansion of Habsburg power, so it supported Maximilian in the Palatinate possessions that had been awarded him by the Emperor, at the same time agreeing that Maximilian could vary the treaty if any of its provisions conflicted with his first allegiance, which was to the Emperor. The secret deal's main thrust was a mutual defensive pact between France and Bavaria, which, given the reservation about which obligation had the greater importance for Maximilian, looks like a peculiarly empty provision.

7

The Swedish Apogee

As GUSTAVUS MADE inroads in northern Europe, his military opponent Tilly bided his time, waiting for the return of the Imperial troops which had lately sacked Mantua. They were back under his command by the middle of January 1631, and ready for more action. At this juncture Gustavus invaded Mecklenburg, having given up the effort to negotiate with its citizens, and easily captured it. In the entire region of Pomerania and Mecklenburg the Imperial forces retained a weak hold only of three fortresses – Greifswald, Kolberg and Demmin – and these Gustavus now captured too. By March the whole area was under his control.

It was at this moment that Georg-Wilhelm of Brandenburg and Johann-Georg of Saxony convened the Leipzig Colloquy in hopes of avoiding war being fought across their territories by other people's armies. Also attending, apart from the academics and divines who debated the Lutheran–Calvinist doctrinal differences, were the minor Protestant princes, bishops and rulers of the Imperial Free Cities. They resolved on an alliance, which they called the Leipziger Bund, and the establishment of a defensive armed force. Johann-Georg of Saxony raised an army 40,000 strong and put it under the command of the man who had been Wallenstein's second-in-command, Hans-Georg von Arnim. Some of the other Protestant rulers, chief among them Bernhard of Saxe-Weimar, provided smaller forces. Then the Bund sent a memorial to the Emperor saying that if he would revoke the Edict of Restitution they would ally themselves with him against the Swedes.[1]

Ferdinand II rejected the Bund's proposal. He had been convinced by his confessor Lamormaini that he would do better to lose cities than his hopes of salvation, and that these latter were closely tied to the Edict of Restitution. But while the Bund awaited Ferdinand's decision, Gustavus was in a quandary; if he struck westward to relieve the siege of Magdeburg, only to find the Leipziger Bund allying with the Emperor, he would be cut off from the Baltic. So he delayed, and the delay was fatal for Magdeburg. On 20 May 1631 it fell, its women were raped, 30,000 of its citizens were slaughtered, and the city itself was put to the torch.

News of the event went like wildfire through a horrified Europe. Magdeburg was the principal Lutheran city of the German world, and its destruction at the hands of Catholic forces galvanised the Protestants yet again. Those minor Protestant princes who had yet to raise troops for the Leipziger Bund – the rulers of Swabia and Franconia for example – now did so, and sent them post haste to von Arnim.

Gustavus was as galvanised as the rest; he no longer wished to wait to see which way the Leipziger Bund would jump, but decided to ensure that it jumped his way. He marched his army through Brandenburg to its capital Berlin and camped under its walls, by his presence encouraging Georg-Wilhelm to agree an alliance. As the Bund's approach to Ferdinand II shows, the German Protestant princes were not over-eager to ally with Gustavus, whose intentions they mistrusted – rightly, because a major reason for his presence in northern Europe was not just about saving Protestantism. It was just as much a matter of repairing Swedish finances by getting more territory (i.e. more tax income). It was with some reluctance therefore that Georg-Wilhelm of Brandenburg put pen to parchment, agreeing the alliance and the level of subsidies to the ever money-hungry Gustavus.

Tilly remained in camp beside the smoking ruins of Magdeburg until June 1631, waiting for more Imperial troops to join him. Then he invaded Saxony. He occupied Merseburg and Halle, and sent a message to Elector Johann-Georg offering him a choice: Swedish King or Holy Roman Emperor. If the latter, Tilly told him, he would have to disband the army he had gathered, and then quarter and provision the Imperial army in his fertile Saxon lands. This gracious offer helped Johann-Georg to make his mind up swiftly: he chose the Swedish King. A treaty between the Saxons and Swedes was concluded on 30 August 1631, and Tilly now found himself outnumbered by their joint forces.

Tilly did not want to engage in direct battle with the Swedish alliance therefore, but chose instead to lay siege to Leipzig, hoping to weaken the alliance by attrition. But his irrepressible cavalry commander, the Graf zu Pappenheim, forced him into a set battle against his better judgment. On 7 September 1631, as the opposing forces converged on Leipzig, Pappenheim and his cavalry went on a sortie against the Protestant forces, partly as reconnaissance and partly to slow them down while Tilly approached the city itself. But when fighting started Pappenheim sent a message saying that he was unable to disengage and needed help. Very reluctantly Tilly obliged, the opposing armies meeting on a plain near Breitenfeld, a village lying about eight kilometres from Leipzig's walls.

To begin with it seemed that Pappenheim's ploy would succeed; his seasoned cavalry made short work of the inexperienced Saxon conscripts, who broke ranks and fled. But Gustavus was a commander of great skill. He moved his forces quickly and astutely, outmanoeuvring the Imperial effort to turn his flank. His cavalry made a brilliant foray against the Imperial artillery, capturing it all; the guns were immediately turned on the Imperial forces and contributed to the devastating defeat now inflicted on them. The Imperial commanders retreated, Pappenheim to Westphalia and Tilly to the Upper Palatinate, leaving Gustavus supreme in the German lands.

This was the high point for Gustavus. His Swedish forces marched rapidly into the Main and Rhine valleys, capturing the wealthy Catholic Archbishoprics of Würzburg and Mainz – he had promised his troops rich plunder in 'priests' alley' as these territories were collectively known – and taking the Lower Palatinate. Meanwhile his Saxon allies marched east and captured Lusatia, Bohemia and Moravia, taking Prague without a fight.[2]

Gustavus' rapid and decisive victories alarmed the French, who had paid for them but now disliked having his army so close to their own borders. Moreover the Swedes had not kept to their agreement to leave Catholics unmolested. Their promise not to fight Catholic League forces if the latter remained neutral had anyway been nullified by the fact that those forces, in combining with the Imperial armies, had not remained neutral. What worried the French even more was that some of the Catholic princes were minded to ally themselves with Gustavus because the Emperor appeared not to be able to defend them. France's diplomatic efforts to get Gustavus to relinquish control of some of the Catholic territories he had overrun – cannily, of course, the ones closest to France's own borders – were partially successful, the benefit for Gustavus in return being a promise that Catholic League troops would be reduced in number and returned to their home territories. The promise was not kept, however, because Maximilian I of Bavaria would not agree.

At the same time France 'offered protection' to a number of cities in Alsace, and the cities accepted; French garrisons were installed, as a measure of defence should Gustavus choose to tear up the Treaty of Bärwalde and march on France itself.

As the Saxons invaded Bohemia, Wallenstein decided to return to public life. He contracted his former comrade von Arnim to open discussion with the latter's new master, the Elector of Saxony. It was not clear whether Wallenstein was offering his services to the Swedish alliance or trying to entice the Saxons back to the Imperial cause. In any event Ferdinand II, in desperation because of the Swedish victories, was now himself a party to negotiations with Wallenstein; he wanted him back, and Wallenstein was prepared to re-enter service provided he could have carte blanche in the conduct of war and any peace negotiations arising as a consequence of it. Ferdinand II agreed, and Wallenstein set about raising a grand army of 70,000 men.

While these arrangements were in process Tilly and Maximilian joined forces and attacked the bishopric of Bamberg, which was held by a Swedish garrison. They drove the garrison out and congratulated themselves on a victory, only to find that Gustavus had immediately started to march towards them with his whole army – to Maximilian's alarm, for it was clear that Gustavus was intent on invading Bavaria.

Tilly chose the River Lech near the city of Rain as his place to confront Gustavus. On 15 April 1632 the Swedes attacked, mounting a furious and withering artillery bombardment on the Imperial forces. They forded the river in a frontal assault on Tilly's troops, who were dazed by the bombardment, and overpowered them. Tilly himself was fatally wounded by cannon fire, and died two weeks later in Ingoldstadt where loyal soldiers had taken him.

The way to Munich now lay open to Gustavus. Maximilian fled to Salzburg, the Swedes helped themselves to Bavaria, and would have enjoyed the fruits of conquest longer were it not for Wallenstein. He had raised and equipped his new army, had easily recaptured Bohemia from the Saxons, and was now on his way south to join the remnants of Maximilian's army. Gustavus, understanding the danger, tried to get between the two forces to prevent them from uniting, but when he found that he could not do so he decided instead to position himself at Nuremberg, which he hastily fortified. Wallenstein arrived outside the fortifications and camped, choosing to lay siege rather than to mount an assault, leaving it to disease and starvation to deal with the Swedish army. To this end he started building a huge fortified camp outside the city. But Gustavus was not prepared to let either disease or starvation do Wallenstein's work for him, so after launching an attack on the Imperial camp he escaped from Nuremberg and headed for Coburg. Wallenstein did not pursue, but took his army northwards instead.

The reason for these manoeuvres was the same in each case. Gustavus' plan was to attack Upper Austria, thinking that a direct threat to the Habsburg hereditary heartlands would force Wallenstein to direct battle. Wallenstein had the same idea in the opposite direction: threaten Saxony, ruled by Gustavus' important but unreliable ally Johann-Georg, and Gustavus would have to come to Saxony's defence. In each case the general was thinking about where and how he would like to stage a decisive battle.

It was Wallenstein whose intuitions proved to be more accurate. Gustavus hurried north to protect the Saxons, but also to keep open his route to the Baltic – this was all-important to him: Wallenstein, recognising this, had placed himself exactly in Gustavus' way to the sea. The resulting Battle of Lützen, one of the bloodiest and grimmest of the war, was a victory for the Swedes and their allies, yet at the same time a defeat for both sides. Wallenstein's bruised army was forced to retreat into Bohemia, the Swedes held the field and preserved the Saxon alliance; but they lost their King, and the Protestant cause its unifying and guiding centre – for Gustavus was killed in the battle. A dramatic painting by Carl Wahlbom shows Gustavus falling backwards off his horse in the midst of a deadly mêlée, already moribund. Every year to this day on the anniversary of the battle, 9 November, the Swedes remember Gustavus, who led their country to the greatest power and influence it has ever known.

Gustavus was succeeded by his six-year-old daughter Princess Christina. Her mother Maria-Eleonora of Brandenburg was insane and unable to act as regent. Power was therefore transferred to a council of Swedish nobles, with Axel Oxenstierna at their head. But the personal momentum given by Gustavus was lost, and the first result of the more cautious policy pursued by Oxenstierna was withdrawal of Sweden's troops to the Baltic coast, leaving the German princes to consolidate Gustavus' gains in the Rhineland. A meeting of the Protestant princes, though with the electors of Brandenburg and Saxony refusing to attend, was held at Heilbronn in April 1633 to form a new league, its chief decision being to provide a large subsidy to Sweden to maintain its military endeavour.

Talk of subsidies was not quite the same thing as their being paid. In some cases arrears of pay in the Swedish army stretched back five years and more. Mutterings about mutiny forced Oxenstierna to act; he offered some of his senior officers titles and grants of land in lieu of pay. One of the chief beneficiaries was Bernhard of Saxe-Weimar, who was made Duke of Franconia. To pacify the soldiery the only option was to pay cash, so Oxenstierna forced the League to part with some of the money. All-out mutiny was thereby averted, but narrowly.

Richelieu sent an ambassador to Heilbronn, to argue that the King of France should be co-guarantor of the League of Heilbronn along with the infant Christina of Sweden, that the Treaty of Bärwalde should be reaffirmed, and that France's subsidies to Sweden should be redirected into the coffers of the League of Heilbronn. These terms were accepted. But France was not the only bargainer in the picture. Johann-Georg of Saxony was still unhappy about his alliance with the Swedes; he continued to refuse to join the League of Heilbronn, and he kept his lines open to Wallenstein in the hope of making a separate peace. Oxenstierna and the League could not however do without Johann-Georg, for Saxony was unignorable geographically, financially and militarily. In December 1632 Oxenstierna visited Leipzig and persuaded Johann-Georg to participate in the planned spring campaign against Wallenstein. Johann-Georg agreed on strict conditions: that the fighting be done across the border in Silesia and not in his own lands, and that command of the Swedish army be given to Matthias Thurn, the hero of the Defenestration of Prague fourteen years before. Command of Johann-Georg's own Saxon forces remained with von Arnim.

By the end of the campaigning season of 1633 Wallenstein had given Johann-Georg even more reason to get out of the war. He cannily persuaded the League to grant him a succession of truces, during which he strengthened his forces and prepared them for a devastating strike against the Swedes and their allies. In September he overran Thurn's camp in Steinau, inflicting a punishing defeat which led to his taking 8,000 Swedish prisoners and recapturing all the northern Silesian towns that the Swedes had occupied. Then he raided into Saxony and Brandenburg, thereby increasing Johann-Georg's desire for peace.[3]

These were momentous years not just in the war but in other respects. In 1630–1 Venice, already in decline from its greatest years, suffered a deadly visitation of the plague. Estimates of the numbers who died vary, the best of them fixing on a third of the population. As a result the Senate of Venice voted to build a church to express the gratitude of the survivors: this is the striking Santa Maria della Salute on the Punta della Dogana which stands at the confluence of the Grand and Giudecca canals.[4] Opinions about its qualities differ; it is certainly imposing, if overcooked, though its dome is beautiful and attracted the admiring attention of many notable artists including Canaletto and Turner.

Even more significant for subsequent history, however, was the publication in 1632 of Galileo's *Dialogo sopra i due massimi sistemi del mondo* (*Dialogue Concerning the Two World Systems*) which led to his arrest and forced recantation. In histories of the conflict between science and religion this is one of the key moments – in fact, the last great push by the Church to stem the advance of science in its confutation of the literal interpretation of scripture. The book was placed on the *Index of Forbidden Books*, in company with almost all the world's greatest or most important literature. The Church fully revoked its condemnation of Galileo in 1992, though it did not condemn the judges who had condemned him, saying that they had acted 'in good faith'.

One of the forgotten features of Galileo's trial was that his accusers refused to look through his telescope because they knew what they were being invited to look at could not exist; scripture said so. His views were described by the Inquisition as 'foolish, absurd, false in theology, and heretical', and he was sentenced to life imprisonment. His sentence would have been death if he had not recanted. Life imprisonment was soon commuted to perpetual house arrest – a more comfortable form of life imprisonment – and he was ordered to remain perpetually silent on scientific matters.[5]

Reading the *Two World Systems* now, one is surprised at how little effect a rational argument can have. In Day Two of the book, Salviati talks of the motions of the heavenly bodies: why would nature move all the many tens of thousands of them rather than – more simply and economically – the single relatively small object, the earth itself? Given their distance, the heavenly bodies would have to be moving inconceivably fast to complete a rotation in just twenty-four hours of the point occupied by earth. And what would happen to the heavens' movement if the earth is removed from the picture?

As the Venetians began to build the Santa Maria della Salute, as Galileo prepared his book for publication, and as the Swedes enjoyed their successes in the fighting in Europe, so a group of English colonists were founding a town on the eastern seaboard of America which was to play a large role in the continent's history: Boston. The land on which the town was built was bought from its first English owner, one William Blaxton. Its first Governor, John Winthrop, called it 'a City upon a Hill' in allusion to its perceived status as a new Jerusalem. As this suggests, from the outset Boston viewed itself as a special place chosen by the deity for the eager settlers, who were zealous in their own moral protection. Church attendance was compulsory, as was rigorous training in scripture, sin was vehemently punished – not least by public whipping – morality enforced, and dissenters from the Puritanism of the place were punished or expelled.

Such expulsions were the cause of new colonies being founded; Roger Williams was driven from Salem in Massachusetts for being too tolerant, and therefore founded Providence in Rhode Island as a place for 'loving friends and neighbours'. Williams was before his time; he learned native American languages, protested at slavery and argued that it should be abolished in all thirteen colonies, and cherished the idea of freedom of religion. He had been born in London and educated at Cambridge where his command of languages extended from the classical tongues to Hebrew, French and Dutch. Before going to America he was chaplain to Sir William Masham, baronet, grandfather of the third baronet Sir Francis Masham whose wife, Damaris, Lady Masham, was the platonic love-object of the philosopher John Locke, who lived at the Mashams' home in High Laver, Essex. (She was also the daughter of Ralph Cudworth, the Cambridge Platonist whose views on innate ideas Locke so roundly criticised in the first Book of his *Essay Concerning Human Understanding*.) Such are the connections and coincidences that wind their way through history; as a great war raged, life went on in these other ways and places.

8

From Wallenstein to Breisach

Roger Williams' time in the Massachusetts colony during the first half of the 1630s was a troubled one, in which he was constantly at odds with his fellow colonists over Church matters, thus compelling his departure in 1635 for Rhode Island. But his fate was not as louring as that of the great Wallenstein, whose destiny in the same period, back in the tumultuous trials of Europe, was far grimmer.

The Spanish, in concert with Duke Maximilian's Bavarian forces, had spent part of the early 1630s in planning and then attempting to reopen the Spanish Road between the north of Italy and the Spanish Netherlands. When they embarked on the military effort itself they met a section of the Swedish army under the command of the Swedish general Gustav Horn and Bernhard of Saxe-Weimar, who pushed them back, and then followed them into Bavaria where they captured Regensburg.

This was a serious blow to the Emperor and Maximilian, a blow made worse by the fact that they had asked Wallenstein to come south in defence of the city, but Wallenstein had refused. Suspicion of Wallenstein's motives and loyalties grew, and Ferdinand II regretted recalling him and agreeing to give him such plenary powers. Accordingly he sent a peremptory order to Wallenstein to take his army into Bavaria, to which Wallenstein responded by making all his officers swear an oath of allegiance to himself personally. On hearing this the Emperor required that the oath of loyalty to Wallenstein should be binding only while Wallenstein was in Imperial service. Wallenstein refused again.

The overmighty subject was heading fast for his fall: on 18 February 1634 Ferdinand gave orders for Wallenstein to be stripped of his command, and for that office to be transferred to Archduke Ferdinand, the Emperor's son. Accordingly Wallenstein's senior officers – notably the generals Gallas and Piccolomini – and practically all the soldiery deserted him. Wallenstein fled to Eger, now at last openly proposing to join the Swedes and Saxons. But on 25 February 1634 the garrison there turned on him and murdered him, along with the few loyal supporters who had accompanied him.

Saxony and Brandenburg were no longer in the mood to continue the war, and began direct negotiations with the Emperor. The Imperial forces were in need of a new commander; Ferdinand II appointed Ferdinand King of Hungary, who immediately laid plans for combining his forces with the Spanish army under Ferdinand Cardinal-Infante of Spain. The plan was to clear the Spanish Road and defeat the League of Heilbronn, consisting now mainly of the south-western Protestant princes. The joint Imperial–Spanish forces recaptured Regensburg in July 1634, then set off west along the Danube, capturing Donauwörth and laying siege to Nördlingen.

Fatally for the Swedish forces, its generals Horn and Saxe-Weimar had agreed a bizarre arrangement by which each took it in turns on alternate days to be supreme commander. This clumsy deal resulted in delays and muddle when the Swedes reached Nördlingen, where victory would have been theirs if they had attacked soon upon arriving. Instead they were too disorganised to do so, and by the time they were ready the Imperial and Spanish forces had been heavily reinforced. The result of the Battle of Nördlingen was destruction of the Swedish army; by nightfall on the day of the battle, 27 August 1634, it simply did not exist any more. Horn was a prisoner of the Emperor, and Bernhard of Saxe-Weimar a refugee, sending messages to his garrisons in various places to join him for a last stand on the Rhine.

The extinction of the Swedish army at Nördlingen meant the effective end of the Heilbronn League. Imperial and Spanish forces swept into Franconia, Swabia and Württemberg, meeting hardly any resistance.

Heilbronn itself fell, and Stuttgart; the Spanish section of the force advanced rapidly towards the Rhine, taking Aschaffenburg and Schweinfurt. By the end of October 1634 the north German Protestant anti-Imperial resistance was geographically cut off from the south-western Protestant anti-Imperial resistance, and it was years before they were again in geographical connection.

The defeated Heilbronn League and their Swedish allies had only one resort in their emergency: France. In the strong negotiating position he now occupied, Richelieu was able to dictate the terms of the resulting Treaty of Paris, signed in November 1634. He offered further subsidies to the Swedes and Heilbronn League members for their military efforts, and undertook to supply an army of 12,000 for the German theatre of conflict, but this latter was only to act if France officially declared war on the Emperor. He said that the members of the Heilbronn League were to tolerate Catholicism wherever they encountered it, and were not to make war on anyone whom France regarded as a friend or ally. Finally Richelieu required recognition of France's entitlement to keep troops in Alsace.

The League members agreed, but Oxenstierna did not. He continued to negotiate, seeking better terms for Sweden. The result was the Treaty of Compiègne, signed in April 1635, in which Oxenstierna gained recognition of Swedish control of Mainz and Worms, and toleration for Protestantism.

Treaties are not the same thing as soldiers and firepower. French and League troops did not have much success against their Spanish–Imperial foes, who were able to pin them to the left bank of the Rhine and to keep them there for years. Part of the reason was France's distraction over the question of Triers, whose Archbishop-Elector was under its protection. At the end of March 1635 the city was attacked and both it and its Elector were captured by the Spanish. France declared war on Spain; the two countries remained at war until 1659, a drain on both and a distraction from the main event.

Four months earlier, in November 1634, Johann-Georg of Saxony had reached an accommodation with Ferdinand II known as the 'Preliminaries of Pirna'. It was immediately followed by an armistice between the Saxon and Imperial armies. The chief sticking point for Johann-Georg as for all Protestants was the Edict of Restitution. Ferdinand's attachment to it, fostered as we saw by the influence of his confessor Lamormaini, was beginning to weaken now that peace with Saxony hinged on it, so he began to consult more widely. His wife's confessor Don Diego de Quiroga was not so sure that Ferdinand's immortal soul hung in the balance over the Edict. Ferdinand consulted twenty theologians and his fellow Catholic electors, and was persuaded by their collective opinions to temporise: in the Peace of Prague which resulted, signed on 30 May 1635, the Edict was suspended for forty years; there were to be no more restitutions of church property for that time. This was kicking the ball out of play as an expedient – leaving it to a later generation to have its own wars, perhaps, over the matter.

The Peace of Prague was good for Johann-Georg. It was peace, he was ceded Lusatia, the Edict was suspended, some lands which had been returned to Catholic control now returned to Protestant control again. For Ferdinand II the gain was that the treaty's signatories undertook not to form leagues against him, were not to sign treaties with foreign powers, and were to place their militaries at Imperial disposal. The treaty was open to any prince who cared to sign, in return for amnesty and restoration of titles. The only exceptions to the latter were the heirs of Frederick V of the Palatinate and those of his first ally, the Duke of Baden-Durlach. All but one of the princes signed the treaty; the one hold-out was Wilhelm of Hesse-Cassel, who declared neutrality. The Peace of Prague effectively ended the civil war aspect of the Thirty Years War, though certain of the Imperial estates at times allied themselves to the foreign powers – France and Sweden – who were now the Empire's principal enemies.[1]

Another brief glance away from the war is merited by mention of the year in which the Peace of Prague was signed. If 1635 was good from the point of view of ending the civil war aspect of the Thirty Years War, it was good for education and learning too. It saw the establishment of the famous Latin School of Boston, the first public school in America and today the United States' oldest existing such school. It also saw the founding in Paris by Cardinal Richelieu of the Académie Française. The Académie grew out of a salon of savants and literary folk who had been meeting at the Hôtel de Rambouillet for more than a decade, and who had attracted the patronage of Richelieu. The Académie's 1635 letters of royal patent specified its task, which was to purify the French language, specify its rules and make it fit for literary and scientific purposes. Richelieu was inspired by the model of the Accademia della Crusca in Florence, which had existed since the 1580s and which had the same object in regard to language, thereby establishing Tuscany's dialect as the standard form of Italian.[2]

The Holy Roman Emperor had much trouble persuading some of his Catholic allies to accede to the Peace of Prague. He had to resort to bribery to get them to do it. Duke Maximilian of Bavaria, always independent-minded despite being a supporter, did not like the requirement that his armed forces were to be subsumed into the Imperial army. He had to be seduced into signing the treaty by the offer of marriage to the Emperor's daughter, Archduchess Maria Anna, by the granting of the Bishopric of Hildesheim to his brother the Elector of Cologne, and by a promise that the Bavarian forces in the Imperial army would have a degree of autonomy.

To the Protestant elector Georg-Wilhelm of Brandenburg a different and mistaken promise had to be made: Ferdinand had to say that when the Swedes were defeated, Pomerania would be given to Georg-Wilhelm. Because the Swedes so avidly wished to retain Pomerania, this clause was a guarantee that the war would continue.

It will be remembered that in 1629 Richelieu had succeeded in bringing Sweden into the war by arranging a truce between Gustavus and his cousin the King of Poland, thus releasing the Swedes to pursue bigger fish. Now in 1635 Richelieu had to get the truce renewed to ensure that Sweden would not be distracted into revived hostilities in the east of Europe. He sent ambassadors to Sweden and Poland to arrange an extension of the truce, and succeeded; it was renewed for twenty-six years.

The terms were not so advantageous for Sweden as they had originally been, for the Poles now understood that they had a bargaining position. Before the ink was dry the Swedish garrison in Poland under Field Marshal Lennart Torstensson gathered themselves and hastened towards Germany, where the need for them was sore, for in October 1635 Saxony declared war on Sweden, threatening to realise the Swedes' worst fear, which – rather like that of the ancient Greeks – was to be cut off from the sea. In the event Torstensson beat back the Saxon threat, and the Swedish hold on Mecklenburg and Pomerania was secure.

Matters were not progressing so well on the western and southern fronts of the war, where France had launched major offensives against the Spaniards in the Low Countries and Spain itself, and in Italy. All three offensives failed. Bernhard of Saxe-Weimar, in need of French support and waiting for the French Rhine army which, thus distracted, could not go to his aid, was in an exposed position in Spiers. He had to retreat, leaving Kaiserslautern, Heidelberg and Mainz to fall to the Imperial army.

Richelieu was much shaken by the defeats suffered by the French armies, and realised that the only reliable force available for defence of the Rhine was the experienced army under Bernhard. The latter at the same time realised that because the Swedes were weakened, and the Protestant princes who had joined the Peace of Prague were lost to the anti-Imperial cause, he had to establish a new alliance. Accordingly he and Richelieu held talks, and agreed that the French would pay him a million livres annually to maintain his forces, that he would be Margrave of Alsace, and that he could wield sovereignty over any territories he conquered. The deal was signed on 19 November 1635. By entering this agreement Bernhard was reneging on his obligations to Sweden, and the Swedes were naturally angered that France had – as they saw it – stolen him away. But in the state of affairs obtaining at the close of that year – a difficult year for the anti-Imperial cause – no one was in a position to do otherwise.

The war was now, in 1636, in a state of what might paradoxically be called bloody and vigorous stagnation, much to the harm of the lands and people over which the contending forces trampled back and forth.

France and Bernhard made progress in Alsace, Spain's Cardinal-Infante invaded northern France from the Spanish Netherlands and was driven back with difficulty, the Swedes regathered themselves and went on the offensive down the Elbe.

That was the pattern all year. The combined armies of the Emperor and Saxony met the Swedes at Wittstock in Brandenburg on 4 October, and a fierce battle ensued. It was fought over marshy ground, which made manoeuvring difficult. Casualties were great on both sides. It was decisively won by the Swedes, who were quick to exploit their success; they occupied the rest of Brandenburg and pushed forward as far as Eisenach. The effort to reattach Georg-Wilhelm of Brandenburg failed because the Elector chose to observe the terms of the Peace of Prague. The Swedes ventured into Saxony and laid siege to Leipzig, unsuccessfully; in January 1637 they therefore retreated to Torgau until the next campaigning season.

In February 1637 Ferdinand II died, to be succeeded by his son Archduke Ferdinand.[3] This Ferdinand had been titular head of the Imperial armies since the fall of Wallenstein. His father had at last succeeded in having him elected King of the Romans in December 1636, so he now became Holy Roman Emperor, as Ferdinand III.

The change at the top of the Empire had no marked effect on the war, except perhaps to return it to the back-and-forth stagnation that every succeeding campaigning season seemed to involve. In the north the Swedes were pushed back by the Imperial forces, losing all their gains and more of the previous year, so that after a series of encounters they found themselves confined to a corner of Pomerania – the least territory they had held since Gustavus Adolphus first invaded. Meanwhile in the south-west Bernhard made gains along the Rhine, capturing the Forest Towns and by the beginning of 1638 getting himself in position to besiege the great fortress at Breisach, which was the lynchpin of Imperial power in the Vorosterreich, the Imperial lands of the Rhine.

After reinforcing his army and beating off attempts by Imperial forces to prevent him establishing the siege, Bernhard settled down to starve the Breisach garrison out of their otherwise impregnable position. Ferdinand III made a number of further attempts to relieve the fortress, all sporadic and each easily rebuffed. When at last the fortress surrendered Bernhard learned to his horror that some of his men who had been prisoners in the fortress had been obliged by starvation to eat their own dead comrades.

The loss of Breisach was a major blow to the Imperial cause. While the fortress was under siege Sweden's Oxenstierna had been contemplating his choices: whether to make a separate peace with Ferdinand III, or persuade the French to give more financial support. In March 1638 the drawn-out negotiations over the latter possibility came to an end in the Treaty of Hamburg; the French were to pay a million livres annually to the Swedes in return for two things – a guarantee that the Swedes would not seek a separate peace with Ferdinand III, and continued military endeavours by them in the eastern Habsburg territories. Oxenstierna sent 14,000 freshly raised troops from Sweden to join the forces in Pomerania under the command of his general in the field, Johan Banér.

Given this new impetus Banér was able to regroup, and in the spring of 1639 he again advanced. He recaptured all of Pomerania and Mecklenburg, and pursued the Imperial forces into Silesia and Bohemia after inflicting a crushing defeat on them at the Battle of Chemnitz on 14 April, in which the Imperial troops were commanded by the Emperor's brother, the Archduke Leopold-Wilhelm. Another equally crushing Swedish victory at Brandeis opened the way to Prague; by May Banér was under its walls, but because he was insufficiently prepared for a siege he chose to withdraw to the Elbe.

The gods on either side of this war seemed, like the Olympians at Troy, to be sporting with the opposing sides. As the Swedes made gains on the eastern side of the conflict, their allies on the western side fell into disarray. First, the son of the Winter King Frederick V, Karl-Ludwig, had at last raised an army paid for by money from Charles I of England, and led an invasion against the Empire down the Ems. It was stopped at Hochfeld by an Imperial force, and completely destroyed. Meanwhile Bernhard of Saxe-Weimar and the French had fallen out over which of them could lay claim to Breisach. Bernhard argued that it fell within his Margravate of Alsace, to say nothing of being his by right of conquest; the French disagreed, saying that Breisach was part of Breisgau and not Alsace, and that anyway the original agreement excepted the Alsatian fortresses from Bernhard's control should he capture them. Any appearance of inconsistency here – that Breisach was not in Alsace, but as an Alsatian fortress it was exempt from the agreement – is to be attributed to the natural human desire to win an argument at any cost.

In anger Bernhard withdrew his forces to the Franche-Comté to overwinter. In the event, he stayed too long; he was still there with his army in June 1639 when plague broke out among his troops. He caught the disease too, and died on 11 July.

Command of the Saxe-Weimar forces fell to Bernhard's second-in-command, Johann Ludwig von Erlach, who thought differently about matters from his erstwhile commander. He promptly entered into negotiations with all three of the French, Swedes and Ferdinand III to see who would pay most for his loyalty. All three were highly interested given the seasoned and experienced nature of the troops he commanded. In October 1639 he decided to stay with the French, and combined his forces with theirs. The enlarged army immediately enjoyed a number of successes along the Rhine, and crossed it at Bacharach, a significant blow for the Emperor.

9

Towards Westphalia

AWAY FROM THE war history was proceeding along its many separate paths. In August 1639 the British East India Company bought a strip of land from the Nayaka of Vandavasi, and secured his permission to build a fort and trading post there. This was the beginning of Madras, now called Chennai, the first British post in India and today one of the subcontinent's most flourishing cities. Close to the land bought by the East India Company was a little fishing village called Madraspatnam, hence its original name. The city stands on the Coromandel Coast of Tamil Nadu, a stretch of seaboard which already harboured Portuguese and Dutch trading factories; the British were not the first to arrive. But their foothold was to prove the most consequential by far.

If India seems a long way from the fighting on the Rhine and in Bohemia, the planet Venus is even further still. It will be remembered that it was in 1639 that Horrocks and Crabtree observed a transit of Venus, excitedly watching the little black dot of its shadow traversing the face of the sun. In Paris the Académie Française was inaugurating work on a dictionary of the French language. These peaceful and constructive avocations seem far from the grim and repetitive struggles devastating central Europe, but in fact the first hints of a possible peace were visible there too.

The military successes of the Swedes in 1639, together with those of the renewed French–Saxe-Weimar allied army on the other wing of the war, promised well for the anti-Habsburg cause in 1640. But rather than constituting a platform for further gains and the linking of the two anti-Imperial wings, no further advances, at least of a major kind, were made on either front. But more heartening were the first tentative signs that peace might come. Peace after a fashion, of course – the century was never really peaceful – but peace at least in the struggles between the pro- and anti-Habsburg contenders. It was not to come for another eight years, and there was plenty more fighting to be done. But by calling a Diet to be held at Regensburg in September 1640 Ferdinand III showed that he was anxious to agree with the suggestions of his electors – reached at the Nuremberg *Kurfurstentag* in February of that year – that there could be a more general internal peace in the Empire, of the kind sought by the Peace of Prague, if a broader amnesty were announced.

Hopes for the Regensburg Diet were high at first. Ferdinand III gave safe conduct to ambassadors from those Protestant states of the Empire which had been in armed revolt for practically the whole war to date – Hesse-Cassel and Brunswick-Lüneburg, and even to the 'Winter Queen' Elizabeth Stuart herself. The Diet announced a general amnesty, and set to work discussing the prospects of a more general settlement. But then two things happened that derailed the process. One was the publication of a pamphlet called *Dissertatio de Ratione Status in Imperio nostro Romano-Germanico*, written by someone calling himself 'Hippolithus à Lapide' – a pseudonym believed to hide the authorship of a Swedish citizen with the non-Swedish name Bogislav of Chemnitz. It argued that the Imperial constitution gave the Emperor fewer powers than everyone supposed, and that Ferdinand III and his predecessors regularly exceeded the authority they were entitled to, in pursuing their own interests at the expense of their subordinate rulers in the Empire. The pamphlet had the effect of stirring unrest and suspicion among the Empire's junior rulers, with Ferdinand III as the target.

Perhaps because of this, the new Elector of Brandenburg, Friedrich-Wilhelm, who had succeeded on the death of his father Georg-Wilhelm in December 1640, was not persuaded by the irenic sentiments expressed in Regensburg.[1] To the surprise and dismay of Emperor

Ferdinand and his fellow electors, he announced that he would take no further part in the Diet, and made public a truce he had agreed with Sweden. Both moves had the effect of detaching the more junior Protestant princes from the Regensburg process and attaching them to Brandenburg instead. It was a sign of the increasingly important position that Brandenburg was to take in the future of the northern German-speaking peoples.

Despite the failure of the Diet to achieve its aim, the fact that it had been called at all, and that the Emperor had granted safe conduct to inveterate enemies so that they could attend it, was the first major indication that a peace process was possible. In June 1641 France and Sweden reaffirmed the Treaty of Hamburg first signed three years earlier, and then they jointly sent an invitation to Ferdinand III, Spain and the estates of the Empire, to discuss peace in conferences to be held in Westphalia.

There were to be two sets of overlapping talks in both of which the Emperor and his Spanish cousins were to take part. The Emperor and the Spanish were to meet at Osnabrück with the Swedes, the Dutch and the Protestant princes of the Empire. The Emperor and the Spanish were to meet separately at Münster with the French and the Catholic princes of the Empire. The two sets of talks were to open in May 1642.

Ferdinand and his Spanish cousins agreed, but at the same time Ferdinand recognised that if he could secure internal peace in the Empire he would be in a stronger position to negotiate with the foreign powers. To this end he proposed a Deputationstag to meet at Frankfurt in the hope of getting his Imperial subordinates to reach a compromise with him.

Neither of these initiatives stopped the fighting. The Swedes under Torstensson began an offensive in the spring of 1642 which had great success at first. They defeated the Saxons at Schweidnitz, then marched south into Moravia and captured its capital Olmütz in June. Torstensson fortified the city, making it the pivot of Swedish operations in the region. It served this purpose for the rest of the war.

Olmütz was too close to Vienna for Ferdinand not to act. He put Piccolomini and Archduke Leopold in charge of a large force and sent it against the Swedes. Torstensson fell back to Breitenfeld outside Leipzig, drawing his pursuers to the plain where the first Battle of Breitenfeld had been fought. Here he suddenly turned and attacked the Imperial troops as they were trying to arrange themselves in battle order. His victory was decisive; half the Imperial army was destroyed, and Leipzig itself yielded to a brief siege.

Among the reasons why the dynamic of events in central Europe was changing was that players on the margins of Europe were changing too, in ways that variously weakened them or made them more introverted relative to those wider affairs. Portugal became permanently independent of Spain in 1640, and in that year too the celebrated Long Parliament convened in London, shortly to set to work on limiting the powers of Charles I, whose refusal to accept any limitations precipitated the English Civil War. Indeed England had been distracted for some time; Charles had been frustrated in his attempts to raise funds for his wars in Scotland, and had dissolved the Long Parliament's forerunner as a result. His was an unhappy pair of kingdoms, shortly to be unhappier yet.

In the view of Christopher Hill and other historians, the activities of England's Long Parliament set a course for reform and liberty that eventually blossomed in the French, American and subsequent democratic revolutions of the Western world. In this respect the events in Westminster in 1640 and 1641 were as consequential for global history as the first proposals for the Westphalian peace process.[2]

There were other significant events in these war-logged years. The *Meditations on First Philosophy* by René Descartes was published, and has never been out of print since. He cannot have imagined that this book would sustain his reputation, chiefly as a result of being almost the first classic text of philosophy put into the hands of undergraduate students of the subject on every continent of the planet. The book he regarded as his most important contribution was his *Principles of Philosophy*, by 'philosophy' meaning physics; in it he advanced a theory of the structure and properties of the material universe which, despite some French patriotism, was rapidly superseded by the theories of Newton in less than half a century.

Focus on Europe and its wars and internecine intellectual struggles, even if the focus includes the far-flung parts of the world that Europe was changing through its trading and colonising activities, can make one forget events elsewhere. The Yuan dynasty was in its final years in China, the auguries of its loss of the Mandate of Heaven including earthquakes, epidemics, floods and famines, these in turn prompting civil unrest and uprisings. The great epidemic of 1641 which raced along the Grand Canal from Beijing through the provinces of Hebei and Shanxi, killing up to half the population in some of the crowded cities along the route, was the worst of these occurrences. According to J. N. Hays' history of epidemics, the one that afflicted the Chinese in that year was probably not bubonic plague, but a variety of coincident epidemic diseases which seized on a population already weakened by famine, and devastated it. Smallpox, anthrax or other fungal diseases, malaria, typhus, dysentery and influenza in combinations of several at a time would easily have arisen in the crowded living conditions and close proximity to animals which frequently shared the humans' living quarters.[3]

Richelieu died on 4 December 1642, to be succeeded by Cardinal Mazarin.[4] The disruption of a change of government in France was minimised by two factors, one being that Mazarin shared Richelieu's views about France's war aims, while the other was that the proposed opening of the Westphalian peace conferences had perforce been delayed until the following year, 1643, because of internal disputes in the Empire. The delay made a material difference to the eventual conduct of the conferences, because Louis XIII of France died in May 1643, leaving his infant son Louis XIV under the regency of Anne of Austria. She was of course a Habsburg, and sister to Philip IV of Spain. The immediate expectation was that France would now adopt a more pro-Imperial stance, but this hope was based on a misunderstanding of Anne, who was intent on protecting her infant son's interests – which meant the interests of France – above all else. She therefore allowed Mazarin to continue Richelieu's anti-Imperial policy unchanged.

This meant pursuing the war as before; and as before French arms met with mixed success. After advancing into Swabia and capturing Rottweil, in December 1643 the French army lost the city to a vigorous counter-campaign by the Bavarians, who had heavily defeated France's allies, the late Bernhard's Saxe-Weimar troops, at the Battle of Tuttlingen in the previous month. The French forces had to retreat in much depleted condition to the Rhine. Repeated Bavarian assaults resulted in further French losses, among them Breisgau; well into 1644 the Bavarians had the upper hand. But determined efforts by France's general, Henri vicomte de Turenne, to retake Freiburg were successful and reversed the tide. In August the Bavarian army withdrew to its bases, and the French advanced after them into the Lower Palatinate and invested all of its cities except Frankenthal.

Such was the oscillating nature of campaigns fought by armies living off the land in campaigning seasons – from spring to autumn, when roads and countryside were just about passable, and outdoor living conditions just about tolerable.

In the north the Swedes had been distracted from their successes of 1642 by the outbreak of the old hostilities between Sweden and Denmark. Oxenstierna learned that Christian IV of Denmark had opened secret negotiations with Ferdinand III. He decided on a pre-emptive strike. In September 1643 he ordered the Swedish army to abandon the siege of Brno in Moravia and cross Germany to Jutland as rapidly as it could. At the same time a Dutch fleet – the Dutch were allied to the Swedes – attacked the Danish peninsula and ports, and Oxenstierna mounted raids against Danish island territories close to Sweden's shores. Christian asked Ferdinand III for help, and an Imperial force was dispatched from Bohemia – but too late; with Jutland lost and the Swedes and Dutch pressing hard, Christian sued for an armistice. It was signed in November 1644. It was another humiliation for a ruler whose judgment and capacities were severely tested by the exigencies of the time, and always found wanting.

In the east a revolt by the Hungarians under Stephen Rákóczy added to the difficulties of the Imperial side. Ferdinand III had to recall forces from the Danish front to reinforce his troops in Austria, and Sweden's Torstensson followed them, harrying them as they passed through country stripped too bare by years of war to provide food and supplies for the troops and their horses. By the time the Imperial forces reached Bohemia they were a mere tenth of the size they had been in the north. This compelled Ferdinand to negotiate with Rákóczy, at the same time successfully persuading the Ottomans to withdraw their support from him. But Torstensson, keen to recover the areas of Bohemia and Moravia he had left in order to participate in the Danish actions, pushed on and captured Budweis and Pilsen. As he approached Tábor he was met by a force that Ferdinand had managed to assemble with Maximilian's help, commanded by Count Götz. The Swedish and Imperial armies clashed at Jankau near Tábor on 6 March 1645; at the end of a day of bitter fighting the Imperial army was destroyed, having lost half its men, among them Götz himself.

Vienna was only fifty kilometres away, with no defences. Ferdinand III fled the city, taking refuge in Graz. Rákóczy broke his agreement with the Emperor and resumed hostilities. At this perilous moment for Ferdinand the Habsburg heartlands looked as if they were about to be conquered. But Torstensson, perhaps thinking he had time to secure Moravia before finishing off Ferdinand, turned his attention to Brno and besieged it. By August 1645 it was clear that the siege was going to fail, so Torstensson decided to attack Vienna after all. By this time the Imperial forces had regathered, and Archduke Leopold Wilhelm was powerfully in command of the Danube line. Torstensson saw that he had lost his chance and took his army back into Bohemia; the threat to Vienna was over, and the great opportunity gained by Torstensson at Jankau was lost.

When the French received news of the Swedish victory at Jankau they attacked Bavaria. Turenne was confident that the Bavarians were now too weak to offer resistance, and accordingly divided his forces as if to occupy rather than fight. At Mergentheim his main corps was given a bloody nose by Bavarian troops under Graf von Werth, and had to withdraw to Hesse-Cassel. The army of Hesse-Cassel's redoubtable ruler, Amalie-Elisabeth, together with a contingent of Swedish troops, joined

Turenne and the combined forces marched south again, outnumbering the Bavarians they met at Nördlingen on 3 August 1645 and there defeating them. The Bavarian general Franz von Mercy was killed in the battle, and Maximilian – left practically without resources – offered France separate peace terms.

The Swedish troops which had participated in the second Battle of Nördlingen now turned their attention to Saxony. Already devastated by the long war and the repeated marches of armies across its territories, it was again and further ravaged, having no defences. Johann-Georg surrendered, signing the Armistice of Kotzschenbrode on 31 August 1645 which gave the Swedes right of free passage through his dominions together with subsidies in money and supplies. Saxony was no longer part of the war.

The fighting did not altogether stall preparations for the Westphalian conferences. Mazarin sent two ambassadors, who arrived in Osnabrück in April 1644. History relates that the two – Abel Servien, the marquis de Sablé, and Claude, comte d'Avaux – loathed each other heartily, and spent more time conspiring to cause each other discomfiture than in representing France's interests. This did not much matter at the outset because all parties were in preliminary mode, wrangling over arrangements and protocols, jostling over precedence and who should sit where and what titles they should be addressed by. Opening lists of demands were not presented until December of that year, and even then they too were only preliminary.

Ferdinand's Deputationstag at Frankfurt was still meeting and had come to a compromise that had great significance for internal Imperial politics. It agreed that the Imperial Aulic Court should consist half of Protestants and half of Catholics, instead of one-third Protestants and two-thirds Catholics as hitherto. That was a major reform, and a promising one. The Aulic Court – the Reichshofrat – consisted of the Emperor's personal advisers, and was superior to the supreme court of justice in the Holy Roman Empire, the Reichskammergericht. The latter had been founded by Maximilian I in 1496, who added the Aulic Court in 1497 to serve as a counterbalance to the supreme court. Both survived until the dismantling of the Holy Roman Empire by

Napoleon in 1806. By the seventeenth century the members of the Reichskammergericht were all doctors of Roman law, and their remit was not just the usual supreme court business of appeals relating to crimes and violations of such civil liberties as Imperial subjects enjoyed, but also disputes between vassals of the Empire – for example, territorial disputes between electors and princes of states within the Empire – though these latter were often bitterly contentious and required the mediation of the Aulic Council for their resolution.

Even this, however, did not help to abbreviate the famous lengths of time that Reichskammergericht cases took to reach a verdict – in disputes between princes and electors some cases took hundreds of years, indeed some were still unresolved when Napoleon abolished the Empire. The principle that justice delayed is justice denied did not seem to apply in this laborious structure. The Aulic Council was located in the Emperor's palace in Vienna, while the Reichskammergericht met in Frankfurt or Worms, a mark of the two courts' respective roles: the Aulic Council's job was to advise the Emperor, the supreme court's task was to administer the law as independently of the Crown as it could.

At last, in June 1645, the French and Swedish ambassadors at the Westphalian conference began issuing their demands. The first was that the Empire should be returned to the *status quo ante*, the way things were before hostilities started in 1618, all lands returned to their original rulers or ruling houses (which would mean, among other things, return of the Palatinate to the family of Frederick V the Winter King), and a general amnesty. A significant demand was that questions of taxation, war and peace were to be decided by Imperial Diets, not by the Emperor alone; and the estates of the Empire were to have autonomy in making alliances among themselves and with foreign powers. France, Sweden and some of the small Protestant estates were to be compensated for the expenses of the war. The Swedes added a demand that Calvinists were to be recognised on the same footing as Lutherans.

After several months of deliberation Ferdinand III rejected these demands. His counter-proposals were in effect no more than an iteration of the Peace of Prague terms. In November he sent one of his closest advisers, Count Maximilian von Trauttmansdorff, to conduct the negotiations on his behalf, and bargaining began in earnest. Sweden now demanded sovereignty over Pomerania, Kammin, Wismar, part of Lusatia, and the bishoprics of Verden and Bremen, while France demanded all of Alsace, Breisgau, Sundgau and the fortress of Breisach. It also demanded that French troops be allowed to garrison Philippsburg.

Trauttmansdorff accepted the French demand for Alsace and a Philippsburg garrison, and a preliminary treaty to that effect was signed between France and the Empire in September 1646. The terms of the treaty were ambiguously couched, leaving it unclear whether the Empire had ceded sovereignty or just usufruct. For the time being the ambiguity was allowed to ride, in the interests of helping the peace talks make some progress. For even as they continued, so too did the fighting.

In the campaigning season of 1646 Imperial forces succeeded in dislodging the Swedes from Bohemia, only to displace them to Paderborn, which they captured. There the Swedes were joined by a French army under Turenne, and the combined force marched south, threatening Bavaria. This caught the Imperial forces off balance; the latter had been hoping to confront the Swedes in the region of Hesse-Cassel, but the Franco-Swedish army did not turn back to engage them, continuing south and thus cutting the Imperial force off from Bavaria, to the great alarm of Duke Maximilian. He urgently requested that the Imperial army should return, but it was too late; the Franco-Swedish troops invaded Bavaria and devastated every part of it other than Munich and Ingolstadt.

That was enough for Maximilian. He sued for peace, and on 15 March 1647 signed the Treaty of Ulm with Sweden and France, yielding garrison rights to their forces in most of Bavaria's cities. At this point France should have been in victorious mood, but the playful gods of war were still unsatisfied; at just this juncture the United Provinces of the Netherlands and Spain concluded a peace treaty after their eighty years of war, thus releasing Spanish forces in the southern Netherlands to turn their attention to France. Mazarin had to order Turenne to march quickly north to confront the threat, but the general's best troops – the Weimaraners who had been led by Bernhard of Saxe-Weimar – refused to fight outside the borders of the German world, and abandoned Turenne to ally themselves to the Swedes instead.

It was not just the Weimaraners who proved resistant to change. Ferdinand III hoped that he could persuade Bavaria's cavalry to join the Imperial army, but they refused. He needed them; the Swedes were on the move again, back towards Bohemia where they captured the city of Eger. It was with relief therefore that he received overtures from Maximilian of Bavaria, who now regretted the Treaty of Ulm given France's renewed difficulties with the Spanish. Maximilian accordingly returned to his alliance with Ferdinand, signing the Treaty of Pilsen with him in September 1647 and sending his army to join the Imperial troops in Bohemia.

These oscillations of alliance and treaty-breaking played a major part in prolonging the war. No one could blame Maximilian for breaking the Ulm treaty obligations when, in signing the Treaty of Münster with the Spanish on 30 January 1648, the Dutch were likewise in breach of their 1644 agreement with France not to make a separate peace with Spain.

The final campaigning season of the war began in March 1648 when French and Swedish forces combined to attack Bavaria yet again, determined to punish Maximilian. They defeated the Imperial and Bavarian forces at Zusmarshausen, and drove them beyond the River Inn. The Emperor asked Piccolomini to resume command of the Imperial troops – he had been with the Spanish forces in the Netherlands – and Piccolomini was able to stop the Franco-Swedish advance. But in the areas of Bavaria under their control the Franco-Swedish troops subjected the towns and countryside to vicious depredations, leaving swathes of damage to farms and villages.

While this was happening in Bavaria a small section of the Imperial army was fighting its way into Prague, having laid waste all the regions of Bohemia it passed through. With Swedish reinforcements promised, and stout resistance from the citizens of Prague, the Imperial force was in an exposed state. It was at that moment that the Peace of Westphalia was announced, all the main players suffering from a combination of war-weariness and anxiety: the Emperor was militarily hard-pressed, Mazarin was confronted by the Fronde rebellion in France, the Swedes had likewise had enough, wanting to conclude matters while the Empire was weak, and not wishing to risk waiting for another campaigning season before which Ferdinand III might again raise fresh forces.

Accordingly, the Treaties of Osnabrück and Münster, together constituting the Peace of Westphalia, were signed on 24 October 1648, and the war was over. There was no clear victor, though the French and Swedes were at that point on top and Ferdinand III and his allies on the bottom – and indeed they lost most under the terms of the treaties. Nevertheless their foes did not have a definitive enough grip to ensure that the Empire could not strike back, so they were just as keen for peace.[5]

A dominoes-game of land transfers was initiated by the treaties, with Sweden getting much of Pomerania and other north European territories, as it desired, and France getting Alsace. The son of the Winter King, Karl-Ludwig, got half the Palatinate back – while the other half, the Upper Palatinate, remained with Maximilian of Bavaria – and an eighth electorate was created so that he could have it. The constitutional structure of the Empire was further loosened and made incoherent by the grant of further liberties to the vassal princes. Sweden's demand for recognition of Calvinism was agreed, as was resecularisation of estates which had been returned to Catholicism during the war, with the proviso that no more secularisations of Catholic territories would occur. Money changed hands in multilateral arrangements.

Perhaps no one was completely happy with the various provisions of the treaties of Osnabrück and Münster, but the least happy was the Pope. Infuriated by the concessions to Protestantism and the losses to Catholicism he condemned the treaties as 'null, void, invalid, iniquitous, unjust, damnable, reprobate, inane, empty of meaning and effect for all time'.[6] A papal bull no longer had the effect it had had in medieval times; the blast from the Vatican changed nothing. But his condemnation is of great historical significance in this respect: it marks recognition that the divisions in western Christendom created by the Reformation were permanent. The Catholic aim of recovering all Europe for its version of Christianity had been defeated, and there was now no chance of it ever happening.

The Peace of Westphalia did not of course result in peace. Fighting continued among European states for the rest of the century and beyond, though each of the wars after 1648 was recognised by its combatants as being about something different from the preoccupations of the Thirty Years War. The real importance of Westphalia, apart from the end of Catholicism's hopes and with it the end of religion as a *casus belli* for Christianity, was the difference it made to Europe's understanding of the international and national orders thus created. The idea of sovereign states in whose internal business other states should not interfere was enshrined in the removal of powers from the Emperor and their vestiture in the governments of the separate states. The Holy Roman Emperors had attempted to assert a monarchical control over the Empire, but Westphalia created a federal alternative. There were about 300 princes in the Empire to whom power now devolved, and the Empire itself – because of the land grants to Sweden and France (whose border with the Empire was indefensible by the latter) – had shrunk by 40,000 square miles. But Austria, Bavaria and Brandenburg – soon to be Prussia – had been set on the path of growth as major European states by their liberation from the preceding Imperial arrangements.

As ever, the true meaning and nature of the Westphalian settlements is a matter of an entire scholarly industry. The standard view, that it created 'a society of states based on the principle of territorial sovereignty',[7] has by other scholars been dubbed a 'myth'.[8] The dispute seems fruitless; a glance at the map of Europe after 1648, and a survey of European history since, plus the increasing growth of nationalistic sentiment everywhere in the world thereafter (though especially from the nineteenth century), tells us that the treaties constituting the Peace of Westphalia made a profound difference to global history in the centuries that followed.

10

In the Ruins of Europe

THE THIRTY YEARS War was devastating. On some estimates one in every three German-speaking people died because of it. Some of the states lost as much as three-quarters of their populations, others a half. Overall figures for deaths directly attributable to the war vary widely, from 3,000,000 to 11,500,000.[1] Fighting, famine and disease were the causes; towns and countrysides were ravaged, many of them taking more than a century to recover. The Swedish armies alone are said to have been responsible for the destruction of 1,500 towns, nearly 2,000 villages and 2,000 castles. A principal reason for the devastation was the actions of marauding mercenary armies. 'Rape and pillage' is a mere phrase; the actuality it denotes is dire beyond telling. Refugees took disease with them as they flooded into neighbouring towns when their own towns were sacked. Typhus, dysentery and plague were the commonest diseases, but injuries suffered from beatings, rape and general atrocity exacted a toll besides.

The social and psychological effects took horrific turns also, as witness the increase in witch-hunts. The failure of crops, military defeat, pestilence and epidemic disease – the general suffering of the time – were often blamed as much on supernatural causes as on the depredations of mercenary troops. Purges, torture and mass burnings of witches occurred in many of the Empire's states, particularly in the first phase of the war, as noted earlier; they followed the routes of the Imperial armies' successes, and had an explicit sectarian aspect, Catholics treating Protestants as a source of satanic influence.

The economic and social dislocation of the war, worse in some areas where destruction was near complete, was exacerbated by the huge expense incurred by the raising and maintaining of armies. The tax burden on peasants and working people was onerous, and occasioned frequent riots.

One of the sources of contention about the aftermath of Westphalia is whether it shifted the focus of politics from the religious to the secular, with decreased influence of the former not just on national but on international politics. A cursory view across the landscape of the centuries since Westphalia would suggest that this is emphatically so; the contentions profession of history being what it is, naturally this has been challenged.[2]

What was the world like in the years 1648–50, in the immediate aftermath of the war? A few indicators hint at the changes that had taken place independently of its direct results. Estimates of population say that by then Istanbul had became the largest city in the world, taking over from Beijing. The English Civil War was coming to an end, with defeats of Charles II at the battles of Inverkeithing in Scotland and Worcester in England. Jews were allowed to return to France and England. René Descartes died in Sweden in 1650, where he had briefly been Queen Christina's Court philosopher. Nell Gwyn, future mistress of Charles II, was born in that year, and so was John Churchill, first Duke of Marlborough, and William III of Orange, future King of England. All these events point forward, not just to the later part of the seventeenth century but to the century beyond. When one thinks of the War of Spanish Succession in the years 1701–13 – the first world war, if one thinks of how many international powers were involved in it, and how widespread the fighting was – and Churchill's part in it, one is thinking of a different history altogether; the beginning of the eighteenth century is so utterly unlike the end of the sixteenth as to prove every point about the transformative nature of the century between.

But many of the elements of that new history were shaped by events at the end of the Thirty Years War. For one major example, Louis XIV of France was twelve years of age in 1650, shaken by the danger to his mother and himself in the revolution of 1648 known as the Fronde, and by the experiences of his uncle Charles I and first cousin Charles II of England in being ousted by Parliament. When he attained his majority he was determined that matters would be very different under his rule, and so it proved.

Who now remembers that Charles II sold the town of Dunkirk to Louis XIV for £400,000 in 1662, having no use for it any longer, and needing money? People talk of Mary I having the name 'Calais' inscribed on her heart after its loss in 1558, but Calais was not the last English possession in continental Europe, and one wonders what sentiment would be in Britain today if parts of the continent still belonged to it. In any event, such a sale would have been unthinkable before the Thirty Years War. That is another measure of the war's impact on the mind of the time.

11

The Maritime Conflicts

WITHOUT DIMINISHING EITHER the importance of, or the suffering in, the other wars of the war-riven seventeenth century, it can plausibly be said that the Anglo-Dutch Wars were second only to the Thirty Years War in real significance for subsequent history. The two maritime nations were increasing their overseas trade and dominions, and were in serious competition therefore. Hypothetical speculation about what character the world might have had after the seventeenth century if the Dutch had won decisively, or if the House of Orange had not provided a King of England in William III, can take any number of shapes: but the fact is that the series of wars, if not all the battles fought in them, eventually benefited the English side of the argument, with what followed being – as they say – history.

The first Anglo-Dutch War of 1652–4 was not desired by either side, and given the similarity between the two countries should not have occurred at all. Both had relatively new governments – that of De Witt in the United Provinces and Cromwell in England – both were Protestant, both were Republican, both were on their guard against the dynasties they had overthrown, both were supported by merchants and traders eager to expand overseas and thus to profit from the fading influence of Portugal and Spain. Indeed, Cromwell was keen not merely to form an alliance with the Dutch, but even contemplated seeking a union of the two countries.

His somewhat idealistic aspirations on the political and foreign relations front did not accord with the pragmatism of the commercial interest in the Rump Parliament, which succeeded in getting a Navigation Act passed, designed to stop the Dutch trading with English colonies. The Act, which provided that only English ships could carry goods imported into England from abroad, was the manifestation of something that proved much more enduring and formidable than the Cromwellian interregnum itself, namely, the determination of English businessmen to get and keep as much world trade for themselves as they could. They were conscious of the success of the Dutch in exploiting Portuguese weakness in the East Indies, where the Dutch now controlled the lucrative spice trade. Dutch shipbuilding was also a major factor, producing good vessels cheaply and supporting the rapid growth of Dutch seaborne commerce everywhere from the Baltic to the Far East.

Charles I had attempted the perilous task in 1631 of making a secret treaty with Spain intended to limit Dutch sea-power, even as England was supposed to be on the Protestant side of the war. The chief reason that England did too little at first in contesting the rise of Dutch maritime influence was the Civil War; distracted, impoverished and weakened by that conflict, England was for a time not in a good enough position at sea to keep pace with Dutch advances.

Dutch reaction to the Navigation Act of 1652 was exacerbated by other irritations. These included Cromwell's requirement that a levy be paid for herring caught within thirty miles (fifty kilometres) of England's shores, and the demand that shipping in the Channel must salute English warships. The immediate trigger for fighting was an order by the commander of the Dutch war fleet, Martin Tromp, to refuse to salute the English navy. The response of the commander of the English navy, Robert Blake, was to open fire on the Dutch fleet. Over the next few months a series of battles followed, the first two of which were won by Blake, the third by Tromp. In the following year, 1653, the Dutch fared worse. At the Battle of Portland – sometimes called the Three Days' Battle – Tromp lost twelve warships and fifty merchantmen. Admiral Blake was wounded in the action, which gave him time while recuperating to meditate on the encounters with the Dutch and to write his celebrated *Fighting Instructions*, a major advance in the science of naval warfare. At the Battle of the Gabbard in June 1653 the commander of the English ships, George Monk, put the *Instructions* into practice, and achieved a decisive victory; at the following Battle of Scheveningen the English crushed the Dutch fleet. Tromp died in that battle.

The war ended with England having destroyed much of the Dutch navy and holding a thousand Dutch merchantmen captive.

The second Anglo-Dutch War began much further from either country's home shores. Dutch slavers were undercutting the price of English-shipped slaves from West Africa, so a squadron of English warships attacked and captured two West African ports used by the Dutch. That happened in 1663; the following year the English captured New Amsterdam on the east coast of America and renamed it New York. This second incident precipitated a full naval war which lasted until 1667. In 1665 the Duke of York (later James II) led a naval force to victory over the Dutch off Lowestoft in the North Sea. In return the Dutch engaged the English fleet in the grim Four Days' Battle which, though it ended in far greater losses for the English – including capture by the Dutch of the great ship *Prince Royal* – was claimed by the English as a victory because the Dutch fleet withdrew first. The English achieved a number of further victories, including the Sack of Terschelling, but when Charles II was obliged to cut back on naval expenditure because of his poor management of his country's economy – which had been further hit by the outbreak of plague in 1665 and the Fire of London in 1666 – the Dutch took their chances. In an audacious attack they sailed up the Thames into the Medway and destroyed the English fleet at anchor there, towing away England's two most prized ships, the *Unity* and the *Royal Charles*.

While these hostilities were occurring on the European side of the Atlantic, the celebrated buccaneer Henry Morgan was enjoying himself in the Caribbean. His adventures continued after the war ended, laying him open to charges of piracy, which resulted in a spell in prison when he was remanded back to England in chains. But when the third

Anglo-Dutch War broke out in 1672 he was given a knighthood and sent back to the Caribbean as Governor of Jamaica. His story exemplifies the continuation of the often semi-private, semi-autonomous nature of the seventeenth-century conflicts that were officially regarded as wars between states.

It is well to remember that these tussles between the English and Dutch had much independent background to them. For Anglophone readers the often murderous and introverted obsessions of the people in the British isles are familiar; yet by regicide and civil war they had brought the future forward at a faster pace than anywhere else in the world at that point. With hindsight it is clear that the new political thinking in England – discussed later in these pages – and its contest between people and monarchy had laid the foundation for what happened in the great revolutions of the eighteenth century and their own sequels.

But the Dutch too had a strenuous and formative legacy; they had endured eighty years of war with Spain to secure their full independence, and their navigators and merchants had been determinedly successful in making their nation prosperous. Wealth flowed like a river from the seas into the canals of its cities; the expression 'the Dutch Golden Age' scarcely does justice to this period in their history. The ebullience of its art is well known; less well known is the fact that it was the southern Netherlands of Brabant and Flanders, for long more urbanised and industrialised than the United Provinces when these latter broke away, that had been the rich part in the late sixteenth century, having led Europe economically – mainly because of its textile industry – since late medieval times. But the industry of the northern provinces in fishing, agriculture and shipping provided the basis for expansion into a great maritime trading empire in the seventeenth century, so when the United Provinces unilaterally split from Spain, the exodus of Protestants from the southern Netherlands to the northern maritime provinces provided an impetus of experience and enterprise that spurred yet further the northern provinces' energies.

The shipping trade of the northern provinces had carried salt, cloth, brick and tiles, and brought slaughtered meats from Denmark and timber and grain from the Baltic, grain transportation being the major source of the United Provinces' revenue in their early years. The Dutch fishermen in the North Sea caught over 30,000 metric tons of herring a year, outpacing Scottish fishing by a substantial margin. Protestant weavers who fled to the northern provinces after the split between north and south in the 1580s soon made Leiden one of the premier industrial cities of Europe.

But once the expansion of maritime trade and colonisations began, the Dutch Golden Age truly flowered. From sugar to spices the Dutch were in control of lucrative commodities; their principal markets in the Baltic – the Hanseatic cities, conduits to and from the interior of Europe – absorbed a large part of what they brought back from around the world. Until shortly beforehand the spice trade had relied on the laborious overland routes of the Middle East, but European navigation by the three sailing nations – Portugal, the Netherlands and England – had circumvented Arabia and the Ottomans, and the Netherlands were at the outset the most successful and vigorous of the three.

Travellers and exiles in the Dutch Republic, as it became, were impressed by the order, cleanliness, comfort and tolerance of its people and cities. Apart from the unpleasant matter of the Gomarists and Arminians in the early decades of the century, the northern Netherlands was an oasis of internal peace in those troubled times. But its success prompted both rivalry – as with the English – and covetousness – as with the French, whose Louis XIV doubtless often reflected on what a milch cow the Netherlands would be as part of a larger continental empire.

Somewhat for the reason just mentioned, the third Anglo-Dutch War was not of a piece with the first two. France was at war with the Dutch, and Charles II saw a chance; an alliance between England and France against the Netherlands, and English naval support for a French invasion, was intended to dent the Dutch commercial threat in the wider world. But the Dutch had a superb naval commander in Michiel de Ruyter and a canny military tactician in William of Orange, against whom the combined efforts of the two powerful states proved unavailing. It was in this war that the Dutch famously flooded the polders around Amsterdam to halt a French invasion; it was in this war too that the Dutch entered an alliance with their old enemies the Spanish, because the Spanish were at odds with the French: 'the enemy of my enemy is my friend' indeed.

Anti-war sentiment in England was strong, however, because there were suspicions that Charles II was using the war as a stalking-horse for Roman Catholicism to get back into England. The futility and stalemate of the war gave anti-war advocates an upper hand. The Treaty of Westminster in 1674 marked the end of hostilities. It included among its terms the requirement that the Dutch Republic pay England an indemnity, and that William of Orange marry Mary, Charles II's daughter (and William's cousin; he was Charles II's nephew). Fourteen years later William of Orange was King of England, having fought against his other cousin, Mary's brother, the man who became James II and whose vacant throne William took. While James was Duke of York he was an effective naval commander, and had led English ships to several victories over the Dutch. That is why New York, captured from the Dutch in 1664, was named after him.

It has been astutely pointed out that historians of England are prone to neglect the Anglo-Dutch Wars, relegating them to a position of relative insignificance in the march of English and then British naval power in the centuries after the seventeenth century.[1] But the fact that their overall outcome was to establish England as the dominant commercial global power has a meaning that cannot be ignored. These wars were fought in the interests of a class of men in England who had risen to influence in the Civil War – middle-class commercially minded men, the men (I am using the male term advisedly) whose triumph was completed by the constitutional settlement of the 'Glorious Revolution' in the 1680s when Parliament, their instrument, became supreme. The model of that Parliament, the political principles which justified its nature and powers (see the discussion of Locke in Chapter 19 below), and the central importance to civic life of the interests of the commercial middle classes, were exported to a world-wide empire policed by naval supremacy, an empire that was the chief world power for a large part of the next three centuries. The acorn from which this oak grew was the capturing of an unrivalled position at sea. In the Dutch Golden Age the fleets and seamanship of the Dutch were as good as and (from the English point of view) at times – and too often – better than those of the English. But the outcome of these wars, though it was not the result of obliterating naval victories as such, was to allow British sea-power to surpass all contenders.

In the nineteenth century the British navy and the *Pax Britannica* it imposed was predicated on the concept of the 'two-power standard', which is the measure of how great British maritime supremacy had become. The two-power standard embodied the idea that the British navy had to be big enough and powerful enough to beat not just the next most powerful navy in the world, but the *next two* most powerful navies in the world *combined*. The rise to this pre-eminence, the ability to project force anywhere in the world at will, is explicitly attributed by maritime historian Glen O'Hara to the Anglo-Dutch Wars. His discussion 'traces the rise of [English then British] naval dominance to the mid-seventeenth century, a time of ideological and economic disputation with the Dutch Republic that ended in three wars and that helped put England on the road to maritime supremacy'.[2]

This is why in every continent today there are institutions, political practices, attitudes to the administration of law, education systems, even games and sports such as cricket and rugby, which are the residues and deposits of what, quite literally in British ships, was carried from the small islands off the west coast of Europe to large parts of the rest of the world from the seventeenth century onwards. This is not a chest-beating remark, though there are British historians (and politicians) today who cannot forget the greatness – nor remember the bad aspects of it too! – that British naval supremacy and determined commercialism together achieved. It is just a statement of fact. And it is a fact that is one of the legacies of the seventeenth century, and specifically of this series of naval wars that were relatively minor in themselves but had a huge consequence.

Taken together, then, the Thirty Years War and the Anglo-Dutch naval wars, chief among all the conflicts of the century, have a role in the epoch under consideration that equals that of the intellectual advances happening at the same time. The wars and the ideas connect in many ways, directly and otherwise. One of the direct ways is that the wars permanently freed large parts of Europe from the attempted hegemony over thought and enquiry of the Roman Catholic Church. Another direct link is the interplay of science and technology in the development of weapons, and of the effect of war on economies; see the final sections of Chapter 18 below. Another unexpected, indirect but important link is the topic of the next chapter.

PART III

THE CUMULATION OF IDEAS

12

The Intelligencers

THE WARS OF the seventeenth century were horribly destructive of lives and property, as we have seen, and the burden laid on people over whom armies trampled, seeking food and lodging, horses, wagons, recruits – and likewise women to rape and valuables to steal – was immense. It has been said that the German-speaking parts of Europe suffered as much devastation as the Third Reich in the Second World War. The figure attached to those who, in the Holy Roman Empire, died in direct and indirect ways attributable to the Thirty Years War, is, again as mentioned, one out of every three people. As a measure of the wreckage to lives, land and material welfare in central Europe, that is a tragic number.

Yet, alas, times of disruption and destruction are also times of opportunity for some; the bleak saying 'it is an ill wind that blows no one any good' reminds one that bad times are good for those who can profit from them. Yet it is not just a matter of who might profit: there are also genuine opportunities – for new ideas, for the breaking down of barriers that had prevented exchanges of ideas beforehand, and the fresh inspirations that such exchanges bring. This happened in the unsettled condition of Europe in the seventeenth century, aided by the happy accident that the means of communication – chiefly: the sending and receiving of letters – was not harmed but in fact enabled by the greater uncertainty of the time.

To make sense of this aspect of the seventeenth century requires lifting its floorboards to peer beneath. Somewhat unexpected aspects come to light, such as the role of a French Minim monk, a Polish-German war-refugee, and the story of postal services. These latter play a significant part in what made the intellectual debate of the seventeenth century flourish. Without them the role of 'intelligencers' such as Mersenne, Hartlib and others, collecting and resending correspondence at the hubs of postal networks of enquirers, could not have existed.

The significance of Mersenne to the intellectual history of the seventeenth century has not been properly acknowledged.[1] Histories of mathematics remember him for his contributions to geometry and the study of prime numbers, histories of musical theory remember him for his work on oscillating strings, and studies of Descartes cite him as the correspondent who kept the philosopher in touch with friends and rivals during his most creative years. Those years were lived by Descartes in privacy (actually, for much of the time, in secrecy) in the Netherlands; his correspondence with Mersenne was a necessity for him. But Mersenne's significance is greater than that. To employ a wholly anachronistic metaphor which nevertheless does not stretch matters, he – as with others of the intelligencers who played a similar role – can be described as the seventeenth century's closest thing to an internet server, in a way to be demonstrated below.

Mersenne was born in 1588 at Oizé in the north-western region of France then called Maine (divided during the French Revolution into the now existing departments of Sarthe and Mayenne). His family were poor peasants, but the intellectual gifts he manifested early in life gave him the chance of an education. He studied locally at first, then at the nearby newly established Jesuit college of La Flèche, then the best school in France.

After completing his education in Paris at the Collège Royal de France and the Sorbonne, Mersenne entered the Order of Minims, founded in 1436 by St Francis of Paola. The order still exists today in rump, but in the early seventeenth century it was flourishing. It is a mendicant order of friars, contemplative nuns and lay persons who attempt to live its discipline of simplicity, poverty and veganism. The name 'Minim' derives from Italian *minimo* meaning 'least' or 'smallest', St Francis of Paola having described himself as *il minimo dei minimi*, the 'least of the least' as a poor hermit and devotee of St Francis of Assisi. In addition to the usual three monastic vows of chastity, poverty and obedience, the Minims adopt a 'Lenten' diet excluding all meat and dairy products except in case of illness, and they dedicate themselves to contemplation and study.

The Minims' simplicity of life and devotion to scholarship is what attracted Mersenne. He entered the order in July 1611 and was ordained to the priesthood in 1612. After three years teaching philosophy and theology at a monastery in Nevers he returned to Paris, remaining at the Place Royale monastery with only a few forays abroad until his death in 1648.

Although his interests lay principally in mathematics and musical theory, Mersenne's first published works were attacks on scepticism and atheism: *L'Usage de la raison* and *L'Analyse de la vie spirituelle.* His first major work was *Quaestiones Celeberrimae in Genesim*, published in 1623. Ostensibly a commentary on the Bible's Book of Genesis, it is in major part a sustained attack on magic, cabalism, astrology and other like 'arts', and forms part of the important moment in the history of ideas when the transition from thought's obeisance to the demands of religious orthodoxy passed through a period of inflated hopes for mystical or magical short-cuts to the universe's secrets (and therefore of the means to transmute base metals into gold, to secure immortality or at least longevity and eternal youth, and the like) – and thence to the triumph of the more accurate methods of mathematics and empirical enquiry which have given rise to today's sciences. Mersenne's attack on magic, Cabala and the rest was of a piece with the efforts by Bacon and Descartes to distinguish, each in his own way, science from those magical forms of thinking, by describing and enjoining methodologies better destined to arrive at knowledge. Of this important matter, and Mersenne's part in it, more in the next chapter.

It's a telling fact about Mersenne's character that he began as a staunch defender of the Aristotelianism attacked by Descartes and other leaders of the seventeenth-century intellectual revolution, but very soon joined the ranks of Aristotelianism's critics when he had learned more about their reasons. Likewise in the early 1620s he was a severe critic of

Galileo, whose views he said should be condemned; within a decade he was one of Galileo's chief supporters, conveying news of the scientist's work to other savants in Europe.

Perhaps Mersenne's chief technical contributions to science are those included in his *Traité de l'harmonie universelle*, published in 1637. In this book, apart from introducing major improvements to the design of mirrors for use in reflecting telescopes, he stated what are known as 'Mersenne's Laws' describing the oscillation frequency of a taut string. The ancients knew that the frequency of a taut string is inversely proportional to its length, but Mersenne noted further that the frequency is inversely proportional also to the square root of the stretching force, and to the square root of the mass per unit length. The practical application of these insights relates to the construction and operation of stringed instruments such as violins, harps and pianos. They all require that the tension force of the component strings has to be maintained at the right level to yield the correct pitch, and Mersenne's Laws explain the science of why lower-pitched strings are thicker and require less tension, while higher-pitched strings are thinner, require more tension, and can be shorter.

He also made empirical tests of Galileo's law of motion for falling bodies, and enquired into the principles of the barometer, in the course of which he discovered that the density of air is about one-nineteenth that of water. It is quite likely Mersenne who suggested to Pascal, Roberval, Périer and others the experiment soon afterwards carried out on the Puy de Dôme volcano to see whether the height of the mercury column in a barometer is determined solely by air pressure.

Mersenne is remembered by mathematicians for his work on the curved line known as the cycloid – an example is the figure traced by a point on a rolling wheel as it moves along – and especially on prime numbers and a related application of them now made to computing and cryptography.

Prime numbers – numbers that are divisible without remainder only by themselves and one (all other numbers are called 'composite') – have always been a mystery and a fascination to those interested in numbers as such. The innocuous description of prime numbers just given disguises their extraordinary significance in the number universe and indeed the physical universe (for a striking example of this latter: cicadas of the genus *Magicicada* only emerge from their grub stage, lived underground, every seven, thirteen or seventeen years, each of these numbers being prime; entomologists surmise that this is to protect them from predators which would co-evolve to feed on them if they emerged from underground at more regular intervals). Mersenne wished to find a formula for generating all primes, and although he did not find a wholly general device for doing this, the formula he proposed yields a sequence with interesting and still puzzling properties, and their role in number theory (and latterly in cryptography) makes them a target of much study, not least by the Great Internet Mersenne Prime Search or GIMPS conducted by 'distributed computing' – linking millions of personal computers – to hunt for them. To date fewer than fifty have been found, and the first sequence claimed by Mersenne himself contained errors; but in the search for ever greater cryptographic security a Mersenne prime whose period is known as the 'Mersenne twister' has become a standard random number generator.

This interest in number theory was occasioned by Mersenne's editorial work on the mathematical treatises of the ancients, among them Euclid, Apollonius and Archimedes. His wide range of interests, his intellectual gifts, his generosity and encouragement to others, his dedication to the cause of science, and his evident personal charm which attracted and kept together a large and disparate group of sometimes prickly clever people make him a key figure in the seventeenth-century story.

The role Mersenne played was described above as a kind of one-man human internet server. The simile is apt. He was the recipient of letters from almost all the great savants of the day, which he then multiply copied and disseminated to spread news, opinions, discoveries and conjectures around Europe. Copies of his correspondence were available in his lodgings for any visitor to read, and as Paris was a major intellectual centre, many came to him as to a library to get news of the latest scientific ideas. The reputations of some of the century's leading minds – Hobbes, Descartes, Gassendi – were created by Mersenne in this way. Thomas Hobbes became famous long before he published a book as a result of the esteem in which he was held by Parisian intellectuals who read his letters in Mersenne's lodgings. The same was true of Descartes; Mersenne had in effect made him famous through their correspondence well before the appearance of the philosopher's first publication, the *Discourse on Method*. Likewise Descartes would not have remained so closely in touch with the course of debate in the period between the late 1620s and the end of Mersenne's life (in 1648) without this invaluable relationship, because – for reasons one can speculate about[2] – he lived in near-exilic private circumstances in the Netherlands for almost the whole period between 1628 and 1649, the year before his death.

It is pertinent and of interest to know the background to letter-writing and the post in Mersenne's time, and how it came to be so. The story is not an obvious one; in our age of instant electronic social media, letters are a very diminished form of communication. In the pre-email age, and despite the advent of the telephone, they were still the principal way to be in touch with those at a distance. Before the telephone this was even more emphatically the case; Victorians wrote several or more letters a day – and had them delivered that same day if they lived in a city.

In the seventeenth century the mails were not quite so frequent or convenient as in Victorian times, but letter-writing had long been re-established as a common means of communication – 're-established' because of course it had been common enough among educated Romans, but was lost with the near-total destruction of intellectual culture in the 'Dark Ages'.[3] A common practice of letter-writing requires a literate class, pens, ink, parchment or paper, and a postal service; it was only in late medieval times that this congeries of means started to be available once again, though in partial and stuttering fashion at first. Even so, as illustrated by the administrative affairs of Henry I of England (1068–1135), royal messengers carried an average of 4,500 official letters a year – meaning that an average of a dozen letters were being written and sent every day by the King and his ministers alone.

By the beginning of the fourteenth century a number of factors had come together to make letters a principal means of connecting the European world with itself. The needs of banking and commerce involved not just direct communication about orders, invoices, financial transactions, instructions on credit lines, and the like, but information; and letters about these things were typically written in vernacular tongues. The classical languages remained the resource of humanists and scholars as they communicated the fruits of their studies of antiquity and the recovery of texts, and debated matters of philosophy and theology. Politics and diplomacy, centralised military structures, tax raising, judicial functions and administration necessitated a professional class of notaries and secretaries and a reliable postal network for the sending and receiving of every kind of document.

By the end of the sixteenth century all the elements were copiously in place for a flourishing culture of letter-writing, abetted by two developments: the availability of inexpensive paper made from pulp – water-powered pulp mills were invented in Italy as early as the fourteenth century – and the widespread availability of printed books among which letter-writing manuals and compilations of models of classical and rhetoric-based epistolary styles abounded.[4] Cicero was taken as the outstanding example of a letter-writer, and schoolboys were coached in his manner. Europe was criss-crossed by a variety of postal services from imperial and royal to local and private, the messengers of the official royal mails supplementing their incomes by taking personal letters for a fee on the side.

In the seventeenth century, accordingly, there existed a fully formed overlapping network of postal services, and it sustained an unofficial and informal *respublica litterarum* – a Republic of Letters largely based upon exchanges of letters – itself constituting an elaborate network of communication which was as important a way for savants to spread their ideas and secure their reputations as publishing them in book form. 'There were two ways in which the ideas of a philosopher could come to be known in this invisible republic,' writes Daniel Garber, using 'philosopher' in the then general sense of enquirer, thinker, scientist; 'one was of course the appearance in print of his ideas, but the other was through the remarkable network of letters which writers across the continent exchanged with one another. European scholars had always been busy letter-writers; Erasmus complained that he had to write more than ten a day' – and that was a century before the period under consideration.[5]

The seventeenth-century republic of letters was an 'international, unstructured' association for which the letter post was the practical bond. 'The posts across the continent were surprisingly efficient; it is very rare to find any seventeenth-century scholar complaining that a letter had been lost in the post, and the post between major cities was fairly quick (Paris to The Hague in a week or ten days, and Paris to London the same).'[6] The idea of there being an efficient, reliable and regular postal service in the seventeenth century seems an unlikely one perhaps, but its existence and character are fundamentals of the story. How this came to be the case is well illustrated by the history of the Taxis family.

In the early fourteenth century the couriers in the service of the Signoria of Venice were largely drawn from members of a single extended family which hailed from the Bergamo valley in the Italian Alps.[7] They derived their name, the Tassi, from their habit of fastening the pelt of a badger (*tasso*) to their horses' heads as a means of protection against the whip of tree branches and the risk of falling stones in the Alpine passes. The Tassi extended their expertise as messengers and postmen from Venice to Milan and Rome over the course of the next two centuries, at length appearing in the records of the Holy Roman Emperor Maximilian I at the end of the fifteenth century, in Innsbruck where Maximilian kept his court. There were three Tassi family members in Maximilian's service – they were there known by the German version of their name, Taxis – and one of them in particular, Baptista, was already rich and influential, having graduated from Chief Postmaster of the city to Imperial Court Postmaster. The phrase 'rich and influential' scarcely does him justice; he was in a position to make loans to the Emperor, who in gratitude ennobled him. Thenceforth the family were no less than (and in time much more than merely) 'von Taxis'.

There were soon von Taxis in a number of imperial cities, including Vienna. Although they were officially carriers of imperial mail, they also took private commissions, and their wealth steadily increased. Another of the von Taxis at Innsbruck was Francesco or Franz, who served as private courier to Maximilian's son Philip, who on his father's behalf ruled over part of Spain, the Netherlands and Burgundy. Philip required a line of communications both swift and sure between his Spanish and Dutch dominions, and gave Franz von Taxis the task of establishing it. Franz offered to set up a full-blown postal service with Philip as his main customer, and Philip agreed. The resulting network linked Flanders, Paris, Castile, Vienna and Rome, and was based on a relay system in which horses and their riders were changed at each post. The mail pouches were sealed and the postmen carried a book known as a *Standenpass* or 'hour book' to record the time at which a mail pouch was handed over. The swiftness of the system is attested by the fact that it took a mere ten and a half days for the mail to get from Brussels to Rome in summer; in winter it took twelve days.

Franz von Taxis' service carried private mail also, and the logbooks show how voluminous that traffic was, and how quickly it grew. The mail routes were also the principal travel and commercial routes, and as the population of Europe doubled from 30 million to 60 million between the years 1500 and 1600, with growing literacy and trade alongside, the volume of mail rose steeply. It was expensive to send letters; a Taxis postman earned 8 gulden a month, out of which he had to keep his horse too, whereas it cost anything between 25 and 80 gulden to send a letter by the Taxis post, depending on distance.[8] The von Taxis accordingly became even richer as demand for their services burgeoned. And burgeon it did; in the Exchequer archives of England's Henry VIII are records of substantial payments to 'Master of the Posts Francis de Taxis' for mail services to France and Italy.[9] It is no surprise therefore that Henry VIII's celebrated portraitist, Hans Holbein, also painted Franz von Taxis' portrait.

Franz built himself a palace in Brussels, and when he died in 1517 he was buried in the city's church of Notre Dame de Sablon to which he had donated four magnificent tapestries, each worth 6,000 gulden, into one of which was woven his own portrait three times over.

So far had Franz enhanced the patrimony of his name and its trade that through the succeeding centuries the family went (mainly by purchase for large sums from indigent monarchs) from barons to counts to marquises to dukes and eventually to princes – different branches of the family, depending on the country they lived in, varying the name from von Taxis to de Tassi to di Tasso, and intermarrying with other great aristocratic families to yield combinations such as von Thurn und Taxis, de la Tour et Tassis, della Torre e Tassi, and magnificently resounding strings such as Prince Vicenz von Zapata und Taxis, Duke of Saponara, and Don Iñigo Vélez Ladrón de Guevara y Taxis. The basis of the family's vast wealth remained postal services, and the family itself evolved into something like a sovereign state with which actual states or their rulers entered into treaties; in 1844 France entered such a treaty with the Taxis, the signatory parties being respectively described as 'His Majesty the King of the French and His Most Serene Highness the Prince de la Tour and Taxis.'[10]

Bit by bit, as the Holy Roman Empire decayed through the wars of the seventeenth and eighteenth centuries and was given its deathblow by Napoleon at the beginning of the nineteenth, so the extent and power of the Taxis postal services declined. The last post for the Taxis was played when the Prussian state purchased the one remaining Taxis franchise for 3 million thaler in 1867 (perhaps about 8 million US dollars today). But by then the Taxis dynasty was well beyond mourning its commercial beginnings in the smell of leather and horse sweat; they were in different spheres altogether. In 1912 a German history of postal services was dedicated to 'His Highness Albert Maria Joseph Maximilian Lamoral, Ruling Prince of the House of Thurn and Taxis, Duke of Wörth and Donaustauf, Prince of Buchau, Prince of Krotoscyn, Princely Count of Friedberg-Scheu, Count of Valsassina and of Marchthal and Neunheim . . .' and so on 'for thirteen more lines of print'.[11]

It was not just the demand for postal services that underlay the aristocracy-engendering commercial success of the Taxis post in the period to the seventeenth century, but also the fact that the Holy Roman Emperors granted and renewed near-monopoly status for its operations in all their parts of Europe, and in 1615 made it a fief so that it was heritable by succeeding generations just as if it were land. It had of course functionally been a fief for a long time by then, and making the fact official was merely a recognition that the Taxis network was the blood and sinews of continental communications. In 1628 that network reached its apogee; more than 20,000 postmen in the Taxis blue and silver livery galloped between its relay stations from the Mediterranean to the North Sea, from the Atlantic coast to the Holy Roman Empire's precarious border with the Ottoman Empire.

One drawback of the Taxis post's close connection with the Empire was that as spying on the mails increased with the increasingly tense state of European affairs in the sixteenth and seventeenth centuries, so concerns about the security of the mails grew. Many of the Taxis relay stations had 'lodges' in them, staffed by Imperial agents tasked with scrutinising the mail pouches and opening any letters they regarded as suspicious.

By the seventeenth century, then, the Taxis system was extremely well established and flourishing, with an associated network of co-operative local services to carry mail into provincial nooks and corners. At the same time it had stimulated rivals, smaller services regarded as less accessible to spying, which made arrangements among themselves to carry each other's mails onward. Postal companies were also often passenger coach companies, the post sometimes coming first and sometimes the passenger service. The commercial viability of all these operations depended on reliability, which explains why there were so few complaints of lost letters.

Almost certainly, the savants of the seventeenth century used these smaller mail services for the bulk of their correspondence. They included town services, university messengers, private carriers, guilds, merchant groups, rich nobles with their own messengers who would deliver letters for savants living on their patronage, and the like. The Taxis network was not allowed to gain dominance in France because of French suspicion of the Habsburgs, so it was in France that one of the earliest state postal systems developed. That however was not until later in the seventeenth century, so the spider's-web of correspondence which had Mersenne at its centre chiefly consisted of the numerous smaller rivals to the Taxis post. In France the Holy Roman Emperor's grant of monopoly facilities to the Taxis did not apply, so whereas in Habsburg dominions no other postal service was allowed to operate by relay, in France there had long been such services. Louis XI (1461–83) is credited with having established a relay post in France, and there is an evocative entry dated 1480 in the town archives of Tours for a payment for torches 'to light the watch gathered every night at the drawbridge to admit the couriers called posts'.

It is against this background that we can understand the ease with which Mersenne became the centre of a republic of letters in both the figurative and literal senses of 'letters'. By being a *poste restante* and human internet server, he drew about him a group of some of the most distinguished minds of the century. He corresponded with – and in many cases personally knew and collaborated with – Descartes, Pascal, Pierre Petit, Gassendi, Beeckman, van Helmont, Roberval, de Peiresc, Hobbes, Giovanni Doni, Torricelli, Constantijn Huygens, Galileo and many others. It was indeed Mersenne who made Galileo's work more widely known outside Italy, just as he had made Descartes known across Europe. In 1635 he gave his circle of acquaintance a semi-formal institutionalisation as the Academia Parisiensis (Académie Parisienne; friends sometimes called it the Académie Mersenne) which had nearly 150 corresponding members, among them all the leading mathematicians, astronomers and philosophers of the day. It was in effect the embryo of the Académie des Sciences which Jean-Baptiste Colbert set up in 1666, and arguably also part of the inspiration for the Royal Society of London founded in 1660.

An example of Mersenne's role as a focal point for the republic of letters is afforded by Descartes' visit to Paris from his exile in the Netherlands in 1647. He stayed only for four months, but that was long enough for him to meet Pierre Gassendi, proponent of a version of an atomic theory of matter, Thomas Hobbes, author of the *Leviathan* published four years later, and Blaise Pascal, the mathematical prodigy. Pascal was close to Roberval and Fermat, with both of whom Descartes had clashed bitterly, so neither of the two expected to become friends, and this proved right. Descartes was curious about Pascal, though, because he had heard much about his mental powers, and had been struck by the genius of an essay that Pascal had written on conic sections at the age of sixteen. For at least that reason he welcomed the encounter.

Descartes met Hobbes and Gassendi at a dinner especially arranged by Mersenne to effect a rapprochement between the three, because the two men had been severely critical of ideas in the *Meditations*, their criticisms appearing in the 'Objections' which Descartes had openly invited, through Mersenne's good offices, from anyone interested enough to comment. Always sensitive to criticism, Descartes had been very annoyed by their objections, and he had formed the view, as he told Mersenne tartly, that Hobbes was profiting from the opportunity to criticise his *Meditations* as a way of promoting his own reputation. When the day of the dinner arrived Hobbes and Claude Clerselier were present along with Mersenne, but Gassendi was unable to attend because he was ill. When the dinner was over, therefore, the four men went to Gassendi's home to wish him well.

Mersenne was also instrumental in putting Descartes together with Blaise Pascal. At the time of Descartes' visit Pascal was aged twenty-one. Descartes had two meetings with him, during the first of which the young man was feverish and confined to bed. Roberval was there too, which irritated Descartes, who wished to talk with Pascal alone. Nevertheless Pascal showed Descartes the calculating machine he had constructed – not perhaps the first ever computer, for the Chinese abacus might count as such – but cleverly based on knitting-machine technology. When Descartes left to keep a luncheon appointment Roberval accompanied him; they both climbed into the coach Descartes had hired, and argued vigorously with each other as they crossed Paris.

This first meeting between Descartes and Pascal was recorded by the latter's sister Jacqueline, who commented dryly on the way it ended: 'Monsieur Descartes took [Roberval] away with him in a grand coach, where the two of them were all alone, insulting each other, but somewhat louder than here.'[12]

The next morning Descartes and Pascal met again, tête-à-tête, and were therefore able to talk uninterruptedly. Descartes urged his view of the plenum on Pascal, suggesting an experiment to settle the conflict between his theory and that of Torricelli, which invoked the concept of a vacuum to explain atmospheric pressure. This was the same debate to which Mersenne contributed, and which resulted in the Puy de Dôme experiment to resolve the question.

Mersenne was not of course alone in facilitating the intellectual intercourse of the continent. Another of the intelligencers was Samuel Hartlib (1600–62).[13] Like Mersenne he was the centre of a voluminous correspondence among European savants, and was the first to have the sobriquet 'intelligencer' applied to him, in fact by the compatriots of his adoptive land, England. He had been born at Elbing on the Baltic coast of the German-speaking part of Poland, and was educated at the Albertus University of Königsberg (the 'Albertina'). He was in effect a refugee from the Thirty Years War, for in 1628, when Imperial armies took up positions in the west of Poland and the threat of invasion from Sweden was growing, he chose to leave. He settled in England, perhaps drawn there because he had an English grandmother (who had once been the head of an English trading post at Elbing), studying briefly at Cambridge then unsuccessfully attempting to establish a school at Chichester in Sussex.

Despite the failure of this project he maintained an active and enduring interest in education and educational reform, under the influence of both Bacon and Comenius. John Milton dedicated his own tract *On Education* to Hartlib in 1644, having been encouraged by him to write it. Hartlib's most ambitious educational endeavour was the effort to set up an institute of advanced study on the model of Bacon's 'Solomon's House' as outlined in *The New Atlantis.* So large a project required public funding, which Hartlib failed to get. Nevertheless his campaigning on education was instrumental in persuading Cromwell to increase the number of elementary schools in England, and it also played a significant role in the founding of the short-lived New College at Durham, which was staffed largely by Hartlibians.

A number of distinguished men gathered round Hartlib in his efforts at educational reform – Milton and Kenelm Digby included – forming the nucleus of the 'Hartlib Circle' or 'Invisible College' which was a primary source of the Royal Society. He encouraged a group of gifted young men, Robert Boyle and William Petty among them, who were influenced by his belief that if knowledge is to be truly valuable it must have useful applications.

Hartlib's association with the Parliamentary cause in the Civil War led to his exclusion from the Royal Society when it was founded in 1660, because of course the Society was under the patronage of Charles II who had no time for rebel sympathisers. The pension Cromwell had given Hartlib was also therefore discontinued – altogether a poor reward for the contribution Hartlib had made to the development of the century's mind.

He also made significant contributions to social welfare thinking. With his close friend the Calvinist divine John Dury he set up the 'Office of Public Address', a semi-charitable project aimed in part at being a labour exchange and putting poor people (whether intellectuals or labourers) into contact with possible benefactors. It was also intended to be a clearing house for news of all kinds including scientific and philosophical developments, a point of contact for merchants from all over Europe, and a place at which new inventions, technologies and schemes could be demonstrated and discussed. Above all it aimed to promote education and entrepreneurship of all kinds, applying Hartlib's educational ideal of combining the practical and theoretical.

Hartlib was a polymath like Mersenne, but had even broader interests than the latter, among them agriculture (extolling crop rotation and the use of nitrogenous vegetables for increased soil fertility), fruit-farming and bee-keeping. His proposal for a glass beehive (the designs for it were provided by Christopher Wren) was one of the highlights of his book *The Reformed Commonwealth of Bees*. He took an active part in the political debates of the Civil War, urging religious toleration and publishing proposals to achieve it. So wide was the range of his interests that the diarist John Evelyn dubbed him 'Master of innumerable curiosities',[14] and it is unsurprising to find him discussing by letter with Henry Oldenburg clocks, perpetual-motion devices, lanterns, medical prescriptions, chemical formulae, agricultural machinery, and much besides.

A major contrast with Mersenne was Hartlib's interest in ideas drawn from alchemy – he read the alchemical literature with interest – and sympathetic medicine. He was indeed receptive to ideas from anywhere, including speculative and fanciful sources, though he was not an uncritical thinker and was always prepared to experiment. It is likely that he hastened his death by drinking sulphuric acid to see if it would dissolve the kidney stones that plagued him.

Like Mersenne, Hartlib occasionally travelled in pursuit of his intellectual interests, and in the course of a visit to the Netherlands in 1634 met Descartes at the house of Princess Elizabeth Stuart, the daughter of James I and 'Winter Queen' to the hapless Frederick of the Palatine.[15] As this shows, the circuit of letters and their writers was a constantly overlapping one.

When Hartlib died he left over 25,000 folios of correspondence and notes, including 4,250 letters from 400 different correspondents mainly but not exclusively in England, the Netherlands and France. The collection is now housed in the Sheffield University library, which has made it digitally available.[16] He accordingly furnishes another example of the way that the seventeenth-century revolution in thought was carried out: by a level of communication and an open exchange of ideas unprecedented since the Edict of Thessalonica – the *Cunctos Populos* – in 380 C.E. ordered all subjects of the Roman Empire to profess the faith of the bishops of Rome and Alexandria, thus making Christianity the Empire's sole official religion.

Over a thousand letters sent and received by Mersenne are extant, but these are almost certainly only a part of his correspondence. He was known to contemporaries as 'the Mailbox of Europe', which implies something about the volume of letters he handled, even if not as many as another of his fellow intelligencers whose full collection of letters survives: this was Nicolas-Claude de Peiresc (1580–1637), whose extant correspondence numbers close to 14,000 items.

Peiresc's sobriquet was 'the Prince of Erudition', high praise for anyone in the seventeenth century. He was an astronomer, collector and archaeologist; among his chief contributions to science were his telescopic identification of the Orion nebula, and his measurement of differences in the longitude of locations across Europe and around the Mediterranean Sea. By the precision with which he collated observations of the lunar eclipse of 28 August 1635 he was able to determine that the Mediterranean is a thousand kilometres shorter than had hitherto been thought. Among the extensive and varied collections kept at his home in Aix-en-Provence were a number of cultural treasures, including the Barberini ivory, now in the Louvre, and a copy of the Codex Luxemburgensis, itself a copy of an illuminated manuscript made in 354 CE known as the Calendar of Filocalus.

But his greatest contribution was the correspondence network he created. He is said once to have written forty-two letters in a single day. He had nearly 500 correspondents across Europe, among them Mersenne, Galileo, Tommaso Campanella and Pierre Gassendi.

Another of the scientific revolution's intelligencers was the mathematician and astronomer Ismaël Boulliau (1605–94), who left a collection of 5,000 letters dating from the period between the years 1632 and 1693. Born into a Calvinist family, Boulliau converted to Catholicism as a young man, and was ordained to the priesthood. With the brothers Jacques and Pierre Dupuy he helped to build the collections of the Royal Library in Paris. In 1667 he was elected a foreign associate of the Royal Society of London on the strength of his work on planetary motion, involving the 'conical hypothesis' relating to the planets' orbits, and his discovery of the inverse square law which states that an effect's intensity (e.g. the effect of the gravitational force, or of illumination) changes proportionally to the square of the distance between a given point and a source. This law, as applied to gravitation, is chiefly associated with Newton, for which reason Boulliau is described as the law's 'finder but not keeper'.

The Royal Society's first Secretary, Henry Oldenburg (1619–77), was also a copious correspondent, even before his official duties as Secretary required it of him. He earned the sobriquet 'the Clearinghouse of Science' in consequence. His correspondence fills thirteen volumes, and the geographical spread of his correspondents was even greater than that of his fellow intelligencers – it ranged across Europe, the Levant and North America. As editor of the Society's *Philosophical Transactions*, for which he invented the practice of referring submitted manuscripts for peer review, he is a key figure in the transition between the first and second halves of the seventeenth century in the way that science was communicated and debated. In the first half of the century this was done by private correspondence between individuals, whose networks were informal and dispersed; in the second half of the century it was done by groups of scientists in state-sponsored institutions publishing their findings in printed journals.

Mention of the Winter Queen – Princess Elizabeth Stuart, daughter of James I of England – brings to mind a particular example of an intellectual exchange of letters; that between René Descartes and the daughter of the Winter Queen, namely Princess Elisabeth of Bohemia (note the mother's 'z' in Elizabeth and the daughter's 's' in Elisabeth).

When Hartlib met Descartes at a soirée held by the Winter Queen, Princess Elisabeth was only sixteen. She was however at that point being sought in marriage by King Władisław IV of Poland, an offer she rejected on the grounds of the difference in their religions – he was Catholic, she Calvinist – for unlike Henri IV of France, she did not think conversion a price worth paying for a crown.

Elisabeth and her mother and siblings were living in the Netherlands because, as a previous chapter relates, that is where her father, Elector Frederick V of the Palatinate and briefly King of Bohemia, had chosen to go into exile. His wife the Winter Queen was cousin of the Prince of Orange, who honoured the family tie by giving the exiles two substantial houses and a pension. Frederick died of the plague in 1632, leaving his family wholly to the Prince of Orange's charity – and his political acumen: while the Electorate of the Palatine had a legitimate Protestant claimant, Habsburg control of it was incomplete, and that served the Netherlands well.

The Winter Queen had eight children, four of each. That was quite a burden for an impoverished exile, but although her brother was Charles

I of England and she could have claimed refuge with him, she decided to stay where she was. For one thing Charles I was preoccupied with his own troubles, but for a more important thing she calculated – in line with the views of her cousin of Orange – that her eldest son's Palatinate claims were best served by staying geographically close to them in the Netherlands.

Such were the conditions in which Princess Elisabeth of Bohemia was raised.[17] She was a highly intelligent and gifted individual who loved to study. She made very good use of her otherwise unpropitious circumstances to acquire six languages, among them Latin, and mathematics, at which she excelled. She read Descartes' *Meditations* and the *Discourse* and wished to talk to him about the ideas they contained. She asked Alphonse de Pollot, a Piedmontese member of the Prince of Orange's staff, to find out if Descartes would be willing to meet her. Descartes was always ready to meet royals, and was flattered to be noticed. Moreover he had heard of her intellectual reputation and was interested.

They met in 1642, in the autumn. Descartes travelled from his home in Endegeest to her home in The Hague along a canal which passed through beautiful countryside and wealthy suburbs, a circumstance he particularly remembered because, he said, of the importance to him of the relationship that began that day.[18] He visited her again in the following spring, and a lively and increasingly warm exchange of letters began. The probing questions Elisabeth asked in her letters eventually obliged Descartes to write a book he would not otherwise have written, *The Passions of the Soul*.

This short treatise arose directly from Elisabeth's dissatisfaction with Descartes' inability to solve the mind–body problem. She was puzzled as to how substances defined as *essentially* different – mind was 'thinking stuff' and body 'spatial stuff' according to Descartes' *Meditations* – could mutually interact. She therefore asked him to explain 'the manner of [the soul's] actions and passions on the body'. She wrote on 6 April 1643,

> Given that the soul of a human being is only a *thinking* substance, how can it affect the bodily spirits, in order to bring about voluntary actions?

> The question arises because it seems that how a thing moves depends solely on how much it is pushed, the manner in which it is pushed, or the surface-texture and shape of the thing that pushes it. The first two of these require *contact* between the two things, and the third requires that the causally active thing be extended. Your notion of the soul entirely excludes extension, and it appears to me that an immaterial thing can't possibly *touch* anything else. So I ask you for a definition of the soul that homes in on its nature more thoroughly than does the one you give in your *Meditations* – that is, I want a definition that characterizes what it *is* as distinct from what it *does*.[19]

In replying on 21 May Descartes acknowledged the acuity of her question, and provided a lengthy response offering a somewhat fudging attempt at a solution, which is that the notion of a *physical thing* x moving a *physical thing* y is different from the notion of a *mental event* x moving a *physical thing* y: there are, Descartes claimed, two different senses of 'move' in play. Of course the second sense of 'move' requires an explanation, and Descartes attempted a partial one, saying that if in accounting for how a rock moves, for example by falling, we single out the *weight* of the rock as the significant factor, we do not imagine that weight is a *thing* like the rock of which it is a property. 'How do we think that the weight of a rock moves the rock downwards?' he asks; 'We don't think that this happens through a real contact of one surface against another as though the weight was a hand pushing the rock downwards! But we have no difficulty in conceiving how it moves the body, nor how the weight and the rock are connected, because we find from our own inner experience that we *already* have a notion that provides just such a connection . . . I believe that this notion was given to us for conceiving how the soul moves the body.'

This was not an explanation calculated to satisfy a sharp mind. Elisabeth replied on 10 June, 'I don't see how the idea that you used about weight can guide us to the idea we need in order to judge how the (non-extended and immaterial) soul can move the body. To put some flesh on the bones of my difficulty: I don't see why we should be persuaded that a body *can* be pushed by some immaterial thing . . .' She went on to say that she found it easier to attribute extension to the soul than to conceive of an immaterial thing acting materially on a material thing. As we know, Descartes in the end was obliged to confess that he did not know the answer either.

Elisabeth's interest was practical as well as theoretical, for she noted her emotions' effect on her health, writing on 24 May 1645, 'My body is awash with many of the weaknesses of my sex; it is affected very easily by the troubles of the soul and doesn't have the power to restore itself when the soul is restored . . . It doesn't take long for sadness to obstruct the spleen and infect the rest of the body by its vapours. I imagine that this is the source of my low-grade fever and dry throat . . .'

She had raised the problem of mind–body interaction at their very first meeting in 1642. At last, in a letter of September 1645, she demanded that he provide her with 'a definition of the passions'. From this came Descartes' little treatise dealing with that subject.

In an account of their relationship Léon Petit suggests that Descartes and Elisabeth were in love with one another.[20] Others, including Geneviève Rodis-Lewis, agree, though in Rodis-Lewis' opinion it was not a sexual relationship. It did not really have time or opportunity to be such before Elisabeth was sent by her mother to live with other relatives, the family of the Elector of Brandenburg in Berlin. Elisabeth left the Netherlands in August 1646 soon after she and Descartes had their last ever meeting together. But their correspondence continued, sometimes on intellectual matters and sometimes on less recondite topics such as Elisabeth's rashes, headaches and even bowel movements.

In dedicating his *Principles of Philosophy* to Elisabeth – he regarded it as his *magnum opus*, the definitive statement of his scientific views – Descartes wrote,

> when I consider that such a varied and complete knowledge of all things is to be found not in some aged pedant who has spent many years in contemplation, but in a young princess whose beauty and youth call to mind one of the Graces rather than grey-eyed Minerva or any of the Muses, then I cannot but be lost in admiration . . . together with your royal dignity you show an extraordinary kindness and gentleness which, though continually buffeted by the blows of fortune, has never become embittered or broken. I am so overwhelmed by this that I consider that this statement of my philosophy should be offered and dedicated to the

> wisdom which I so admire in you – for philosophy is nothing else but the study of wisdom. And indeed my desire to be known as a philosopher is no greater than my desire to be known as your Serene Highness's most devoted servant, Descartes.[21]

That was in 1644. In 1648 he said of *The Passions of the Soul* that he had written it 'only to be read by a princess whose mental powers are so extraordinary that she can easily understand matters that seem very difficult to our learned doctors'.[22] Elisabeth's sister, Princess Sophie, wrote, 'My sister, who is called Madame Elisabeth . . . loves to study, but all her philosophy cannot keep her from chagrin when the circulation of her blood causes her nose to turn red . . . She knows all the languages and all the sciences, and has a regular commerce with Monsieur Descartes, but this thinker renders her a bit distracted, which often makes us laugh.'[23] Reference to the 'circulation of the blood' shows how alert these young women were to up-to-date currents in science; William Harvey's book on the subject, completely overturning what had been thought about blood and the heart and proving by experiment that blood is conserved and circulates, had been published in 1628.[24]

Elisabeth lived with her boring cousins at the Court in Berlin for twenty-one years. In 1667 she entered a Protestant convent at Herford in Westphalia, and after a time became its abbess – a job suitable for one who might have been a queen, considering that the convent employed 7,000 people in its factories, farms, mills and vineyards. It is notable that while Elisabeth was abbess the convent became a refuge from religious persecution for people from any religious background. She died in 1680, at the age of sixty-four.

It was mentioned a few pages ago that Mersenne was a significant contributor to that important moment in the history of thought when, at first in supplementation of, and then gradually freeing itself from, obedience to religious orthodoxy, thought passed through a phase of hope in magical and Cabalistic short-cuts to a knowledge of the universe's secrets, before settling to the disciplined scientific and philosophical approaches which have marked its best endeavours since, giving us via technological applications computing, space flight, television, modern medicine and so much besides, as well as astounding advances in understanding of nature and the universe. This passage in the history of method – for that is what it really is – and the role in it of Bacon, Descartes and Mersenne himself, merits mention; which the next chapter offers.

13

The Short Ways to Knowledge

HISTORIES OF THOUGHT, and especially histories of science, do well to remind us of two matters that subsequent progress makes us forget. One is the role of scientific instruments, sometimes originating in fairground attractions and novelties. Without them the seventeenth century's forward leaps would not have been possible. The examples of both the microscope and telescope are especially pertinent. Magnification was known in antiquity; Seneca wrote in the first century CE of how tiny objects could be enlarged by looking at them through a glass globe filled with water. But enquirers then and before, and for centuries afterwards, had none of the fuller knowledge, the skill or the technology to produce and improve lenses to a point where they could be applied in either practical or scientifically informative ways.

By the thirteenth century CE the principles of refraction of light (again: first estimated by Claudius Ptolemy in the second century CE, but not applied to lenses), and the way to grind lenses to produce corrective effects, were sufficiently well understood for spectacles to make their appearance. The English Franciscan friar Roger Bacon, who taught at the universities of Oxford and Paris in the second half of the thirteenth century, is often cited as the inventor of these useful devices.[1] In the sixteenth century a father and son team of spectacle manufacturers in the Netherlands, Hans and Zacharias Janssen, discovered the magnifying properties achieved by juxtaposing two lenses; and the true history of microscopes began.[2]

The story of instruments and their powerful effect on the progress of science is a rich tale in itself.[3] It needs to be told alongside other enabling developments, such as the adoption of Arabic numerals, advances in mathematics and the availability of mathematical tables, accounting systems, cheap paper, printing and more accurate and more uniform systems of weights and measures. When one wonders why the ancients did not develop means of magnification for studying nature, and failed to apply Claudius Ptolemy's insights about refraction of light by water and glass, the answer becomes apparent: a discovery of these kinds makes a practical difference to understanding and application only when there is a confluence of other factors to make that happen.

The second matter that histories of thought do well to remind us of – and this is the theme of the present chapter – is the fact that science emerged from a period in which many enquirers were deeply involved in magic and occult practices and beliefs. Whether the 'occult sciences' were the precursors of what we now think of as genuine science, or something quite separate from science, or a sometimes helpful and sometimes unhelpful admixture in the early development of science – in short: quite what the relationship is – is a matter of controversy. Scholars of Renaissance thought take sides on the question. For Frances Yates, Deborah Harkness and others, occultism was one of the progenitors of science proper, and an important one. For them science was the achievement of men who were at the same time dabbling in Cabala and magic, in Hermeticism, astrology and angelology. Yet for others – Brian Vickers, Paolo Rossi and more – occultism and science were distinct, and indeed distinct in the minds of sixteenth- and seventeenth-century thinkers themselves; and their argument is that those who practised science rather than the occult arts won the day.[4]

Whichever view is right – and what follows in recounting this story is in fact consistent with either, though inclines to the former view – the effort to extricate science from the entanglements of occultism, whether by some thinkers from other thinkers or within the selfsame thinker engaged in both, took a great deal of work by people whom we now remember for their achievements in this respect. By contrast, almost all of those who remained keen on the occult route to knowledge are now remembered, if they are remembered at all, only as dead-ends in the story.[5]

The words 'almost all' are particularly appropriate in that last sentence, however, because among those keenest on the occult route were some of the period's greatest scientists, including Isaac Newton and Robert Boyle. Newton's seminal contributions to proper science occupied far less of his time than his studies in alchemy and biblical interpretation. He thought the Bible was written in a secret code which, if cracked, would explain all nature. The Book of Revelation especially interested him because he believed its prophecies were genuine windows into the future. And like all alchemists before him he wished to find the Philosopher's Stone, the magic mineral which would transmute base metals into gold and give us eternal youth.[6]

John Maynard Keynes bought Newton's papers in 1936, and found to his astonishment that by far the greatest number of them concerned alchemical and magical speculations. In an address written for the Royal Society's celebration of the 1942 tercentenary of Newton's birth, Keynes said that the discovery did not make him think less of Newton and his achievements in genuine science, for he was certainly a genius; but it did make him realise that Newton was very different from the picture history had drawn of him.[7] 'In the eighteenth century and since,' Keynes wrote,

> Newton came to be thought of as the first and greatest of the modern age of scientists, a rationalist, one who taught us to think on the lines of cold and untinctured reason. I do not see him in this light. I do not think that anyone who has pored over the contents of that box which he packed up when he finally left Cambridge in 1696 and which, though partly dispersed, have come down to us, can see him like that. Newton was not the first of the age of reason. He was the last of the magicians, the last of the Babylonians and Sumerians, the last great mind which looked out on the visible and intellectual world with the same eyes as those who began to build our intellectual inheritance rather less than 10,000 years ago. Isaac Newton, a posthumous child born with no father on Christmas Day, 1642, was the last wonderchild to whom the Magi could do sincere and appropriate homage.

This characterisation of Newton rather overstates the case; Copernicus and Galileo lay between Newton and the Babylonians, and of course made it impossible for him to see the universe or observable nature in quite the same way as those archaic watchers of the skies. But there is enough right in Keynes' view – for as he put it, Newton indeed 'regarded the universe as a cryptogram set by the Almighty' – to make us see him with a more ambiguous eye.

For example, on the basis of his 'interpretation' of Revelation – that apocalyptic last book of the Bible with its terrifying vision of final things – Newton calculated that the world would not end before 2060:

> So then the time times & half a time [*sic*] are 42 months or 1260 days or three years & an half, recconing twelve months to a yeare & 30 days to a month as was done in the Calendar of the primitive year. And the days of short lived Beasts being put for the years of [long-]lived kingdoms, the period of 1260 days, if dated from the complete conquest of the three kings A.C. 800, will end A.C. 2060. It may end later, but I see no reason for its ending sooner.[8]

Newton thus offers an interesting example of how enquirers even of his great gifts could fail to distinguish genuine from spurious knowledge as we now understand this distinction. His interest in nature and its constituents was not divided, as it would so clearly be now, into physics and chemistry, and chemistry was still sufficiently entangled with alchemy that it makes it impossible even now to allocate, definitively into one or other of these categories, many of the experiments then being made and theories offered.

Surprisingly perhaps, this applies also to Newton's contemporary Robert Boyle, discoverer of Boyle's Law on the inverse relationship between the pressure and volume of gases. Boyle's work falls clearly into the field of chemistry, and his book *The Sceptical Chymist*, published in 1661, is a foundational text in that science. His researches into sound waves in air, the expansion of water when it freezes, electricity, colour and much besides, was firmly based on experimentation, making him a paradigm of an early leader of genuine science. But Boyle was also interested in the possibility of transforming metals, to the extent that he helped to campaign for the repeal of a centuries-old law against 'proliferating gold and silver' that in effect criminalised alchemical efforts to get gold from base metals. He was critical of the kind of alchemists whom he called 'vulgar Spagyrists' – a term first coined by Paracelsus to denote those who separate and purify the elements in substances – and he was therefore careful to distinguish the concept of 'mixtures' from that of 'compounds' and to insist on their proper analysis. In contrast to the Spagyrists who claimed that 'Salt, Sulphur and Mercury' are the 'Principles of Things', Boyle took a corpuscularian view, which is that matter is composed of ultimately irreducible particles or 'corpuscles' (which means 'little bodies' – the Greek-derived word we now use is 'atom', from *atomos* 'indivisible').

But this did not make Boyle an enemy of alchemy. On the contrary, like Newton he hoped that alchemy would provide a means to understand the nature of the physical world, and to achieve the great desiderata of wealth, health and even immortality. The Enlightenment and subsequent histories of science have concealed or at least deliberately understated this part of Boyle's story, just as they did with Newton's story.[9] We now know, as a result of extensive biographical investigation into the work and interests of both men, that the picture is more complicated. Just how complicated can be seen from the fact that Boyle allowed himself to be duped by a conman claiming that if he would send a large sum of money to Turkey he would receive in return a number of alchemical secrets. Boyle sent the money, but of course received no secrets. And he was even duped into thinking he had witnessed – actually witnessed with his own eyes – a case of transmutation of lead into gold: in a letter to Gilbert Burnet he wrote, 'The man had a crucible in which was contained some lead. He put in a bright powder and put the crucible on the fire to heat. He removed it and when it was cold I was surprised to find not lead but gold, which, after testing, turned out to be true gold.'[10]

Yet despite these interests and aberrations, Boyle's own work was scrupulously empirical and experimental, and he laid the foundations of modern chemistry as a result. Newton made little use of Boyle's work, but devoted himself to his own alchemical researches with a single-minded and exclusive passion that resulted in a nervous breakdown. Just how much alchemical work he did cannot now be known, because – famously (or allegedly) – a fire in his laboratory, caused by his dog Diamond knocking over a candle, destroyed an unknown quantity of his writings. It has been speculated that the illness he experienced might have resulted from the lead and mercury he used in efforts to find the Philosopher's Stone.[11] But what remains of his work, more than a million words of it, sufficiently attests to his devotion – no lesser word will do – to the occult and mystical. He wrote a book about Solomon's Temple interpreting it as a source of mathematical knowledge and information about the size of the universe and the place of mankind in it. In an annotation of an alchemical treatise he wrote, 'This philosophy, both speculative and active, is not only to be found in the volume of nature, but also in the sacred scriptures, as in Genesis, Job, Psalms, Isaiah and others. In the knowledge of this philosophy, God has made Solomon the greatest philosopher in the world.'[12]

Even Greek mythology suggested to Newton a secret code for explaining the world. In the story of the adultery of Aphrodite there was, he thought, an alchemical message: Helios the sun saw Ares the god of war sneaking into the chamber of Aphrodite, goddess of love, while her husband Hephaestus, god of the forge, was out at work. Helios told the divine but lame blacksmith that he was being cuckolded, so Hephaestus made a net and strung it above the bed he shared with Aphrodite, with which to catch her and her lover in the act. They were indeed caught in the act, and the angry Hephaestus summoned his fellow Olympians to witness his betrayal. We are told by Homer that the gods laughed uproariously at the sight – thus 'Homeric laughter', the 'unquenchable laughter of the gods' as recounted in Book I of the *Iliad* (the goddesses, however, all turned away their faces in embarrassment). For Newton there was a deep secret here. Each of the players in this divinely domestic drama is associated either with a metal – Helios with gold, Ares with iron, Aphrodite with copper – or with the power that transforms them, namely fire, as used by Hephaestus in his work. Apparently Newton thought that iron + copper + fire yields the lead-like metal antimony, with its appearance when oxidised of a net-like trigonal lattice pattern. Amateur researches into alloys of copper and iron do not bear this out, though a sulphide of antimony with copper and iron constitutes tetrahedrite, a substance Newton would not have known.[13]

Subsequent history has ignored these extravagances of imagination and concentrated instead not only on the amazing achievement of Newton's serious scientific work, but also on the methodological rules he laid down for scientific enquiry in the *Principia* (remember that 'philosophy' then meant every kind of careful systematic enquiry and therefore also what we now call 'natural science'):

> RULE I.
> *We are to admit no more causes of natural things than such as are both true and sufficient to explain their appearances.*
>
> To this purpose the philosophers say that Nature does nothing in vain, and more is in vain when less will serve; for Nature is pleased with simplicity, and affects not the pomp of superfluous causes.
>
> RULE II.
> *Therefore to the same natural effects we must, as far as possible, assign the same causes.*
>
> As to respiration in a man and in a beast; the descent of stones in *Europe* and in *America*; the light of our culinary fire and of the sun; the reflection of light in the earth, and in the planets.
>
> RULE III.
> *The qualities of bodies, which admit neither intension nor remission of degrees, and which are found to belong to all bodies within the reach of our experiments, are to be esteemed the universal qualities of all bodies whatsoever.*
>
> RULE IV.
> *In experimental philosophy we are to look upon propositions collected by general induction from phaenomena as accurately or very nearly true, notwithstanding any contrary hypotheses that may be imagined, till such time as other phaenomena occur, by which they may either be made more accurate, or liable to exceptions.*

> This rule we must follow, that the argument of induction may not be evaded by hypotheses. For since the qualities of bodies are only known to us by experiments, we are to hold for universal all such as universally agree with experiments; and such as are not liable to diminution can never be quite taken away. We are certainly not to relinquish the evidence of experiments for the sake of dreams and vain fictions of our own devising; nor are we to recede from the analogy of Nature, which uses to be simple, and always consonant to itself.[14]

These rules have been part of the backbone of science – 'real science' we can say – ever since. It is a matter of controversy how Newton could regard them as consistent with biblical interpretation and alchemy, but evidently he did; to him these were somehow not 'dreams and vain fictions' – and he thus exemplifies the entanglement of science and the putative occult routes to ultimate knowledge that so fascinated many in the period before and up to his time.

The interest in alchemy and mystical fantasies displayed by Newton and to a lesser extent Boyle comes at the tail-end of these distractions. The soon-following Enlightenment did both men the kindness of ignoring this aspect of their interests, concentrating instead on their outstanding contributions to real science. But the fact that they were still dabbling with alchemy – and in Newton's case with other even less plausible occult matters – at the end of the seventeenth century, means that it is no surprise to find that a century before them it was even more difficult for people to make the right discriminations between science and nonsense. Just how muddy the waters were is illustrated by the case of many sixteenth-century thinkers, illustratively among them the Elizabethan magus Dr Dee, the man to whom is imputed responsibility for Europe's last truly great spasm of *magia, alchymia, cabala* at the beginning of the seventeenth century. I turn to him below.

Let us first clarify *magia, alchymia, cabala*, the concepts of magic, alchemy and Cabala (sometimes 'Kabbalah').

'Cabala' denotes one of several related systems of mysticism, almost all of which have roots in Jewish mysticism and practices of meditation and divination. It contains substantial elements of Neoplatonist philosophy as well as earlier Jewish thought about the supposed hidden meanings of the Torah and Rabbinic teachings.[15] The elaborate doctrines of the Cabala were developed to a high point of sophistication by the Sephardic Jews of Spain in the medieval period. In the last quarter of the thirteenth century CE there emerged from among them the Zohar, a collection of texts on Torah interpretation, the origins of the universe, mystical topics, salvation, prayer, the nature of the soul and of God, and much besides. It was published by one Moses de León, who claimed that the texts were written by a second-century CE rabbi called Shimon bar Yochai, who had hidden from the Romans in a cave during the period of persecutions. There he had received a visit from the prophet Elijah who directed him to write down Judaism's tradition of esoteric teachings which had hitherto been transmitted in oral form only.[16] 'Zohar' means 'Radiance' or 'Light', and the work bearing that name draws richly and widely on many earlier commentaries and mystical texts, as well as on the Talmud and the commentaries on the Tanakh (the Jewish bible) known as Midrash.

A key aspect of the Cabala is the concept of the Sephirot or Sefirot, and its teachings about the mystical significance of the Hebrew alphabet. The Sephirot are the ten chief names of God; the word literally means 'emanations' so they are viewed as manifestations or attributes of the Infinite through which it both reveals itself and creates all things. As attributes they include glory, wisdom, will, goodness, splendour, eternity and virtue – the nature of the manifestations and their ordering in relation to the Infinite depends on which school of Cabala one is studying.

The twenty-two letters of the Hebrew alphabet contain many further names of God. One Sephardi in thirteenth-century Spain, Abraham Abulafia, created a meditation routine of great complexity based on permutations of the Hebrew letters, and they and the alphabet's associated number system (for the letters also stand for numbers) provided the materials for a great elaboration of mystical notions. For example: a feature of the Hebrew language is that individual letters are meaningless on their own, and require always to stand at least in pairs to form a significant linguistic unit. The pairs are known as 'gates', *sha'arim*, and in the Cabala are said to number 231, and are integral to the three-letter roots, *shorashim*, of Hebrew words. Using the same factorial calculation as yields 231, the number of these three-letter roots is 1,540. Here is an example of how these are interpreted Cabalistically: one reading of the word 'Ysrael' is *yesh-rala*, which means 'there are 231 gates'. A second reading of 'Ysrael' – using the fact that Hebrew letters stand for numbers and that *alef* ('a') is similar to *elef* which is the number 1,000 and sometimes substitutes for the numerical value of *alef* which is 1 – yields the result that 'Ysrael' stands for the number 1,540. With time on one's hands one can find many other amazing and significant coincidences and suggestiveness by manipulation of the Hebrew letters and these two numbers, ranging from geometry to the nature of the universe and its deity.[17]

Even before the Jews were expelled from Spain by the joint monarchs Isabella and Ferdinand in 1492, taking their Sephardic traditions with them into their new diasporas, Cabalistic ideas had begun to influence some of the more imaginative Christian minds in Europe. In the thirteenth century the Spanish mystic and Franciscan friar Ramón Lull knew of the Jewish Cabala, and his ideas contain several striking parallels with it. But the individual most credited with introducing Cabalistic notions into a version of Christian thought, marrying them to Hermeticism and laying the foundations of a full-blown Occultism and dignification of 'good' magic, was Pico della Mirandola (1463–94), the brilliant, aristocratic, short-lived protégé of Marsilio Ficino and Cosimo de' Medici.

Pico's *Oration on the Dignity of Man* is often cited as a Renaissance blueprint for the humanistic turn, this being the new insistence – or rather, an insistence renewed from its classical sources – on seeing humankind and its experience as the important focus for humanity's own attention, in contrast to medieval Christianity's denigration of this life as merely a woeful exordium to death, with a correlative fixation on the soul's destiny after death. But in fact Pico's essay is a startlingly clear manifesto of a hotch-potch Cabalistic–Platonist–Neoplatonist–Hermetic–eclectic project, favouring not just the self-creating freedom of man but the legitimacy of magic and a new way of knowing, which he claimed would transform our understanding of the universe.

The *Oration* was written as a preface to a set of 900 theses that Pico wished to debate before the Pope and cardinals in Rome. It begins with the words, 'Most esteemed Fathers, I have read in the ancient writings of the Arabians that Abdala the Saracen on being asked what, on this stage, so to say, of the world, seemed to him most evocative of wonder, replied that there was nothing to be seen more marvellous than man. And that celebrated exclamation of Hermes Trismegistus, "What a great miracle is man, Asclepius!" confirms this opinion.' The humanist tradition takes this eloquent exclamation by Pico, and his subsequent account of God's award to man of self-creating and self-governing powers, as its manifesto; Pico has God tell Adam, 'Whatever place, whatever form, whatever gifts you may, with premeditation, select, these same you may have and possess through your own judgment and decision. The nature of all other creatures is defined and restricted within laws which We have laid down; you, by contrast, impeded by no such restrictions, may, by your own free will, to whose custody We have assigned you, trace for yourself the lineaments of your own nature.' And Pico breaks out in joy at the thought: 'Oh unsurpassed generosity of God the Father, Oh wondrous and unsurpassable felicity of man, to whom it is granted to have what he chooses, to be what he wills to be!' There is scarcely a clearer expression of the Renaissance humanist attitude. It might be summed up in the same words used by Jean-Paul Sartre centuries later: our existence precedes our essence: we are self-creators because we are radically and ultimately free.

But a more attentive reading reveals that Pico is, by this characterisation of God's licence to man and his long dithyramb on the quest for knowledge by former saints and sages, astutely trying to wrest from Church orthodoxy the freedom to explore and apply Cabalistic and Hermetic wisdom. 'I have not been content to repeat well-worn doctrines,' he says,

> but have proposed for disputation many points of the early theology of Hermes Trismegistus, many theses drawn from the teachings of

> the Chaldeans and the Pythagoreans, from the occult mysteries of the Hebrews and, finally, a considerable number of propositions concerning both nature and God which we ourselves have discovered and worked out . . . I have, in addition, introduced a new method of philosophizing on the basis of numbers. This method is, in fact, very old, for it was cultivated by the ancient theologians, by Pythagoras, in the first place, but also by Aglaophamos, Philolaus and Plato, as well as by the earliest Platonists; however, like other illustrious achievements of the past, it has through lack of interest on the part of succeeding generations, fallen into such desuetude, that hardly any vestiges of it are to be found. Plato writes in *Epinomis* that among all the liberal arts and contemplative sciences, the science of number is supreme and most divine. And in another place, asking why man is the wisest of animals, he replies, because he knows how to count. Similarly, Aristotle, in his *Problems*, repeats this opinion. Abumasar writes that it was a favourite saying of Avenzoar of Babylon that the man who knows how to count, knows everything else as well . . . I have also proposed certain theses concerning magic, in which I have indicated that magic has two forms. One consists wholly in the operations and powers of demons, and consequently this appears to me, as God is my witness, an execrable and monstrous thing. The other proves, when thoroughly investigated, to be nothing else but the highest realization of natural philosophy. The Greeks noted both these forms. However, because they considered the first form wholly undeserving the name magic they called it *goeteia*, reserving the term *mageia* to the second, and understanding by it the highest and most perfect wisdom. The term 'magus' in the Persian tongue, according to Porphyry, means the same as 'interpreter' and 'worshipper of the divine' in our language.

One notes the telling remark, 'The other [form of magic, *mageia*] proves, when thoroughly investigated, to be nothing else but the highest realization of natural philosophy.' This claim was firmly and sincerely believed by many subsequent thinkers in the period up to and into the seventeenth century.

Pico's sponsor and admirer Marsilio Ficino (1433–99) was the translator of the recently recovered complete works of Plato into Latin, and an enthusiastic astrologer (here Pico disagreed; he was critical of astrology);[18] but Ficino's chief relevance for present purposes is that he was also the translator of the classic of Hermeticism, the *Corpus Hermeticum*. His translation was made from a Greek text which had been given to Ficino's patron, Cosimo de' Medici, by a monk called Leonardo of Pistoia, who had been sent by Cosimo to search monastery libraries for ancient texts. Pico combined what he learned of Hermeticism with Platonism and the Cabala into a syncretist *mélange*, which encouraged others to adopt Cabbalistic ideas and to associate them with Hermeticism, by that means evolving their own versions of Christian mysticism.

Hermeticism is a congeries of beliefs based on a body of texts said to contain the secrets of all things and supposed to have been produced by a great and wise person or god called Hermes Trismegistus, who either lived in remote pre-antiquity or was a contemporary of Moses. This corpus consists of 9,000 texts, some say; others – aiming at something more modest and precise – say forty-two.[19] Some scholars think that Hermes Trismegistus is a combination of the Greek god Hermes and the Egyptian god Thoth, a blending that might have occurred in the Hellenistic period of Greek influence in Egypt following the Alexandrine conquest in the fourth century BCE. The blending of the two gods would have been a natural one, given that both were the nominated patrons of writing and magic in their respective cultural settings. They were also both 'psychopomps', that is, deities who guide the souls of the dead into the afterlife.

Scholars also suggest that the belief held by some that Hermes Trismegistus was an historical figure might have resulted from association with the Egyptian priest and philosopher Imhotep (lived about 2650–2600 BCE), who was deified after death and mentioned in many inscriptions. Identifying Imhotep and Hermes Trismegistus makes the latter both human and divine, shades of Jesus Christ. Or perhaps the connection is with a much later figure often linked in tradition with Imhotep, namely the celebrated scribe Amenhotep son of Hapu (lived about 1390–1330 BCE), not to be identified with any pharoah of that name. This Amenhotep was as greatly praised as Imhotep for deep knowledge of medicine and nature.

In inscriptions to Thoth the formula 'Thoth the great, the great, the great' occurs frequently, hence Trismegistus or 'thrice-great'; but many other legends and traditions surround the supposed origin of the name and the being thus named. References to Hermes Trismegistus diminished after late antiquity, only to be revived in the high medieval and Renaissance period, when he came to be thought of as an inspired individual contemporary with Moses and author of the mystical texts translated by Ficino.

Whatever the obscure and convoluted origins and character of Hermes Trismegistus, by the time that the Renaissance was in full flow Hermeticism had become a major cultural force, inspiring alchemists and mystics, making magic and astrology credible, and attracting the attention and following of some of the leading minds of the time, ranging from Pico at the end of the fifteenth century to Giordano Bruno at the end of the sixteenth century.[20] A shared view was that the Hermetic writings preserved a so-called *prisca theologia* or pure and primitive theology, given to mankind by God in the remotest of ancient times. The *prisca theologia* therefore underlies all religious beliefs everywhere, but particular cultures had diversified and modified that original truth, corrupting and obscuring it. Newton held this view too.

As with the Cabala among certain sects of Jews today, credulous interest in the Hermetic tradition also continues among some who think that the forty-two key writings still exist, hidden somewhere in Egypt perhaps, with all the universe's secrets contained in them. But the overwhelming Renaissance interest in Hermeticism rapidly dwindled (Newton apart) after the scholar and philologist Isaac Casaubon (1550–1614) showed at the beginning of the seventeenth century that the Greek in which the *Corpus Hermeticum* was written could not be earlier than the first and probably the second century CE. Casaubon's demolition of the *Corpus*'s pretensions to great antiquity occurred in the course of his criticism of the *Annales Ecclesiastici* by Cesare Baronio, a Catholic history of the Church which the Huguenot Casaubon criticised for its fraudulent attempt to bolster papal claims to authority not just in the spiritual but in the temporal spheres.[21] Casaubon was acknowledged by his contemporaries to be their age's foremost scholar of Greek and the antiquities of the Christian religion. He was formidably equipped to identify the least tincture of fakery in texts, as in his edition of an entire collection of fakes, the *Scriptores Historiae Augustae*: 'He revealed some of their many inconsistencies and improbable statements,' Anthony Grafton writes. 'He used considerations of style and content alike to argue that the works ascribed in the manuscripts to Aelius Spartianus, Aelius Lampridius, and Iulius Capitolinus could more plausibly be ascribed to a single author. He showed that the collection had been edited and revised, though the job had been done by an incompetent.'[22] The figure of Casaubon might have provided George Eliot with her model of a bloodless scholar, but that scholarship exploded the Hermes myth, and put an effective end to Hermeticisim.

Casaubon did this not just by showing that the Greek of the *Corpus Hermeticum* could not be earlier than the first or second century of the common era, but that the doctrines were borrowed from familiar Greek philosophy in the period between Plato and the date of composition. It was in short merely an anthology of views from sources as various as Plato's *Timaeus* and Hippocrates' *On Regimen*. 'I would have to copy the whole book here,' Casaubon wrote, 'if I wanted to go through one by one the heads of doctrine that the fake Mercury has turned to his own use from the Greek philosophers. For except for the points derived from Scripture, everything that he has is from them.'[23] The clincher was that 'Hermes' mentions such things as the sculptures of Phidias, which were made centuries after the supposed date of the *Corpus*'s composition. And Casaubon was scathing about the claim that the text was a translation from ancient Egyptian, which he showed to be of a piece with a fashion in the early centuries of the common era to attribute everything to mysterious sources in ancient Egyptian or Eastern traditions, 'the pullulating mass of pseudo-ancient, pseudo-Eastern literature' as Grafton puts it. Quoting Casaubon again: 'We should not then be surprised that in the first centuries of Christianity, when books with false titles were invented every day with complete license, someone barely acquainted with our religion should attempt the same in the science of theology.'[24]

If the story of Cabalistic and Hermetic ideas and their influence were told in full, it would require an account of the writings of Johann Reuchlin (1455–1522) and Francesco Giorgi (1467–1540) who promoted Christian versions of Cabala, and a much longer story about Hermeticism reaching back to Plutarch, Tertullian, Iamblichus and Porphyry in later antiquity, all of whom mention it – though Casaubon's analysis of the *Corpus* proved that its production was contemporary with them rather than earlier. But it is chiefly because of Ficino's translation of the *Corpus* that Hermeticism's life was renewed and became of relevance to the just-pre-scientific ebullition of magical thinking.

For magical thinking itself, however, perhaps the most resonant name of the time is that of Cornelius Agrippa (1486–1535). In histories of occult thinking Agrippa invariably features not many pages away from another luminary of the age, Paracelsus (1493–1541), whose real name was Philippus Aureolus Theophrastus Bombastus von Hohenheim. But whereas Agrippa was avowedly a magus or magician – he calls himself exactly this in the opening of his chief work *De Occulta Philosophia Libri Tres* (*The Occult Philosophy in Three Books*); even though a *good* magician who thinks that magic is merely the manipulation of nature as it genuinely is – Paracelsus was a different man and mind altogether, as arguably the founder of modern medicine and certainly a great contributor to its progress. This is not to say that he did not have interests in alchemy and, in his own modified view of it, astrology; but there was a real scientist at work in his head, and he makes an interesting contrast with his contemporaries in the late fifteenth and early sixteenth centuries.

Agrippa was born in Cologne and became a teacher at Dole University in Burgundy. For a short time he studied with Johannes Trithemius (the by-name of Johann Heidenburg), a Benedictine monk then and for a century afterwards celebrated as an authority on magic. Trithemius' book *Steganographia* was placed on the *Index of Forbidden Books* by the Vatican which believed it to be about its ostensible subject – long-distance communication by the medium of spirits and astrology – but actually it is a work of cryptography.[25] To the intoxicated minds of the time, a work in code seemingly about magic was as nectar to the bee. In any case Trithemius is said to have believed that it was possible to communicate with heaven by magical means, so those who studied with him besides Agrippa – Paracelsus was another – might be forgiven for thinking they were in the presence of a master of occult thought. For this reason Agrippa gave his *De Occulta Philosophia* to Trithemius to approve, which circumspectly Trithemius did, advising him not to put it into print too hastily.

The *De Occulta* was written by Agrippa in his early twenties, and following Trithemius' advice he allowed it to circulate in manuscript copies only. Two decades later he revised and expanded it for print publication.[26] The aim of the work was to restore the fortunes of magic, the understanding and practice of which Agrippa believed had greatly declined since antiquity. Among the various familiar and less familiar sources he drew upon – Neoplatonist writings, the Hermetic texts, Pliny, pseudo-Albertus Magnus, Pico, Reuchlin – he also used *The Aim of the Sage* (*Ghayat al-Hakim fi'l-sih*), better known as the *Picatrix*, attributed to the celebrated mathematician al-Madjriti who lived in Andalusia in the eleventh century CE. The *Picatrix* is one of the largest and most extensive *grimoires* or treatises of magic known. It became influential in Europe after its translation into Latin in the early thirteenth century CE, at the court of King Alphonso 'the Wise' of Castile, who was interested in its contents for practical as well as intellectual reasons. In a disorganised and meandering way the *Picatrix* covers talismans, astrology, magical theory, nostrums and more, but its very manner and scope recommended itself to eager would-be magicians, and it had a substantial influence on Ficino, whose 'spiritual magic' draws from it.

Agrippa opens his *De Occulta* with a letter to Trithemius in which he writes:

> When I was of late (most reverend Father) for a while conversant with you in your Monastery of *Herbipolis*, we conferred together of divers things concerning Chymistry, Magick, and Cabalie, and of other things, which as yet lye hid in Secret Sciences, and Arts; and then there was one great question amongst the rest, why Magick, whereas it was accounted

> by all ancient Philosophers the chiefest Science, & by the ancient wise men, & Priests was always held in great veneration, came at last after the beginning of the Catholike Church to be alwaies odious to, and suspected by the holy Fathers, and then exploded by Divines, and condemned by sacred Canons, and moreover by all laws, and ordinances forbidden.

And the reason, Agrippa argued, was the appropriation of the name and some of the practice of magic by wrong-headed or wicked people, thus giving 'magic' an undeservedly bad connotation:

> by a certain fatall depravation of times, and men, many false Philosophers crept in, and these under the name of Magicians, heaping together through various sorts of errors and factions of false Religions, many cursed superstitions and dangerous Rites, and many wicked Sacrileges, out of Orthodox Religion, even to the perfection of nature, and destruction of men, and injury of God, set forth very many wicked, and unlawfull books, such as we see carryed about in these dayes, to which they have by stealth prefixed the most honest name, and title of Magick.

It is instructive how Agrippa states the rationale for a magical approach to the world, because it shows how the approach he takes – and in this he is representative of those who shared his interests – differs from and yet occasionally has an echo of the proper scientific attitude yet to come:

> Seeing that there is a three-fold World, Elementary, Celestiall, and Intellectual, and every inferior is governed by its superior, and receiveth the influence of the vertues thereof, so that the very original, and chief Worker of all doth by Angels, the Heavens, Stars, Elements, Animals, Plants, Metals, and Stones convey from himself the vertues of his Omnipotency upon us, for whose service he made and created all these things: Wise men conceive it no way irrationall that it should be possible for us to ascend by the same degrees through each World, to the same very originall World it self, the Maker of all things, and first Cause, from whence all things are, and proceed; and also to enjoy not only these vertues which are already in the more excellent kind of things, but also

> besides these, to draw new vertues from above. Hence it is that they seek after the vertues of the Elementary world, through the help of Physick and Naturall Philosophy in the various mixtions of Naturall things; then of the Celestiall world in the Rayes and influences thereof, according to the rules of Astrologers, and the doctrines of Mathematicians, joyning the Celestiall vertues to the former: Moreover, they ratifie and confirm all these with the powers of divers Intelligencies, through the sacred Ceremonies of Religions. The order and process of all these I shall endeavor to deliver in these three Books: Whereof the first contains naturall Magick, the second Celestiall, and the third Ceremoniall.[27]

This work – though of course not alone: there were other significant texts of the period which added to the excitement and interest, such as the *Arbatel de Magia Veterum* (*Arbatel: On the Magic of the Ancients*) by an unknown author – proved immensely influential. Agrippa's most significant reader was undoubtedly John Dee, who took from him the idea that the universe is tripartitioned into natural, celestial and heavenly spheres, and that the key to understanding the nature of each and their relationships is number. Agrippa had lectured on Reuchlin when a young academic in Dole, and his theme had been Reuchlin's linking of Pythagorean and Cabalistic themes. Dee, who was a brilliant mathematician, found these ideas irresistible.

Paracelsus is famous among historians of medicine, and medical practitioners interested in their history, for his seminal remark that 'all things are poison and not without poison; only the dose makes the thing not poison'. It is a remarkable testimony to his influence on the development of medicine that his successors regard what they do as unthinkable without the shaping influence he had on their field of endeavour. He has of course been claimed by the outlying fields of care and cure too: by naturists, homeopaths, herbalists and others in the alternative-medicine field, and with good reason, because it was in these arenas that the only pharmacopoeia available to him was found. But as the 'father of toxicology', the originator of sensible approaches to treatment – for example in advising that wounds not be packed but allowed to drain – the first describer of syphilis and discoverer that mercury can cure it, the reputed recogniser of opium (in the form of laudanum) as a medical analgesic, the teacher of sensible views about antisepsis, his equally sensible view that silicosis ('miners' lung') is caused by breathing dust and not by angry mountain spirits, his innovations in surgery: with all this, his place in the history of medicine is secure. Like too many very clever and innovative people he was not a great conciliator of traditional opinion. As professor in Basle he burned the books of Galen and Avicenna at the University gates by way of statement that they were no longer relevant to the study of medicine. He invited the public to his lectures, contrary to University rules, and at them wore an alchemist's apron instead of an academic gown, at length so irritating the doyens of the University and city that they dismissed him. The last straw may have been an incident in which, having announced that he was going to reveal to the whole city the greatest of secrets about medicine, he produced in a crowded lecture theatre a bowl of faeces. As the audience left in disgust he shouted after them, 'If you will not hear the mysteries of putrefactive fermentation, you are unworthy of the name of physicians!'[28] His iconoclastic, challenging, perhaps arrogant nature is summed up in the by-name he chose for himself: 'Paracelsus' means 'beyond Celsus', the original Celsus being Aulus Cornelius Celsus, a Roman of the second century CE who wrote an encyclopaedia of which the medical part – *De Medicina*, on diet, herbs' surgery and more – is still extant.

A significant fact about Paracelsus is the breadth of empirical background that underlies his thinking. He was born in Switzerland but brought up in a mining town in Austria where his father was a physician and chemist. He had the double benefit of this. He received his earliest medical training in practice at his father's side, helping him also in his compounding and refining chemical substances. At the same time he observed the mining and smelting of minerals in the extraction operations in which, because students of the local school were required to work part-time at the mine, he participated. He thus became familiar with the properties and behaviour of many minerals.

After a period of study at Basle he went to a number of other universities seeking instruction, among them Tübingen, Vienna,

Wittenberg, Leipzig, Heidelberg and Cologne, commenting in characteristic fashion, 'how is it that the high colleges only produce so many high asses'. He travelled extensively, as far as India and Turkey according to some accounts, all the while learning, observing, seeking out physicians, chemists and alchemists. What he saw and learned led him to write, 'The universities do not teach all things, so a doctor must seek out old wives, gypsies, sorcerers, wandering tribes, old robbers, and such outlaws, and take lessons from them. A doctor must be a traveller.' And he concluded with what could be another mantra for science, 'Knowledge is experience.'

Paracelsus' attitude to alchemy and astrology was typically pragmatic. His interest in both was explicitly a matter of what they could do to help in understanding how to deal with nature, not least diseased human nature. He rejected the earth–air–fire–water theory of the elements inherited from antiquity, and adopted the alchemical-derived idea of a *tria prima* – three primary substances – which he identified as needing to be thus: one fluid and mutable, one solid and enduring, and one combustible and capable by its nature of influencing the relationship of all three. Respectively the three substances are mercury, salt and sulphur – mercury the mutable, salt the solid, and sulphur the combustible. Each is a toxin, and diseases are the result of the toxic effects of one or other of them. But small doses of each can be the opposite: a small dose can be a remedy, as witness the effect of mercury on syphilis.

From Hermeticism he took the idea that man the microcosm has to be in harmony with the universe – the universe being the macrocosm – to be well in body and mind. These harmonies were mediated by the relationships between the seven planets, the seven metals and the seven major organs of the human body, for example 'sun–gold–heart', 'moon–silver–brain' and so on. Without knowing as we now know that heavy elements can be forged only at the temperatures found in stars, Paracelsus claimed that poisons come from the stars. However it was not 'forensic astrology' that interested him, but as with alchemy he was interested only in the practical utility of the ideas. 'Many have said of Alchemy that it is for the making of gold and silver. For me such is not the aim, but to consider only what virtue and power may lie in medicines.'[29]

Paracelsus died just a few years after being dismissed from his post at Basle – some say, murdered; the matter is beyond investigation now. It is equally likely that his death was natural, or that he poisoned himself by mistake while experimenting. But murder is not an unlikely explanation, given the opposition he roused among the traditionally minded. He was a difficult and oppositional character, and his very success as a physician was held against him because it smacked of dubitable practices. It was rumoured that he had raised a corpse or two to life, and after his death there were further rumours that he himself had come back to life. His command of the sometimes near-miraculous possibilities of medicine was enough to leave behind him the reputation of a magus. Accordingly the legends accumulated: that Satan had given him a white horse, that he owned a Philosopher's Stone and regularly changed lead into gold. As a result his reputation in the period after his death lent force to the belief that magic, alchemy and the rest were genuine routes to the grails that their aficionados sought: wealth, health, life, knowledge.

14

Dr Dee and the Potent Art

For a clinching example of how the heady mixture of Cabalistic and Hermetic ideas came to be formed into a variety of occult 'science' in the period before the collapse of such thinking in the seventeenth century – leaving aside the last great aficionados such as Newton – none is better than that afforded by the egregious Dr Dee, model for Marlowe's Dr Faustus and Shakespeare's Prospero, and the inspiration for the beliefs and efforts that resulted in the beginning of the end of occult thinking, which the seventeenth century witnessed. In his story one sees the third of *alchymia, cabala, magia* – namely, magic – attempting its utmost.

Dee was educated at St John's College, Cambridge, and was appointed one of the first Fellows of Trinity College, then just founded by Henry VIII. At that time Cambridge was in a state of chaos and decline, largely as a result of Henry's reforms; there were only about thirty students enrolling each year, the University was in debt and having to pawn its candelabra, the departure of the religious orders following the dissolution of the monasteries left buildings empty and decaying, the University and the town were at expensive legal loggerheads which obliged the University to borrow considerable sums of money. Henry's reforms prescribed which subjects and texts could be studied and which could not, abolished a number of degree courses, and obliged dons to fill various University administrative offices for double the usual period of time because there were so few of them to undertake the work.

This debacle followed a period when the University was just beginning to flourish after a previous long period of stagnation. Erasmus twice stayed at Cambridge, the second time as Lady Margaret Professor of Divinity. In 1516, after his first visit, he wrote,

> It is scarcely thirty years ago when all that was taught in the University of Cambridge was Alexander, the Little Logicals (as they call them), and those old exercises out of Aristotle, and *quaestiones* taken from Duns Scotus. As time went on, polite learning was introduced; to this was added a knowledge of mathematics, a new or at least a regenerated Aristotle sprang up; then came an acquaintance with Greek, and with a host of new authors whose very names had before been unknown even to their profoundest doctors.[1]

Erasmus himself was among those responsible for the diffusion of the new interests that were percolating slowly into England's universities.

By the time Dee arrived, however, the tumult of the reforms and Reformation had taken their toll, the advances praised by Erasmus had been reversed, and Cambridge was a very depleted place. It is a mark of Dee's brilliance nevertheless that he was elected at the early age of nineteen to be reader in Greek and Fellow of the newly founded Trinity College.

It was not Greek that was Dee's passion, however, but mathematics, and he relished the quadrivium – the study of arithmetic, geometry, astronomy and harmonics. In two ways these interests fed directly into his subsequent career as a magus. Astronomy was indistinguishable for him from astrology. Mathematics was regarded with suspicion by the authorities, who from time to time burned mathematics textbooks as 'conjuring books' because of the association of maths with 'black arts'. The terms 'calculating' and 'conjuring' were often used interchangeably.[2] The connection between mathematics and magic was clearest in the occult science of numerology. In his *Oration* Pico della Mirandola had cited Pythagoras with approval; this was because Pythagoras was regarded not only as a founder of mathematics but as a magician also, who had recognised the mystical power of numbers and how the simplest of them – the first four positive integers 1, 2, 3, 4 – underlay the fundamental structure of the universe, respectively representing the point, the line, the triangle and the solid, and the harmonic ratios both of music and of the universe itself.[3]

The beginnings of Dee's reputation as a magus rested on his use of mathematics to create an amazing theatrical illusion in a performance of Aristophanes' *Peace* at Trinity College. The main character in this comedy, Trygaeus, wishes to get to heaven to consult Zeus on a military matter, and having failed to do so by ladder decides to conjure a flying creature to get him there. Instead of a handsome winged horse like Pegasus he is scooped up by a maniacal giant dungbeetle which gives him a hair-raising ride. This would be a tricky effect to stage, not least in the dining hall of a Cambridge college; but Dee achieved it to the astonishment and even terror of his colleagues and students, some of whom were convinced he had used supernatural means.

In a work he published in 1570, a *Mathematical Preface to Euclid's Elements*, Dee wrote of what he called 'thaumaturgy' or 'an art mathematical . . . which giveth certain order to make strange works, of the sense to be perceived and of men greatly to be wondered at'. This is a very early use of the word 'thaumaturgy' which standardly means 'magical trickery'. It suggests that his stunning visual effect at Trinity was achieved by mathematically aligning the audience, on one side, with the props and machinery working his tricks, on the other side, so that by concealing the mechanism involved it really looked as if the beetle were flying freely about the room with Trygaeus on its back.

The Trinity flight of Trygaeus might not have been as difficult to achieve as it sounds; in that same century statues were made to talk and move by hydraulics – a great example is the statuary in the gardens of Saint-Denis and Saint-Germain-des-Prés in Paris, which thrilled and unnerved Descartes when he first saw them – and theatres built in the following century had stage mechanisms capable of producing visually stunning effects which, by then, amazed audiences without making them think that magic was involved.[4] In his *Preface* Dee cited non-magical examples of 'thaumaturgy' such as the wooden bird that the ancient Greek founder of mechanics, Archytas, constructed and successfully flew, and the speaking head of bronze said to have been made by Albertus Magnus. Dee saw himself as mining the same vein when he wrote of pneumatics, mirrors, springs and pulleys to illustrate how mathematics (applied in the form of mechanics) could be used to achieve effects that seemed as wonderful as the miracles of God.

In causing such amazement in the audience at Trinity with his flying beetle, however, Dee quickly came to be a figure of speculation among his contemporaries, not a few of whom described him outright as a magician, for they could not believe that he had made use of natural means only. Dee sought to defend himself in his *Preface* against the imputation of being a magician, in at least the bad sense of one who is aided by 'wicked and damned Spirits'. 'For these and such like marvellous Acts and Feats, Naturally, Mathematically and Mechanically wrought and contrived; ought any honest Student and Modest Christian Philosopher be counted and called a Conjuror?' he plaintively asked; 'Shall that man be (in hugger mugger) condemned as a companion of the Hellhounds, and a Caller and Conjuror of wicked and damned Spirits?' The answer to the first of these two rhetorical questions is of course Yes: that is precisely how the enquirers of the sixteenth century were regarded by many, often enough – thinking wishfully – including themselves. The answer to the second question was more equivocal; there was a widespread suspicion that the answer must surely also be Yes – not least by religious authorities of whatever persuasion – but Dee and others were strident in their insistence otherwise. In the case of some (such as Giordano Bruno) this insistence did not save them from the pyre.

Dee was avid for 'thaumaturgy' in his sense of the term, and astrology, and any knowledge he could gather. In 1548 he travelled to the Netherlands, ostensibly to read law at the University of Louvain but in fact to join the group around the mathematician Gemma Frisius. Famous for his development of geometrical techniques of land-surveying, Frisius had also instituted a workshop for the production of accurate measuring instruments. In that workshop Dee met Gerard

Mercator, the geographer, and the two became friends. Mercator gave Dee a beautiful and extremely expensive pair of globes, one of the earth and the other of the sky; in return Dee dedicated his book *Propaedeumata Aphoristica* (*Preliminary Aphoristic Teachings*) to him. There were other enquirers and savants in the Netherlands for Dee to meet, and he spent most of his time with them rather than with the English residents, but he became friends with one of the latter, Sir William Pickering, the Ambassador to the Court of Charles V at Brussels. This association caused him a problem later.

After nearly three years in the Netherlands Dee travelled to Paris where he lectured on Euclid, with great success. Gossip about his 'Aristophanes Scarabeus' had reached the city, and helped to fill to overflowing the halls in which he lectured. On the wings of this success, his reputation already great though he was still only in his twenties, he returned to England in 1551 to present the boy King Edward with two astronomical treatises he had written. The reward was a royal pension, later exchanged for a rectorship which he held as an absentee. His seemingly unstoppable rise was furthered by becoming adviser and astrologer to the Duke of Northumberland, and tutor to his sons. This was Dee's apogee in terms of worldly career for the time being; when Edward died and Mary came to the throne, inaugurating a harsh turn to the re-Catholicisation of England, his association with Northumberland and his reputation as a conjuror at first acted against him.

He was arrested on a warrant of the Privy Council in May 1555. He was under suspicion of communicating with rebels in exile abroad, one of them the aforementioned Pickering. Worse, he was suspected of the 'lewd and vain practices' of 'calculating', 'conjuring' and 'witchcraft'. It was held against him that he had cast horoscopes of Mary and her consort King Philip of Spain – an illegal act, because it suggested the possibility of hexes and spells being cast, or preparations for assassination – and indeed this led to a really serious charge, made by two informers claiming to have secure evidence for their accusation, that he had tried to kill Queen Mary with just such enchantments. One of the informers claimed that Dee had blinded one of his children, and tried to kill another, by the same means.

The charges could not be substantiated, and after a series of examinations Dee was bound over to keep the peace and deprived of his rectorship – which meant that he was deprived of his livelihood. But Mary's officers appeared not to be content; they next charged him with heresy, and required that he be examined by Edmund Bonner, the Bishop of London, infamous for sending so many to the stake in the Marian persecutions. Known as 'Bloody Bonner' for his ferocity in this respect, he earned from Foxe in the *Book of Martyrs* these lines: 'This cannibal in three years space three hundred martyrs slew; they were his food, he loved so blood, he spared none he knew.' By any measure it would seem that Dee was in serious trouble – but here the record of his life degenerates into confusion, for instead of becoming one of the Bishop's victims he was somehow transmogrified into what Foxe called Bonner's 'chaplain', and came to assist in the interrogation of some of those brought to Bonner's attention.

How did this happen? Biographers of Dee appear not to know what to make of it, and speak instead of the fact that Dee not only was neither Protestant nor Catholic in his sympathies, but appeared to have his own distinct and separate views about religion. This would not be surprising for someone keen on Cabala and Hermeticism and the latter's implication of a *prisca theologia*. But the scant evidence seems to suggest a more prosaic explanation: that Dee knew how to save his skin, and did it effectively both in relation to the serious charges preferred against him regarding Mary, and likewise in the presence of 'Bloody Bonner'. Perhaps his individual views on religion made this equally easy and rational – why die for something to which you are anyway indifferent? It did not mean that he was not pious in his own way; his diaries are full of heartfelt religious sentiment, and they record long earnest sessions of private prayer and meditation. But he was definitely a survivor; when Elizabeth I succeeded Mary he was as safe from trouble as he had been in Bishop Bonner's palace in Fulham, and flourished under her reign just as well.

However one interprets Dee's escape in the reign of Mary, it was a complete one. He was soon writing to Mary herself proposing a national collection of books in the form of a Royal Library. He was himself an avid bibliophile, and built a magnificent library of his own, eventually the greatest in England. Among the books he sought were those he needed to help him restore the fortunes of astrology, at that time waning in England because of lack of mathematical knowledge and the correlative rarity of ephemerides (tables of the heavenly bodies), which had to be expensively imported from the continent.[5] Dee's interest was not just the standard astrological one in personal horoscopes, but in how the heavens influenced the sublunar realm in general. The work he produced in this vein was his *Propaedeumata Aphoristica* – the book dedicated to Mercator – in which he introduced a concept, symbolised by a sign he invented for the purpose, denoting the unity of the universe. This was the 'monad', a mystical symbol in the form of the Greek delta 'Δ' destined to play a role in his own later work and that of those influenced by him.

Key to Dee's view was that all things emanate rays, which affect both the souls and bodies of human beings. These rays can be magnified, concentrated, reflected or deflected by lenses and mirrors, and captured and made visible by crystals as in the crystal balls or the 'showstones' of fortune-tellers and 'skryers' or spirit mediums. The rays were derived from the original force imparted to the universe in its creation by God, and Dee thought of the science of these rays as *natural* magic in contrast to the *supernatural* magic that involved consort with demons and wicked powers. He wanted to understand this force, and to be able to harness it: in this general sense he was no different from what we would now call a 'true' scientist, though his premises and methods were ninety degrees different.

They were not ninety degrees different in all respects, however. His interest in cartography and navigation made him an important adviser to merchant adventurers planning attempts on the north-east and north-west passages. He provided them with maps and navigational instruments, and instructed the sailors in the latter's use. He translated Euclid. After Elizabeth I's accession he became one of her intermittent advisers, for example being consulted by her on the legal basis for the foundation of a colony in North America. Indeed he had ambitions for the greater glory of Elizabeth and her realm; he coined the name

'Britannia', dreamed of a global British Empire, and drew up plans for a magnificent navy to gain it and thereafter control it. In the midst of these endeavours he continued his occult and astrological interests as before, for example casting a horoscope to determine the best day for Elizabeth's coronation, and casting a spell on the Spanish Armada and taking credit for the storms that destroyed it – one of the reasons why Shakespeare took him as a model for Prospero.

Then suddenly, in the early 1580s, Dee plunged yet more deeply into occultism, and turned his back on his career as a Court adviser. There was a trigger for this: he was introduced to a new and highly promising skryer – there were any number of these individuals doing the rounds, making a living out of the credulity of the age – on the very day after he had seen a portentous astronomical event: the appearance of a comet, which he took to be the last in a series of signs that something momentous was about to happen, and for which he had been waiting.

The significance of the comet, now known to astronomy as Comet C/1582J1, was that it served as confirmation for Dee that the great thing about to happen applied not just the universe but to him personally too. There was no mere coincidence in the occurrences: the comet alerted him to the fact that the means was at last at hand for him to penetrate the secrets of the universe – the means in question being the skryer who appeared the next day – and it also served as the last and final sign in a series of signs leading up to a highly significant astrological moment of change, in the form of a 'Fiery Trigon'.

The skryer who was to transform his life was a man at first calling himself Edward Talbot, but who soon confessed to the name that subsequent history knows him by: Edward Kelley – one of the most extraordinary and successful liars and charlatans ever to have entered the human record.

The proximate background to this turn in Dee's life stretches back to a point ten years earlier. Late in 1572 a supernova became visible in the constellation Cassiopeia, glowing more brightly than Venus in the night sky. It was observed by many people around the world, and recorded in detail by Tycho Brahe (it is now known as Tycho's Nova, SN1572).[6] It is one of only eight supernovae ever to have been accurately recorded by observers on earth, and it had a seminal effect on astronomy and science, not least by disproving Aristotle's view that the heavens are unchanging – for if a new star comes into existence among the constellations, how could the stars be eternal and immutable? This meant that a new model of the universe was needed, requiring better observations of the skies, and better and more accurate instruments with which to make them. Such was the effect on astrologers and astronomers. More importantly still, and more generally, sixteenth-century beliefs were presented with a crisis by the appearance of the astonishing new star: for, as just noted, either it implied that the received cosmology of both religion and the sages of antiquity was wrong, or if that cosmology were right after all, then the new star's appearance meant that something enormous and unthinkable, and probably disastrous, was about to happen. One can imagine the disquiet this caused in the midst of the Reformation's struggles.

Dee was among those who recorded the appearance of the new star. On this occasion it was not him but the astrologer John Allen who was consulted by Elizabeth I as to the implications. Dee published his observations in 1573, and it is likely that he and Brahe corresponded. The nova remained visible until 1754. Like Brahe, Dee was sure that they had not witnessed a comet with an invisibly small tail appearing in the lower heavens, but a genuine star or star-like object in the remote heavens (the idea that comets appear in the 'lower heavens' is correct – as we now know, by travelling through the solar system in their passage around the sun). Only two 'new stars' had ever been claimed before, once by Hipparchus in 125 BCE – so Pliny claimed; it might have been a genuine supernova – and once in the guise of the 'Star of Bethlehem' in the New Testament. Consequently the phenomenon was a rich and troubling source of speculation.

Dee not only took the appearance of the new star to support the Copernican model, then still officially treated as an heuristic rather than a factual description of the heavens, though unofficially treated by many astronomers as literally correct; but he inferred from the star's variable brightness a theory that was equally revolutionary:

that the star was moving freely in space. The implication of this is that the stars are not fixed to crystalline spheres rotating majestically far from the earth, itself supposed to be lying at the focus of their concentricity, but that they exist at different distances from each other and the earth, like – as one contemporary of Dee's put it – motes suspended in a vast ocean.[7] The variable brightness was also hypothesised to be the result of the earth moving as it swung round the sun, first away from and then towards the star; but this promising suggestion was shown to be incorrect when the new star faded away altogether in 1574.

But the heavens were busy. The next drama to occur in them came soon afterwards, in 1577, with the appearance of the Great Comet (now catalogued as C/1577V1). It passed close to Venus, and therefore not far from earth itself, and was again seen and recorded by many. Brahe's detailed observations of the comet – he made thousands of them – were important to Kepler in the latter's work on the planetary orbits, not least in working out that they are elliptical. A notable feature of Brahe's notes is that they show his recognition that the comet flew above the earth's atmosphere, though he did not know how far above it, and that its coma or head faced away from the sun. Another feature is that in drawing the path of the comet Brahe represented the earth lying at the centre of the orbits of the sun and moon; he was not a Copernican, but a would-be reconciler of Copernicus and Ptolemy, for in his picture of the universe the sun and moon orbit earth but the other planets orbit the sun.

The comet of 1577 terrified all Europe even more than the new star had done, not least because it was far more obvious, it moved across the sky, its very appearance was ominous. Pamphlets appeared, wild in their speculations: the comet was shaped like a Turkish scimitar, which meant the Ottoman hordes were about to ravage Europe. It had appeared in the Seventh House of marriage and partnerships, which implied that religious disunities would deepen, or that the then proposed marriage of Elizabeth I and the Holy Roman Emperor Rudolf II would not take place. The comet had appeared in the west, suggesting something major was about to happen in the New World, though as Brahe observed, its tail pointed east, which suggested that it would instead scatter poison and plague, dissent and division upon the Russians and Tartars.

Dee recorded in his diary that Elizabeth's Court was 'in great fear and doubt' because, like everyone else, the general belief was that the comet signified bad news. He himself linked the comet to the nova, noting in his diary that it had appeared five years almost to the day after the new star had first been seen. Something was in train, he felt; matters were warming towards a highly significant outcome. If further proof were needed, it was supplied in Easter week 1580 in the form of an earthquake felt across the whole of England though seemingly centred on London, whose church bells rang out for two whole minutes with the force of the tremors.

This earthquake is the largest known to have affected northern France and the British isles. Geological investigations during the excavation of the Channel Tunnel suggest that it had a magnitude of about 5.6, and that its epicentre lay south of Calais, about thirty kilometres into the earth's crust – which is very deep, explaining its widespread effects. Cliffs along the south coast of England crumbled into the sea and the sea boiled, buildings shook and some fell. Naturally it was a hair-raising event for those affected, and it added to the general apprehension felt by most – though, for Dee, it was not so much apprehension as excitement. When therefore, a few years later, on that March evening in 1582, he saw the bright light in the sky, and then met Edward Kelley the next day, he felt that The Moment he had been anticipating was imminent.

The Moment in question was the inception of the 'Fiery Trigon'. A trigon is one of the four groups of three signs (Aries, Taurus, Gemini, etc.) which together make up the zodiacal wheel. Every twenty years the planets Saturn and Jupiter fall into an alignment known to astrologers as a 'Great Conjunction' or (more picturesquely) a 'Grand Copulation'. Each twenty years the Grand Conjunction occurs in a different sign; successive Grand Conjunctions stand at 120 degrees from the two preceding, each three Grand Conjunctions in a sixty-year cycle thus forming a triangle. In every ten Grand Conjunctions the signs in which Saturn and Jupiter align belong to the same trigon, though there are never more than four alignments successively in the same sign. But as the cycle repeats, the alignments shift somewhat, so when they recur it is only in the approximate vicinity of the alignment that occurred sixty years before. The occurrence of a Grand Conjunction in a new trigon, which happens every 200 years, is therefore considered important; greatly more important still is the inception of a new cycle after all four trigons have been visited. This happens every 800 years.

And this is what was scheduled to happen in 1583, the last of the Watery Trigon and the entrance of the Fiery Trigon (the trigons being named for the four elements). And of course so great an event was expected to have suitably apocalyptic implications. Such was the general anxiety that a papal bull had to be issued against divination; when twenty years passed – that is, by 1603 – and nothing extraordinary had happened among the usual disasters and conflicts that are mankind's lot, interest in the Fiery Trigon evaporated.[8]

But for Dee in 1582 expectations about the Fiery Trigon were vivid, and the co-occurrence of the comet and Kelley's arrival seemed to him confirmation that he was at an epoch in his life. The secrets of nature – knowledge of which meant access to control over it – and of the future seemed to be within his grasp. And the route to this knowledge lay through what Edward Kelley, by means either of a crystal ball or of a black flat showstone that Dee had acquired, was able to promise him, and seemed almost immediately to deliver: nothing less than regular conversations with angels.[9]

To that point Dee had failed to construct a system which gave him what he wanted; he was frustrated by the insufficiency of the various methods of enquiry he had tried, including those we would recognise as examples of empirical science. So the chance of learning directly from the angels seemed, quite literally, a godsend.[10]

On many occasions over the next four years Dee and Kelley conversed at length with the angels. They began each session by praying earnestly in the chapel in Dee's house, and then Kelley relayed to the eager Dee what the angels said to him. Kelley was not the first skryer Dee had employed; as early as 1581 he reported a session with one Barnabas Saul who gazed into a large crystal globe and said that he saw an angel called Anael. This was a prodigious encounter, too prodigious even for Dee who therefore reacted sceptically, for Anael was one of the seven angels of creation and, at the time of appearing in Dee's crystal globe, was governor of the entire universe as God's lieutenant. Dee tried another showstone, a flat black stone set in a frame, and this time the archangel Michael was named as available for consultation, 'but not until after Christmas', Anael told him.

With Kelley, however, things were different. Kelley seems to have had an amazing imagination, a gift of the gab, a capacity to track Dee's interests by reading Dee's diaries and other writings so that he could feed back to him tidbits that Dee would find credible and exciting. Very early in what was to become an addictive relationship for Dee, Kelley proved his credentials by making contact with the angel Uriel, to Dee's great excitement because Uriel was the angel who had revealed the secrets of astrology to Enoch, and Enoch was important because there was a tradition that he had written a book explaining the original language in which God had spoken to Adam, and which Adam had used to name the beasts and birds. Dee had a copy of a book called *De Originibus* by Guillaume Postel, in which Postel claimed to have been told by an Ethiopian priest that the Ethiopians had a copy of Enoch's Adamic primer. In conversation with Uriel via Kelley, Dee came to hope that a book he owned, *The Book of Soyga*, was in fact a copy of this primer in code. Dee asked if Uriel would interpret the book to him; Uriel said that only Michael could do that. And in order to invoke Michael, Dee would have to have a particular piece of furniture made.

Such was the beginning of the angel conversations, and Dee's rapt absorption in them over the following years. They must have been hideously frustrating because the replies recorded in Dee's diaries are so cryptic and evasive – but often clever, and oftener vivid, given the remarkable talents of the young Kelley, who was only twenty-six years of age when he entered Dee's employment.[11] Dee took the enterprise with immense seriousness. For three days before each session with the showstone he had to avoid sex and over-eating, to wash thoroughly, trim his beard and nails, and then pray. He was rewarded by being told that he would have the Adamic language dictated to him, and that the angels would dig up and deliver to him buried treasure if he would provide small samples of the soil from the places where the treasure lay.

How a man of Dee's gifts swallowed these and like absurdities not merely day after day but year after year might puzzle one, if one forgets the combination of background and desire that generated such credulity. But it was a credulity shared by a wider world than the Dee household. Dee's reputation grew as rumours of his angelological activities circulated, and it was a reputation that was international. In 1583 he was visited by Count Albert Łaski, a Polish aristocrat with claims to the Polish throne, and within a short time Dee and his family, complete with Kelley, travelled to Poland with Łaski. They took up residence in Kraków, there to continue contacting angels and spirits and to pursue researches into transmuting base metals into gold – gold on which Łaski's dwindling (or perhaps nearly non-existent) fortunes depended.

Łaski persuaded Dee to visit Prague, carrying a letter of introduction to the Holy Roman Emperor Rudolf II. The prospect of the journey – eight days by coach – was not as bad as the long journey already exhaustingly undertaken from England via the Netherlands and the unkind seas, but need and the spirits required it – for, coincidentally, the spirits told Kelley to tell Dee that he must go to Prague and give Rudolf an important message. Dee did not invariably believe everything that Kelley said the angels and spirits had instructed, but he believed most of it, this included. Although the angelological activities were supposed to be secret, Dee's ambiguous reputation as savant, astrologer, magician and master of the occult was great and still growing, sending shivers of interest through Polish and Bohemian circles. Comparing Dee's credulous inner life with the grand presence he had in those parts of Europe makes one conscious of the usual paradox of celebrity. Yet some of the mystical residue that still attaches to places like Kraków and Prague – the mysterious legends of sorcerers, monsters and other dark associations lurking along the narrow crooked streets of those cities, misty and ominous in the dead of night – have to do with the fact that Dee passed there in the late sixteenth century, as if he had left a black trail of *magia*, *cabala*, *alchymia* behind him, of contact with demons and dangerous powers, like footmarks across the cobbles and up the steep flights of steps that are still there today, the very same cobbles and steps as in his day.

In Prague Dee lodged with the Emperor's physician, Tadeáš Hájek, at the latter's 'House on the Green Mound' on the corner of Bethlehem Square in the Old Town – the Staré Město. The Old Town lies underneath the castle hill, with the Vltava river flowing close by. Dee's reputation had very thoroughly preceded him and he was visited and fêted, drawing curious crowds. Although neither Łaski's letter of introduction nor his own formidable reputation secured Dee an immediate meeting with the Emperor, he was eventually admitted to the presence, and there delivered the message that Kelley had transmitted to him – a message not in the slightest calculated to please the Imperial ear, because it was – put at its barest – 'If you don't shape up and stop sinning you will come to a bad end and all your kingdoms with you.' Dee arrived for this interview late, having had some sort of domestic problem with Kelley beforehand – a typical occurrence: Kelley was often ungovernable and on this occasion had become entangled in a duel. So they were not the best circumstances in which to deliver the message from God, which was as follows:

> The angel of the Lord appeared to me, and rebuketh you for your sins. If you will hear me, and believe me, you shall triumph, if you will not hear me, the Lord, the God that made heaven and earth (under whom you breathe and have your spirit) putteth his foot against your breast, and will throw you headlong down from your seat. Moreover the Lord hath made this covenant with me (by oath) that he will do and perform. If you will forsake your wickedness, and turn unto him, your Seat shall be the greatest that ever was, and the Devil shall become your prisoner: which Devil I did conjecture to be the Great Turk.[12]

On a scale of one to ten in the matter of how to win friends and influence people, this overture seems well below minus one, but the Emperor was gracious at first. Nevertheless he shortly came to feel the impertinence of the event, after he had sent a valued courtier, Jakob Kurtz, to inspect Dee. When Kurtz arrived at Hajek's House on the

Green Mound he said that Dee's reputation and books were well known to him, so he was pleased to have an opportunity to talk with Dee; an amicable beginning. They spent six hours together, during which Dee explained his ideas and mission to Kurtz, and showed him his recent writings. But when Kurtz left, Dee had an uneasy feeling that he had not made an especially good impression. And sure enough, he was not long afterwards told that Rudolf had taken exception to the 'message from God' and that Dee would not again be welcome at Court. Evidently Kurtz had recognised him as deluded in his ideas and therefore as either a charlatan or (more correctly, as it happened) foolishly under the influence of one.

In the city, as rumours about Dee grew, so with them grew an air of mistrust and hostility. A new Papal Nuncio to the Emperor's court set about discrediting Dee further, with a view to getting the Emperor to deport him. At just that point the spirits and angels intervened again, ordering a return to Kraków. Dee was short of money, his wife had just given birth again and was in need of rest, but the angels – so Kelley said – were insistent. Accordingly they returned to Kraków. Yet not many months later they were back in Prague to meet the Papal Nuncio, who pretended to believe that Dee was indeed in regular contact with angels, and who asked in silky tones if the angels could give some good counsel to the Church, which was much in need of it. It was intended as a trap for Dee, who successfully avoided it by offering blandishments and disavowals in return; but Kelley, ever the loose cannon, annoyed the Nuncio by saying that too many of the princes of the Church lived in a way that brought discredit to the Church, and until they reformed themselves the troubles engendered by the Reformation would continue.

By this time – it was now 1586; the two had been together for four years – Kelley had progressed very far in duping and controlling Dee. Indeed how completely he controlled his employer is illustrated by the 'cross-matching of wives' matter, and the incident in which Dee's books and papers were all burned and then magically restored. Kelley told Dee that the spirits had said that he and Dee should sleep with each other's wives. Dee's wife Jane, who was then thirty-one years of age – they had married when she was twenty-three and he fifty-one – had been a lady-in-waiting to the wife of a nobleman at Elizabeth's court. Dee reluctantly agreed; Jane was even more reluctant, but eventually consented to do as the spirits wished, and may have borne Kelley a son in consequence. It was however Dee who brought the boy up.

The second incident involved the angels giving orders through Kelley that Dee's books and papers should all be burned. With agony of heart Dee agreed, watching bagfuls of his precious work fed into the mouth of a furnace. But a short while later the writings magically reappeared in the garden; Kelley was led to them by a spirit appearing in the guise of a gardener. On some conjectures, the burning of the documents was a ploy by Dee and Kelley to persuade the Nuncio and the Emperor's spies that incriminating evidence of contact with spirits and angels had been destroyed. On other conjectures, this was a typical Kelley manoeuvre in flexing his hold over Dee.[13]

But at this point the question of which of these alternatives is correct becomes irrelevant, for the Papal Nuncio and Rudolf's ministers had lost patience with Dee and his disturbing effect on the city. The former submitted a memorial to the Emperor charging Dee with conjuring, necromancy and other dark arts. Dee urgently sent a plea of innocence, but unsuccessfully; the Emperor issued a decree that he must leave Bohemia within six days.

Here yet another twist in Dee's much twisting tale is required. It has been suggested with some plausibility that he was spying on behalf of the English government. There would be no great surprise if so; travellers provided their own home teams with information as a matter of course, and many notable figures of the time were engaged in conveying messages, collecting and sending information, making contact with helpful agents, and more. Descartes was probably a spy for the Jesuits and the Imperial interest in the Thirty Years War; Peter Paul Rubens was a spy for the Spanish Habsburgs; Huygens father and son exchanged intelligence between the Netherlands and England.[14] During his Prague sojourn Dee made a number of very brief forays to Leipzig and other places to meet English merchants and travellers, suggestive of passing on information or communications. This might well have played a role in his expulsion from Prague.

But Dee was not gone from Bohemia for long. No sooner had his entourage trundled its way into Germany than an encounter with the rich and alchemy-mad William of Rosenberg (Vilém Rožmberk), a Bohemian nobleman who had held high positions at Court in Prague, brought Dee back again – not to William's great castle of Český Krumlov but to a subsidiary estate, at nearby Třeboň, where in its alchemical laboratory William wished Dee to produce gold from base metals.

It was however Kelley who turned out to be the leading craftsman in this respect, appearing to succeed in this grail of alchemical endeavour. Their tenure of Rosenberg's patronage made Třeboň a magnet for visitors, including English visitors, most of whom were eager not for Dee's but, increasingly, for Kelley's advice, help and tutoring in the magic arts of producing riches from nothing, and desiring a taste of his nostrums and medicines. The English government tried to get Dee and Kelley to return home in the interests of filling the Queen's treasury with magically produced gold, but the two refused. Soon Kelley's circle of admirers and clients extended far beyond Bohemia, and he gained the Emperor's good graces also. His association with Dee weakened, then ceased.

The Emperor was as keen as anyone else to accumulate gold, by alchemical or any other means, but his growing interest in Kelley turned on another matter: the desire to escape death. He was obsessed by the fear of death, and the prospect of immortality in the flesh excited him. This is what he wanted from Kelley. As a result of his patronage Kelley became rich, was knighted, fell from grace and was imprisoned a couple of times – for failing to achieve the required alchemical goals – escaped out of windows and the like, and eventually vanished into legend. One fact about him that speaks volumes is that he had no ears: they were lopped off as a punishment for forgery when he was a young man. He always wore his hair long and a cap with the flaps tied down on either side of his head. Despite this considerable inconvenience, his imagination, power with words, chutzpah, cheek, intelligence, cunning and ability to learn fast and plausibly apply what he learned, made him a success in his own terms – at least until whatever end met him, some time before the year 1600.

Dee himself returned to England in 1589, accepting a medium-ranking appointment from the Crown as Warden of Manchester Collegiate Church. He might have ended his days in semi-retirement there had not the devil visited him in his rooms at the College, and left a burned imprint of his hoof on a table (like the *Teufelstritt* in the cathedral in Munich, it can be seen to this day). Dee left as a result of disquiet among his colleagues and congregation because of this incident and his general association with everything dark and unsavoury, and he faded from the record (rather sadly, given that Jane and two of his daughters died – of the plague in all three cases – before he did). What he had left, however, was a reputation and an influence, and it was this that helped fuel the last major outburst of occultism as a force in European affairs. This was the 'Rosicrucian furore' of the decade following the marriage of the Elector Palatine, Frederick V, to the daughter of King James I of England, in 1612 – and which is intimately linked to the outbreak of the Thirty Years War.

15

The Rosicrucian Scare

THE EFFECTIVE DEMISE of the credibility of *magia*, *alchymia*, *cabala*, even though credulousness in them remained (and among a few, remains to this day), can plausibly be attributed to the failure of the supposed 'movement' known as Rosicrucianism in the events that led up to the outbreak of the Thirty Years War. The Rosicrucian panic in the first quarter of the seventeenth century was what in dramaturgical terms would be called the *crisis* of occult philosophy, that is, the last great gasp of an outlook that had overstayed its welcome in the intellectual economy of the age, and in that final fling demonstrated its vacuity. Arguably, the interest in questions of methodology of the two chief formulators of philosophical and scientific method in the seventeenth century – Francis Bacon and René Descartes – was piqued not just by the Aristotelianism they rejected, but by the confusion of alchemy with chemistry, magic with medicine, astrology with astronomy, mysticism with mathematics, that was getting in the way of the advance of knowledge. What they rejected, in arguing for responsible methods of enquiry, was the very *magia*, *alchymia*, *cabala* which had engrossed the preceding century's epistemological and metaphysical imaginations.

Was there actually anything that could be called Rosicrucianism or a Rosicrucian movement in the first decades of the seventeenth century, still less an actual fraternity – 'the Brothers of the Rosy Cross' – with a pedigree reaching back into the preceding century and long before? Some scholars say there never was an organised Rosicrucian movement at all, just a rumour to which hopefuls attached themselves – perhaps thinking that if they supported the putative movement, its members would get in touch and include them. The case is rather that many were intrigued by what they understood to be Rosicrucian ideas, and among these many were those who sympathised with its goals and what seemed to be its principles. Perhaps it is only in this by-courtesy sense that Rosicrucianism was a network among like-minded people, but not a formal or sworn-in cabal or secret society. For convenience therefore the name 'Rosicrucian' might as well be applied to those who felt solidarity with the ideals and ideas associated with the supposed movement.

A first and highly important fact to note is that Rosicrucianism was a Protestant phenomenon. So indeed were all the forms of occultism, alchemy, magic – the esoteric in general. They were supported enthusiastically by Frederick V the Elector Palatine, and although he was not in any official or even financial way their chief supporter, they suffered devastatingly when his brief tenure of the Bohemian throne ended at the Battle of the White Mountain in 1620. His defeat, and with his defeat that of the occultist aspirations linked with him, allowed the Catholic Church – or more accurately its militant wing, the Jesuits, in its vanguard – to devote great energy to suppressing interest in Rosicrucianism and anything occult associated with it. One chief way the Jesuits did this was to spread anxiety about supposed occult activities involving Hermeticism, magic or Cabala, as threatening individuals and cities. This was successfully done in the first half of the 1620s, so well indeed that after the panic about Rosicrucianism in France in 1623, open interest in occultism in general and Rosicrucianism in particular began to fade away.

One of the hammers of the supposed Rosicrucian movement was Marin Mersenne. So emphatic was Mersenne's hostility to occultism that his public contest with Robert Fludd kept the educated populations of Europe riveted for years, and was a major source of occultism's decline. This tale is told in the next chapter.

The immediate source of interest in and fears about Rosicrucianism in the years after 1612 was the publication of three books that gained immediate notoriety. One was the *Fama Fraternitatis Rosae Crucis, oder die Bruderschaft des Ordens der Rosenkreuzer*, printed in Cassel in 1614. It had been known in manuscript for some years, and its interest in Hermetic attitudes to the mystical powers of numbers was well known. The second book was the *Confessio Fraternitatis* or *Confessio oder Bekenntnis der Societät und Bruderschaft Rosenkreuz* published in 1615 also at Cassel. The third was *The Chemical Wedding of Christian Rosencreutz in the Year 1459* (*Chymische Hochzeit Christiani Rosencreutz anno 1459*) published at Strasbourg in 1616. As Frances Yates demonstrates, the aims and ideas of these manifestos were not new, but originated earlier in the familiar Renaissance occultist brew, almost all of the ideas finding their way into the Rosicrucian documents through one identifiable conduit: Dr John Dee.[1]

The manifestos announced that a 'universal reformation of mankind' was imminent, and would be made possible through the mediation of those learned men who followed the lead of 'Frater C. R. C.' – soon identified in the texts as Christian Rosencreutz himself – in the study of the occult sciences. The legend recounted in the manifestos ran as follows. Rosencreutz had lived to a great age – 106 years – and taught a select group of disciples the knowledge he had acquired as a result of studying in the East (note: once again the East, from which all things magical and Hermetic came). He did this because there was no general receptivity for his ideas at the time he lived, which was in the fourteenth and early fifteenth centuries. He had instructed his disciples, just eight in number, to study medicine, remain single, treat the sick at no charge, remain brothers in their secret society, and find a replacement for themselves individually. But now, said the manifestos, after several generations of the Society existing in secret, the opening of thought and greater religious freedom made it possible for them to return to the task of widening membership of their brotherhood and bringing good people into it.

Remembering that occultism was motivated by a Faustian desire to find short-cuts to knowledge and control of the mysteries of nature explains much about the threat it posed to the view – the Church's view – that those mysteries are not mankind's but God's alone to know. From the Church's point of view there was no point in drawing a line between real and occult science. Finding a way of unlocking the universe's secrets was every enquirer's ambition, whatever kind of enquirer was involved – whether by the short-cuts of occultism, or by the empirical and quantitative methods of genuine science. The Church was against both; it did not distinguish them. Again the point presses that neither did all the practitioners themselves. But insofar as occultism was associated with Protestant enquirers and the Catholic Church was at war with occultism as contrary to orthodoxy, there was a parallel between this doctrinal conflict and the shooting war that broke out when Frederick of the Palatine went to Bohemia.

Narrowed to a clash between Catholic religion and Rosicrucianism, the conflict can be seen as having been definitely won by the former before the mid-1620s. The Church's stormtroopers, the Jesuits, so successfully demonised Rosicrucianism, and savants such as Mersenne so successfully discredited it, that if it survived in any sense at all thereafter, it was as an underground rumour and legend merely.

The *Fama Fraternitatis* and *Confessio Fraternitatis* present themselves as invitations to their readers to join what they describe as the revived brotherhood or order which Christian Rosencreutz had founded. It was thereby too an invitation to know the secret wisdom that he had brought back from those extensive travels in the mysterious East. Whereas the *Fama* and *Confessio* were written anonymously, *The Chemical Wedding* has a known author: he was a Lutheran pastor of Württemberg named Johann Valentin Andreae, an accomplished author of other works, among them plays and an autobiography. The geographical aspect of this point is significant.

The state of Württemberg was ruled by Duke Frederick I, an avid Anglophile who had an ambition to be a knight in England's Order of the Garter. To his delight he was appointed to the order by Elizabeth I, after soliciting her long and hard. He was avid also in his alchemical and occult interests, and provided an encouraging environment for the likes of Andreae.[2] Elizabeth indulged him with the Garter as part of her pro-German Protestant policy, which had the same aim as France's policy under Henri IV, namely, that of constraining Habsburg power.

Württemberg abutted the Palatinate, whose Elector Frederick married the daughter of Elizabeth's successor James I in 1613.

The marriage was a spectacular affair, for which plays, songs and pamphlets were written, and lavish festivals held. Actors and musicians accompanied the Elector and his bride back to the Palatinate, performing at the celebrations held at numerous staging-posts on the way to Heidelberg. Frederick was, recall, head of the Protestant Union, and the great noise about his family union with the King of England was meant to be obvious to all Europe. In the end the alliance proved to mean nothing, because when Frederick needed James' help in defending his assumption of the crown of Bohemia, James abandoned him.

Frederick's Chancellor, Christian of Anhalt, was another enthusiast for the occult arts and their promises. He was a patron of a Dee-like figure who claimed himself to be a master of those arts, one Oswald Crollius, who was Christian's physician. Crollius had dedicated a book to Christian, and interested him in his own obsessions with occult ideas.[3] Because of his prime-ministerial position at Frederick's Court Christian was able to foster and indulge these tastes. The influence of Dee and Kelley was palpable in Heidelberg, which Dee had visited on his return journey to England in 1589. His stay in the city created a sensation, with scores of enquirers and noblemen jostling to meet him. Most of the works published in occult fields after his visit bore the stamp of the influence he exerted, especially the influence of the *Monas Hieroglyphica* which laid out his eclectic views on alchemy and occult philosophy.

Two Dee-inspired books which had a more direct influence on the Rosicrucian texts were *The Amphitheatre of Eternal Wisdom* by Henricus Khunrath, and a strange prophetic-seeming work by Simon Studion called *Naometria*, which had been first published in 1604. Studion's book bore on its title-page an image of a rose with a cross at its heart, which many saw as anticipating the Rosicrucian documents that appeared ten years later. The *Naometria* had a special resonance for Frederick of the Palatinate and Christian of Anhalt; it predicted that 1620 was going to be an apocalyptic year, in which the 'Antichrists' – the Pope and Mahomet – would be overthrown. This prediction was unquestionably part of what encouraged Christian to tell Elector Frederick that his proper destiny and that of his cause lay in the Bohemian lands.

Khunrath's *Amphitheatre* was published in 1609, five years after Studion's strange book. Dee's influence on Khunrath is obvious; the latter's views closely shadow those of Dee. In its own turn Khunrath's book had an immediate and no less palpable impact on the Rosicrucian texts. Yates wrote, 'In Khunrath's work we meet with the characteristic phraseology of the [Rosicrucian] manifestos, the everlasting emphasis on macrocosm and microcosm, the stress on Magia, Cabala, and Alchymia as in some way combining to form a religious philosophy which promises a new dawn for mankind.'[4]

When the *Confessio* was published in 1615 it was accompanied by a pamphlet called *A Brief Consideration of More Secret Philosophy*, offered as a gloss or expansion of some of the more obscure themes in the *Confessio*. This pamphlet is in effect a paraphrase of parts of Dee's *Monas Hieroglyphica*, quoting the latter's text frequently and at length. Likewise the *Chemical Wedding* by Andreae has Dee's then instantly recognisable 'Monas' symbol not only on its title-page but in the text itself. Unquestionably, the connection between Dee, the influence he left on the German Protestant states and the Rosicrucian texts is close. The two regions of the Palatinate and Bohemia are where occult philosophy mingles with politics, the controversies of religion, and international affairs. As Yates put it, '[The] Rosicrucian publications belong to the movements around the Elector Palatine, the movements building him up towards the Bohemian adventure. The chief stirring spirit behind these movements was Christian of Anhalt, whose connections in Bohemia belonged right in the circles where the Dee influence would have been known and fostered.'[5]

The very long subtitle of the *Fama Fraternitatis* reads as follows: 'Universal and General Reformation of the whole wide world; together with the *Fama Fraternitatis* of the Laudable Fraternity of the Rosy Cross, written to all the Learned and Rulers of Europe; also a short reply sent by Herr Haselmayer, for which he was seized by the Jesuits and put in irons on a galley. Now put forth and communicated to all true hearts'. The book opens with a resounding claim that 'in these latter days' a great promise is being kept: nothing less than a full revelation of nature's deepest and most recondite secrets. The *Fama* goes on to say that:

> [we may] boast of the happy time, wherein there is discovered unto us the half part of the world, which was heretofore unknown and hidden, but [God] hath also made manifest unto us many wonderful and never heretofore seen works and creatures of Nature, and moreover hath raised men, imbued with great wisdom, who might partly renew and reduce all arts (in this our age spotted and imperfect) to perfection; so that man might finally understand his own nobleness and worth, and why he is called Microcosmus, and how far his knowledge extendeth into Nature.[6]

In recounting the events of Christian Rosencreutz's travels in the East to gather knowledge, the *Fama* emphasises the East's great superiority in epistemological matters, and claims that this superiority arises from the fact that its savants openly communicate their ideas and findings to each other, in contrast to the many 'magicians, Cabalists, physicians and philosophers' in Germany who keep their secrets to themselves, in this way inhibiting the spread of knowledge. This point reminds one of Bacon's argument that science is and should always be a co-operative enterprise, a view urged in his *Advancement of Learning* (1605).

The *Fama* dates Rosencreutz's journey to the fifteenth century, and says that when he returned to Europe he set himself to teach what he had learned; but his efforts were rejected and ridiculed. He therefore started a secret society to preserve what he knew and pass it on. For a long time the tomb where Rosencreutz was buried was kept a profound secret. Its late discovery and reopening – said the *Fama* – thus revealing its treasures and books of secret knowledge, was predicted; this was the moment that Rosencreutz wished everyone to be prepared for. The *Fama* accordingly proclaimed that the time had come for Europe to wake up and undergo a 'general reformation'. The tomb, said the *Fama*, was reopened in 1604.

Between them the *Fama* and the *Confessio* stirred controversy and excitement across the breadth of Europe. They were variously accepted, rejected, quoted, defended, attacked, believed as oracles or vilified as works of charlatanry; but they were read widely, whether by believers or sceptics. Significantly, those who were hostile to the texts were those most alert to the dangerous suggestions of imminent 'alterations' in the Holy Roman Empire, of which the *Fama* talked much; it claimed that the Rosy Cross brotherhood would help to change the Empire greatly 'with secret aid'. These comments were clearly understood to apply to the Elector Frederick as the Protestant Union's head; the *Fama*'s references to the 'Lion' – Frederick's emblem – as the agent of these forthcoming changes made this quite explicit. When Frederick lost his crown at the Battle of the White Mountain a spate of caricatures, lampoons and cartoons pilloried him and Christian of Anhalt together, subjoining mocking references to their Rosicrucian associations.[7]

But although Rosicrucianism had its many enemies, from the Jesuits and the Roman Church generally to responsible scholars such as Andreas Libavius and sharp, well-informed critics such as 'Menapius' and 'Irenaeus Agnostus' – both pseudonyms – it also had a highly enthusiastic following. Literally scores of books and pamphlets followed the publication of the *Fama* and *Confessio*, written by people who hoped to be noticed by the secret brotherhood and to be invited into their number. There were direct appeals from men keen to learn the Rosicrucian secrets and to be part of the movement. There were also publications by people who themselves either claimed to be or seemed to be Rosicrucians, or who clearly knew a lot about Rosicrucian ideas – among them 'Joseph Stellatus' (a pseudonym), 'Julianus de Campis' (also a pseudonym), Theophilus Schweighardt, and more. Yates singled out one apparent Rosicrucian who seemed to have a profound grasp of the relevant ideas, 'Florentinus de Valentia', who gave a careful reply to an anti-Rosicrucian book by 'Menapius' in which he manifested excellent understanding of music, fine arts, architecture, navigation, geometry, mathematics and astronomy. In describing the sciences as standing in need of reform – here displaying the influence of Bacon (an influence that appears also in other Rosicrucian documents) – Florentinus says that astronomy is imperfect, astrology is uncertain, physics is under-supported by experiment, and ethics needs to be examined afresh.[8]

The comments made by Florentinus are astute. They serve as a reminder that despite the alloy of Hermeticism, Cabala and the rest in Rosicrucian ideas, they also contained a serious aspect. Florentinus insisted that it was not impious, other than by the exigent standards applied by orthodox Christians of all kinds, to understand 'God's book', meaning nature. That book, he says, contains everything we need to recover the knowledge that was lost because of Adam's Fall. (This theme – that to study nature was to read God's book – was iterated repeatedly, by among others Newton and in the following century George Berkeley.)[9]

Some historians of ideas take the view that there is a positive side to the outflow of Rosicrucian literature in this period, because they see it as an encouragement to scientific investigation of nature, coupled as it was with rejection of Aristotelian views both in the content of philosophy and in the manner in which it was done. Enquiry into nature and rejection of Aristotle were vigorously opposed by the Roman Catholic Church, which was afraid of what the new sciences were revealing, and which was doctrinally committed to Aristotelian thought. The close connection between Catholicism and temporal power in the Holy Roman Empire made it automatic that opponents of science would anathematise Rosicrucian ideas, which they regarded as subversive of both the religious and temporal orders equally.

The storm of debate about Rosicrucianism, in the form of books and pamphlets on both sides, suddenly ceased in 1620. Yates gives the reason: the failure of Rosicrucian hopes, linked as they were with Frederick's Bohemian ambitions, and both defeated at the Battle of the White Mountain. In 1621 a pamphlet appeared, *Warning against the Rosicrucian Vermin*. It said nothing new, merely iterating the by then standard charges against the supposed brotherhood and its ideas; but what was indeed new and highly significant was its place of publication: Heidelberg, Frederick's erstwhile Palatinate capital, now occupied by Habsburg troops and under the control of Duke Maximilian of Bavaria.

Also in 1621 appeared the *Palma Triumphalis*, a hymn of praise to the Catholic Church and the miracles it performed. It was published at Ingoldstadt, a major Jesuit centre, and it was dedicated to Emperor Ferdinand II. The *Palma* attacked Rosicrucianism's ideas and aims, ridiculing its ambition to 'restore all sciences, transmute metals, and prolong human life'.[10]

Although the political hopes associated with Rosicrucianism died at the Battle of the White Mountain, the 'movement' itself had one big final flourish in it. In 1623 posters appeared in Paris announcing that the Brothers of the Rosy Cross had arrived in town, and were 'making a visible and invisible stay . . . We show and teach without books or marks how to speak all languages of the countries where we wish to be, and to draw men from error and death.' The result was general panic. In his *Instruction to France about the truth of the Rose Cross Brothers* (published in the same year) Gabriel Naudé described the panic as swept along by a 'hurricane of rumour'. The Church responded to the Brothers' supposed presence in Paris by vigorously demonising them, saying that they not only forswore Christianity and the authority of the Church, but bowed themselves down before Satan, who manifested himself to them in glory.

Almost all attacks on Rosicrucianism in the 1623 scare, as beforehand, were vitriolic or hysterical. Naudé's discussion is interesting because it was neither of those things, but instead both well informed and moderate. He placed Rosicrucianism in the Renaissance Hermetic tradition, and in reporting its promise that a new age of discovery was imminent he used the term 'instauration' to describe its conception of a renewal of knowledge. Use of that term demonstrates knowledge of Francis Bacon's writings, among them *The Great Instauration*, which had been published not long before.[11] Naudé's aim was to oppose Rosicrucianism, but by means of careful assessment; after explaining what he took it to stand for he says, 'Behold, gentlemen, the huntress Diana whom Actaeon presents to you naked.' In the myth he alludes to, the goddess Diana, chaste and modest, reluctant ever to be seen naked by a male whether human or divine, was bathing in a pond when the hapless hunter Actaeon stumbled across her. In anger

Diana transformed him into a stag, and made his own hounds tear him to shreds. Naudé's invocation of the myth is clear; Rosicrucians are false philosophers who pretend to reveal truths, but who will be overcome by the real truth. Naudé concludes by agreeing with the Jesuits' condemnation of Rosicrucianism, and he applauds Libavius for refuting them so conclusively.

René Descartes had at least a walk-on role in the Rosicrucian scare of 1623, though in fact it might have been a larger role than it seems. He had been travelling in parts of Europe central to the tumultuous events of the Thirty Years War – a telling fact in itself, if he was in some sense a spy – and appeared in Paris just as the Rosicrucian panic was beginning there. Pierre Baillet's account is worth quoting. When Descartes arrived in Paris, Baillet tells us,

> the affairs of the luckless Count Palatine, who had been elected King of Bohemia . . . and the transfer of the Electorate from Count Palatine to the Duke of Bavaria, which had been made at Ratisbon on the previous 15th of February [1623], were obsessing public discussion.[12] Descartes could tell his friends a great deal about these matters, but in return they told him news of something that was giving them much anxiety, for all that it seemed incredible. It was that for several days there had been talk all round Paris about the Brothers of the Rose Cross, and it was beginning to be said that he [Descartes] was one of their number. Descartes was surprised at this news because such a thing was neither conformable with his character, nor with his inclination to think of the Rosicrucians as impostors and dreamers. In Paris people called them the Invisibles . . . six of them had come to Paris and lodged at the Marais, but they could not communicate with people, or be communicated with, except by joining thought to will in a way undetectable by the senses. The accident of their arrival in Paris at the same time as Descartes could have had an unfortunate effect on his reputation if he had kept himself closeted or lived solitarily, as he was wont to do on his travels. But he refuted those who wished to calumniate him through this conjunction of events, by making himself visible to everyone, and particularly to his friends, who needed no other argument to convince them that he was not one of the Rosicrucians or Invisibles. He used the same argument

about invisibility to explain why he had been unable to find any of them in Germany.[13]

Baillet then adds that Descartes' deliberate visibility and insouciant dismissal of the allegations 'served to calm the agitation of his friend Father Mersenne', who had been particularly upset by the rumours because he did not share others' dismissive view of Rosicrucianism. Mersenne was convinced that Rosicrucians were real and dangerous, because he had read 'what several Germans, and Robert Fludd, the Englishman, had written in their favour', and he believed them.[14]

It might indeed have been coincidental that Descartes arrived in Paris just as the Rosicrucian scare began, after several years of travels around an unsettled and often dangerous Europe, probably looking for Rosicrucians on behalf of the Jesuits to spy on them; and it might be yet more of a coincidence that he was somehow associated with Rosicrucianism itself in the minds of some. But a considerable body of additional evidence – even if it is circumstantial – supports the hypothesis that he was not as uninvolved as he wished his friends in Paris to think. This evidence suggests either that he was indeed an agent, and if so almost certainly for the Jesuits, charged with investigating or watching alleged Rosicrucians; or that for a time he actually was – or wished to be – a Rosicrucian himself. The evidence, ambiguous as between these possibilities, but not quite so ambiguous as to justify some sort of interest, is as follows.[15]

First there is what Descartes wrote in a notebook or diary called the *Olympica*, a work known to Baillet, and also to the philosopher Gottfried Leibniz who owned it and transcribed passages from it, which is why we have those passages now. The notebook was subsequently lost, which is a great pity because it recorded the famously portentous dreams Descartes experienced on 10 November 1619 and which he claimed had shaped his whole philosophical outlook thereafter. The story of that notebook is extraordinary; first, the original was lost after Leibniz made transcriptions from it, then Leibniz's original manuscript transcriptions went missing after a nineteenth-century French scholar published an edition of them. What remains is a

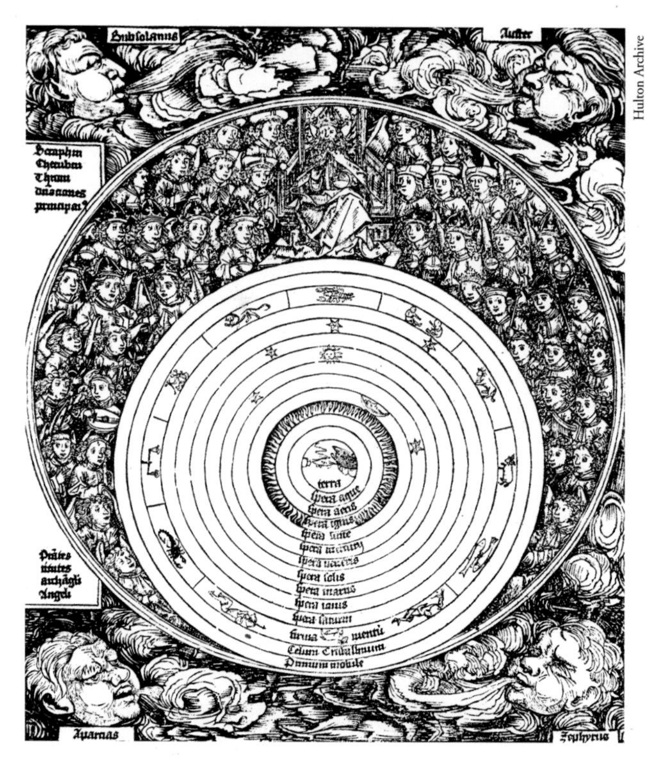

Hulton Archive

Diagram of a geocentric universe from *Liber chronicarum mundi*, 1493.

De Agostini Picture Library

Prognostication auff xxiiii. jar zůkünfftig/durch den hochgelerten Doctorem Paracelsum/Geschriben zů dem Großmechtigsten/Durchleüchtigsten Fürsten vnd Herren/Herren Ferdinanden rc. Römischen Künig/Ertzhertzog zů Osterreych rc.

Mit Kayserlicher vñ Künigklicher Mayestat Freyheyten begnadet/nit nachzůtrucken/on erlaupniß zů keiner zeyt/bey peen/xx. marck lötigs golds.

M. D. XXXVI.

The title page of *Prognostication of Paracelsus*, published in 1536.

Apic, Hulton Fine Art Collection

An anonymous portrait of John Dee, *c.* 1590.

Hulton Archive

Maximilian I, Duke and Elector of Bavaria, succeeded to the dukedom in 1598.

Leemage, Universal Images Group

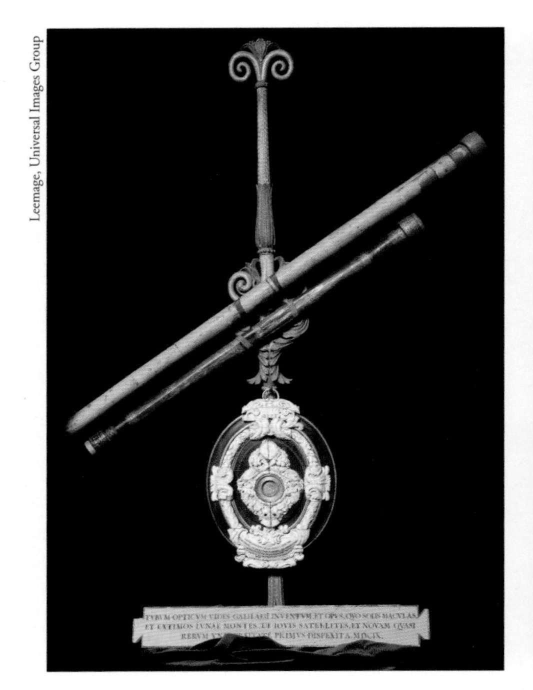

A telescope designed by Galileo Galilei.

DEA / A. Dagli Orti, De Agostini

Portrait of Ferdinand II of Austria by Josef Kiss and Friedrich Mayrhofer. He was Emperor of the Holy Roman Empire from 1619 until his death in 1637.

An etching of Frederick V by Richard Earlom, Charles Turner and R. Dunkarton.

Hulton Archive

The arrival of the imperial armies – a detail from a painting by Pieter Snayers of the first phase of the Battle of White Mountain near Prague in November 1620, during the Thirty Years War.

A. Dagli Orti, De Agostini

Artillery bombardment of the imperial and Bavarian armies before the battle, in the second phase of the Battle of White Mountain – a detail from another painting by Pieter Snayers.

A. Dagli Orti, De Agostini

Gustav II Adolf of Sweden leading his army to victory at the Battle of Breitenfeld (1631) in a portrait by Johann Walter.

Portrait of Cardinal Roberto Bellarmino by Carlo Perotti.

Gustav II Adolph of Sweden imposing an oath of allegiance to his daughter Cristina on the States-General.

Galileo before the Inquisition Court in a painting by Cristiano Banti.

An anonymous contemporary portrait of Rene Descartes.

DEA / G. Dagli Orti, De Agostini

Queen Christina of Sweden surrounded by her court, in a painting from the collection of Musée de l'Histoire de France.

Heritage Images, Hulton Fine Art Collection

An engraving of Marin Mersenne.

Portrait of Thomas Hobbes by John Michael Wright.

Title page of Hobbes's *Leviathan* (1651).

DEA Picture Library, De Agostini

Portrait of Isaac Newton by Godfrey Kneller.

Heritage Images, Hulton Archive

Portrait of John Locke by Godfrey Kneller.

Heritage Images, Hulton Fine Art Collection

Louis XIV, King of France (1638–1715), from the collection of the Musée de l'Histoire de France.

version of them made in the late nineteenth century by Charles Adam, the editor (with Paul Tannery) of the *Oeuvres de Descartes*. Assuming the reliability of the text, here is what Descartes so enigmatically and suggestively wrote:

> Polybius Cosmopolitanus's *Thesaurus Mathematicus* teaches the true ways of resolving all difficulties of this science and demonstrates that the human mind can go no further in this respect. This calls forth hesitation and rejects the recklessness of those who promise to perform miracles in all sciences. It also supports the agonising work of many who (F. Rosi Cruc), entangled night and day in some Gordian knots of that discipline, exhaust their minds in vain. This work is offered again to the savants of all the world, and especially to the most celebrated F. R. C. in G. [Fraternity of the Rosi-Crucians in Germany].
>
> Now the sciences have been masked; they would appear in all their beauty, if their masks were to be removed. For to anyone who sees clearly the chains linking the sciences, it will seem no more difficult to keep them in mind than to remember the series of numbers.[16]

These words suggest that Descartes was planning to write a book with the title *Thesaurus Mathematicus* under the pseudonym 'Polybius Cosmopolitanus', and that it was to be dedicated to the Fraternity of the Rosy Cross. 'Polybius' is a pseudonym Descartes actually used; when he visited Johann Faulhaber at Ulm in the summer of 1620 (Faulhaber described him as 'a clever young French mathematician') he introduced himself using that name. And as we shall see, among Descartes' most urgent concerns was to find a method of enquiry that would lead to certain knowledge. This part of his quest is the one that has remained a live matter for philosophical debate ever since.

Furthermore, the dreams that Descartes describes in the notebook passages bear striking parallels with a Rosicrucian work published by Rudophilus Staurophorus in 1619, called the *Raptus Philosophicus*. In this book a young man pauses at a crossroads, wondering which way to go, is approached by a woman who says that she is Nature and shows him a volume containing all knowledge, but the contents of which have not been put into order.[17] The Descartes scholar Stephen

Gaukroger carefully notes that we have no evidence that Descartes ever read Staurophorus, and equally carefully points out that the conceit shared by their respective dreams is a cliché – a fork in the road on the journey to knowledge, a person (often a woman personifying Wisdom, reminiscent of the goddess Athena) who points the way. Clichés are available for anyone to use.

But even if we discount the *Raptus* of Staurophorus as the model used by Descartes for his seminal dreams, another equally plausible Rosicrucian model is Andreae's *Chemical Wedding* itself. A significant incident in Descartes' dream is that he was startled awake, even as he dreamed, by a loud bang in his ear. In the *Chemical Wedding* the Angel of Truth is announced to Rosencreutz by a trumpet blast. Rosencreutz's way is opposed by a powerfully blowing gale, against which he has to struggle; but he manages to get into a castle where he meets with a number of acquaintances and is shown a huge globe in which the heavenly bodies are visible even by daylight. He also finds an unfinished encyclopaedia, and a voice asks him, 'Where are you going?' The similarities to Descartes' dreams are remarkable.

Descartes reports having three dreams in succession on the same night, or more precisely, two dreams intermitted by the apparently strange occurrence of the loud 'bang' above mentioned, an experience like having an explosion or pistol shot go off next to his ear. All day before going to bed Descartes had been in an excited and overwrought state, thinking hard about what methods of enquiry would lead securely to knowledge. He felt that he was close to discovering what such a method should be. As his notebook relates, and as his peculiar 'second dream' confirms, he went to bed exhausted, in an excited and febrile state, and the first dream came to him immediately he fell asleep.[18]

In this dream Descartes 'felt his imagination struck by the representation of some phantoms', Baillet reports,

> which frightened him so much that, thinking that he was walking in the streets, he had to lean to his left in order to reach his destination, because he felt a great weakness in his right side and could not hold himself upright. He tried to straighten himself, feeling ashamed to walk

> in this fashion, but he was hit by turbulent blasts as if of a whirlwind, which spun him round three or four times on his left foot. Even this was not what alarmed him; the difficulty he had in struggling along made him feel that he was going to fall at every step. Noticing a school open along his route he went in, seeking refuge and a remedy for his problem. He tried to reach the school chapel, where his first thought was to pray. But realising that he had passed an acquaintance without greeting him, he sought to retrace his steps to pay his respects, but was violently repulsed by the wind blowing into the chapel. At the same time he saw another person in the school courtyard, who addressed him by name and politely told him that if he wished to find Monsieur N he had something to give him. Descartes took it that the thing in question was a melon from a foreign country. What was more surprising was that the people clustering around that person in order to talk with him were straight and steady on their feet, although he himself was still bent over and unsteady on the same ground. Having almost knocked him over a number of times, the wind had greatly lessened.

Descartes woke to find that there was, says Baillet, a real pain in his side, which made him think that an evil spirit had caused the dream. He turned on to his other side, therefore, praying to God to shield him against any evil consequences of the dream, and to forgive his sins, which he acknowledged were many and great; for though he had lived in a way that was largely innocent, as any ordinary standard of judgment would have it, he knew that he really merited thunderbolts to fall on his head from heaven.

He could not go back to sleep immediately. After two hours' thinking he fell back to sleep, only to start dreaming again immediately, in a frightening way. 'He thought he heard a sudden, loud noise, which he took for thunder,' Baillet writes. 'Terrified, he immediately woke. Upon opening his eyes he noticed sparks of fire scattered about the room. He had experienced this phenomenon many times before, and it did not seem strange to him that when he woke in the night his eyes sparkled enough for him to see objects close to him.' After a time his fears diminished, and he again fell asleep, again to dream – but this time a peaceful dream, and a highly meaningful one.

Descartes now dreamed that he found a book on his table, not knowing who had left it there. On opening it he saw that it was a dictionary, which pleased him because dictionaries are so useful. He simultaneously noticed another new book next to it, again without knowing who had put it there. It was a collection of poems by a variety of authors, bearing the title *Corpus Poetarum*. When he opened it at random his eye fell upon the line, *quod vitae sectabor iter?*, which means, 'What way in life shall I follow?'

At that point he became aware of a stranger standing near by, who handed him a poem beginning with the words 'Yes and No', and saying that it was an excellent poem. Descartes recognised that the line was a quotation from the *Idylls* of Ausonius, and that this was included in the anthology he had just picked up from the table. To show the poem to the stranger Descartes began searching for it, boasting that he knew the anthology's arrangement perfectly. While he leafed through its pages the stranger asked where the anthology had come from; Descartes said that he did not know, but that just a short while ago he been looking through another book, which had suddenly disappeared, and he did not know who had brought that book either. He was still hunting for the *Idylls* when he saw the dictionary reappear on the other side of the table, and he noticed that it was now no longer as complete as when he had first opened it.

He found Ausonius' poems at last, but 'Yes and No' was not one of them. Descartes told the stranger not to mind, because he knew a better poem by Ausonius, which begins '*quod vitae sectabor iter?*' The stranger was eager to see it, so Descartes began leafing through the pages again. In the process he came across a number of portraits engraved in copperplate, which made him comment on how handsomely produced the book was; but before he could locate the *quod vitae* poem the anthology and the stranger both suddenly disappeared.

Descartes was not woken by this third dream, Baillet says, but even in his sleep he wondered whether what he had just experienced was a dream or a vision, and he set about interpreting it: 'He judged that the dictionary could only mean all the sciences gathered together, and that the anthology of poets entitled the *Corpus Poetarum* represented, in a more particular and distinct way, the union of Philosophy and Wisdom.'

When at last properly awake Descartes analysed his dreams in detail. He interpreted the poetry anthology as representing Revelation and Enthusiasm, 'for the favours of which he did not despair', says Baillet. By 'Yes and No' he understood Truth and Falsehood. 'Seeing that the interpretation of these things accorded so well with his inclinations,' Baillet adds, 'he was so bold as to believe that the Spirit of Truth [God, presumably] had wished, by means of this dream, to open to him the treasures of all the sciences.'

Descartes, in short, understood the dreams to be prophetic. Baillet adds that Descartes had confirmation of their prophetic status that very same day: 'It remained only to explain the little copperplate portraits he had seen in the second book. He looked for no further explanation of them following the visit, later that same day, of an Italian painter.' The idea that Descartes believed in the possibility of foretelling the future is intriguing, for it is at odds with two commitments he was supposed to have made: one, to the teachings of Catholic Christianity which regarded prognostication as sinful, and the other to the rational demands of a scientific world-view. Perhaps the explanation is the date of the dreams – Descartes was still young and not yet finished in his views, particularly as regards scientific method.

The bang that woke Descartes seemed significant both to him and to some who have written about him. Neurology now recognises this phenomenon as a harmless occurrence which it prosaically labels 'exploding head syndrome'. Just as Descartes describes, it involves a subject 'hearing' an explosion inside his head while falling asleep, so loud and unexpected that it jerks him awake. There is no preceding disease or harmful consequences: it just happens, with no outcome other than that its subject is awake and startled. The bangs seem to occur in subjects who are very tired or very stressed. They are most likely some sort of neurological discharge, caused in a similar way to the feeling of tripping just as one is drifting into asleep. The tripping sensation might be a junior version of the exploding experience, if both are ways that the central nervous system reboots itself to keep levels of excitation uniform. Quite a variety of seemingly odd subjective neurological events can occur in the margins of sleep, so it is easy to understand how they might seem significant, until one learns that they are merely common and arbitrary.[19]

The point of this excursus is to demonstrate how similar are Descartes' dreams or 'dreams' – embellishment is always a possibility – to Rosicrucian accounts of awakenings to the path of knowledge. If neither of the texts quoted earlier inspired Descartes' dreams, the similarities are all the more remarkable.

To these coincidences must next be added the fact that Descartes knew a lot of people who either claimed to be Rosicrucians, or stated themselves to be sympathetic to their ideals. One was Jacob Wassenar, who claimed to be a Rosicrucian and – despite or because of which? – with whom Descartes became friendly when he moved to the United Provinces. A 1624 treatise entitled *Historisch Verhaal* explicitly named Descartes as a Rosicrucian; it was written by Nicolaes Wassenar, said to be Jacob Wassenar's father. This book predated Descartes' move to the Netherlands by four years. Another individual with Rosicrucian associations was Cornelius van Hooghelande, a physician who was interested in alchemy. Descartes enjoyed a long and close friendship with him after moving to the United Provinces. As with the Wassenars, both van Hooghelande and his father were open in their adherence to Rosicrucian ideas. When Descartes went to Sweden in 1649 to serve at the court of Queen Christina – his last, and fatal, move – he gave his private papers to van Hooghelande for safekeeping.

Another piece of evidence is that Descartes corresponded with John Pell, an Englishman who was a member of the Invisible College that eventually became London's Royal Society. Pell was an associate of Samuel Hartlib and Theodore Haak who were also fellows of the Invisible College. Haak was a native of the Palatinate; members of his family had been counsellors to the Elector. His family left the Palatinate after the Bohemian disaster. He studied at both Oxford and Cambridge, and on behalf of the English government translated foreign texts and engaged in intelligence-gathering. When Frederick V's son was restored to the Palatinate throne in 1648 Haak was asked to be his secretary, but he turned the offer down because he wished to remain in his adopted country.

Haak's wide continental activities – among many other things he helped Protestant clergymen who had been expelled from Bohemia and the Palatinate after the debacle of the White Mountain – were similar to those of Hartlib, who was likewise a helper of exiles displaced by the Thirty Years War. These exiles were one source of the rich exchange of ideas that fuelled progress in the first half of the seventeenth century, rather as were the Jews forced out of Germany in the 1930s who went to Britain, the United States and elsewhere.

Descartes' numerous and suggestive Rosicrucian associations have prompted some, from Daniel Huet in the 1690s to Charles Adam in the 1890s to Watson in the late twentieth century, to conclude that Descartes was indeed a Rosicrucian. Huet provides a reminder that fanciful theories easily arise: he claims that Descartes did not die in Sweden in 1650, but spread a rumour that he had done so; and then after a fake funeral went to live secretly in Sweden's far north so that he could pursue Rosicrucian studies. As proof Huet quotes letters purportedly written by Descartes to Queen Christina in the years 1652 and 1656, two and six years respectively after his recorded death.

So, was Descartes a Rosicrucian? Or was he a spy on behalf of the Jesuits into Rosicrucian personnel, practices and principles? Much is consistent with the former hypothesis. But much is consistent with the latter hypothesis too. If the latter hypothesis is true, it would still be consistent with his later friendship with the likes of the Wassenars and van Hooghelandes, because by that time the Rosicrucian scare was over, he had himself been obliged to go as an exile to the Netherlands, and he would have found that for all the intellectual posturing of some of the Rosicrucian texts, there were notions in them that were not far from those of serious science anyway.

I go for the second hypothesis. Apart from the difficulty – always worth repeating – that there was probably no formal Rosicrucian movement as such, the claim that Descartes was himself a Rosicrucian, even if he was sympathetic to at least some Rosicrucian ideas, is highly doubtful.

The first point is his Jesuit loyalties, the second is that he never displays anything but opposition to *magia*, *cabala*, *alchymia*, and a third is that his friend and helper Marin Mersenne, educated as he was by the Jesuits at La Flèche, was a vehement opponent of Rosicrucianism.[20] It is true that similarities exist between the Rosicrucian rules and Descartes' own rules about living 'hidden from view', applying his medical knowledge for free, and seeking ways (in his case by natural scientific means) to lengthen life. There is also his urgent desire to find a methodology that would be a secure path to knowledge, and his passion for mathematics. But these ambitions were general, not the possession of Rosicrucians only; so they are far from conclusive.

In my view what settles the matter is Descartes' Jesuit connections. He was loyal to the Jesuits all his life, scrupulously careful to avoid giving them any offence but rather craving their approval, and ambitious to have them adopt his writings as textbooks in their schools.[21] If he had indeed worked as an agent of the Jesuits under commission to find out about Rosicrucian activity and to keep a watch on it, he would have been just one of many they employed for the task. To describe Descartes as a Jesuit spy, travelling around Europe in quest of information about occult activities, would be neither dramatic nor surprising given the situation of Europe at the time. The sort of people most able to travel were scholars, aristocrats, merchants and soldiers, and only the two first were likely to know Latin and thereby have access to the sorts of circles where, if they existed, Rosicrucians might gather. So if the Jesuits knew of a clever young man with interests and skills in many of the same subjects as the Rosicrucians professed, they would be quite likely to make good use of him.

It seems plausible therefore to surmise that Descartes might have been employed in this way when he was a young man. We know that he wandered around Europe between 1619 and 1625, popping up in many of the key places – and some of the most tense places – associated with the early phases of the Thirty Years War. He used pseudonyms, he visited places alleged to be centres of Rosicrucian interest, he was in Bohemia at the time of the crisis, he was in the Val Telline as the likelihood of armed conflict loomed there, he was in Paris at the time of the Rosicrucian panic, all this while rumoured to be associated with Rosicrucians. Moreover, although he had been bequeathed a small farm in Poitou, he was not wealthy, and these years of extensive travel required money. Perhaps he was paid to be in those places at those delicate times.

The final large clue is the reason why he quitted France for exile in the Netherlands, returning only for brief visits years later. While in Paris in 1628 Descartes was invited to a private interview with Cardinal Bérulle, one of the most powerful and influential men in France. The interview took place just as the Jesuits were yet again in trouble with the French government, and just as France was giving renewed diplomatic support – along with intimations of military support – to the Protestant side in the Thirty Years War, the intention as always being to constrain the growth of Habsburg power, which at that point was gaining ascendancy. Immediately after this interview Descartes departed for the United Provinces, and did not set foot in France again for a dozen years, by which time the people and circumstances present when he left had both ceased to exist. In that interview, I surmise, Descartes was told that his connection with Jesuit activities in support of the Habsburg cause was unwelcome to France, and that he was advised to leave the country.

The story of Rosicrucianism is the end-point of what is arguably the gestation period of the modern mind, the period in which enquiry began to enjoy increasing freedom from the heavy constraints of both religious orthodoxy and magical thinking. The process had started in the early Renaissance with the humanistic turn to interest in things of this life in this world, and was dramatically furthered by the Reformation's assertion of liberty of conscience, which quickly became a desire for liberty of enquiry in general.[22] This efflorescence of thought consisted in a mixed luxuriance of what was both good and bad, weeds and crops together, the former all the occult enthusiasms, the latter – with more assiduous cultivation – resulting in the maturation of science and philosophy as we know them now. Thus out of the chaos of ideas constituting *magia*, *cabala*, *alchymia*, with astrology and Hermeticism's mystical employment of number besides – or alongside it, or despite it, but certainly in opposition to it eventually – came science. It is probably most right to see science not as the child of the other forms of speculation, but as being among the speculations that proved worth taking seriously.

If one were asked to put beginning and end dates to this gestation period, a plausible suggestion would be that 'occult science' had its heyday in the period between 1480 and 1620. Perhaps that too neatly gives Rosicrucianism the status of a climax – remember Newton and Boyle – but the latter date has another recommendation: it was the point at which Bacon and Descartes were thinking about method not as the occultists had, but as scientists do; and this, as subsequent intellectual history shows, was the significant thing.

A necessary rider to the foregoing is that rejection of Scholasticism, the philosophical tradition whose roots lay in Aristotle's logic, science and metaphysics, was as much a premise for many of the occultists as it was for the likes of Bacon and Descartes. This adds an interesting complexity to the situation, given that occultists and scientists (especially when the same person was both) shared a number of premises, and those premises were – as noted earlier – at odds with Church orthodoxy. The situation was not therefore one in which there was a two-way fight between occultist and scientific ways of thinking, another two-way fight between religion and occultism, and another two-way fight between religion and science, but a three-cornered relationship which was sometimes a fight and sometimes not, between each of the three and the other two. At the same time as these tricorn intellectual relationships were pulling and pushing, they were doing so against the very present backdrop of the Reformation's religious divisions and the conflicts they generated. It is easy to see therefore why religious orthodoxies on all sides, but especially the Catholic Church, were themselves in a state of difficulty about the new ideas. It was difficult enough for proponents of the real and the occult sciences alike to work out what was fanciful and what was fruitful in what they were doing, but defenders of religious orthodoxy were at a double disadvantage in that all the new ideas threatened their beliefs, but they were not sure which of the threatening ideas were the ones to worry about most. Of course it must have been possible for some of the astuter minds to distinguish between a Dr Dee and a Galileo, but because both Dee and Galileo offered threats to the interests of orthodoxy, both kinds of thinking had to be proscribed. If you put Giordano Bruno on the *magia*, *cabala*, *alchymia* side of things, and Galileo on the proper science side of things, you get a feel for the difficulties, especially as they puzzled the Catholic Church. It burned Bruno at the stake in 1600 and would have burned Galileo in 1632 if he had not recanted, which illustrates the point that no matter what form of unorthodoxy a person then subscribed to, it carried dangers, and that the new mind of humankind had a perilous birth because of it.

PART IV

FROM MAGIC TO SCIENCE

16

From Magic to Method

FOR THOSE INTENT on distinguishing science and philosophy, as we now understand these terms, from the short-cut methods of the occult philosophy, the key question was *method*. As the previous chapter showed, science and occultism – 'natural philosophy' and 'occult philosophy' – shared many aims; it was sometimes impossible to tell them apart in the identity of interests and hopes they frequently manifested. But whether or not one thinks that science was born from occult philosophy, or coexisted in mutual embrace, or was always really separate though the separateness was often difficult to distinguish, the first decades of the seventeenth century saw an explicit disentangling and distancing of one from the other. This was done by means of a focus on method. There were three major figures involved in carrying out this task. They were, in effect, the midwives of the modern mind. They are Francis Bacon, Marin Mersenne and René Descartes.

Bacon's life spanned an era in which England set out on the journey that took it to superpower status over the next several centuries. Its imperial adventure began with the first colonies in Ireland and the New World, and the growth of a supranational consciousness in the union of the English and Scottish Crowns. Agricultural reform and industrial development gathered pace; in the hundred years between 1561 and 1660 the production of coal went from 200 tons annually to 2,000,000 tons annually.[1] Greater energy use marked everything from more industry to a growing population. The release of wealth from the dissolution of the monasteries under Henry VIII, and the harsh system of agricultural enclosures pursued by landowners throughout the sixteenth century, wrought major changes in the economy. In equally consequential ways England was increasingly drawn into the affairs of continental Europe, no longer able to keep aloof from engagement with any but the traditional enemy France.

Bacon played his part in this changing world in several different ways, as a statesman, lawyer, author and philosopher of the new ways of thinking. He was born in 1561 and died in 1626, in a family that had already made its mark in government; his father Sir Nicholas Bacon was Attorney General to Elizabeth I, and his uncle was William Cecil, Lord Burghley, Elizabeth's chief adviser. Bacon had a brilliant mind, which manifested itself early. He entered Trinity College, Cambridge, at the age of twelve, and while there was first presented to Elizabeth, who was impressed by his intellectual precocity. She called him 'the young Lord Keeper'. He entered Gray's Inn to read law, and in 1576 began three years of travels in Europe, studying government and society in France, Spain and Italy, acquiring languages and making useful observations of statecraft.

On his father's death in 1579 Bacon returned to England. Two years later he entered Parliament. His uncle Burghley was useful to him, helping his career at the Bar and appointing him to a lucrative sinecure. He became an adviser to the Earl of Essex, Queen Elizabeth's favourite, who fell dramatically from grace for plotting a coup near the end of her reign. Bacon was required by Elizabeth to be one of Essex's prosecutors. Possibly because he opposed certain Bills in Parliament that Elizabeth wished to see passed, Bacon was baulked in his public career while she reigned. After the accession of James I in 1603 his rise was the next best thing to meteoric. He became Solicitor General, then in 1613 Attorney General as his father had been, and finally attained the position he coveted, that of Lord Chancellor, in 1618. With this advancement in position he enjoyed a correlative rise in status, first being knighted, then created Baron Verulam, then Viscount St Albans.

Bacon's career collapsed in scandal in 1621 when he was charged with two dozen counts of taking bribes from litigants. Opinion is divided as to whether this was a political move, instigated by his old enemy Sir Edward Coke, or an unlucky case of being the one picked for punishment when everyone was doing the same thing; gifts from litigants were a standard emolument of lawyers and judges in that period. Of course the third option is that he was genuinely abusing his office for gain, but the probabilities are against anything so raw, given his character and sentiments. His punishment was severe. He was fined the vast sum for the day of £40,000 and sentenced to imprisonment in the Tower at the King's pleasure. He was banned from holding public office and from sitting in Parliament, and there was a proposal to strip him of his titles. The fact that James I remitted the fine, released him from the Tower after three days and allowed him to keep his titles suggests that the first possibility mentioned – that Bacon was the victim of a putsch by personal and political opponents – has some merit.

From the point of view of subsequent intellectual history, Bacon's expulsion from public life was a plus. It is a little reminiscent of the period Cicero spent rusticating at his villa in Tusculum in 45 BCE, in exile from the politics of Rome, when in a flood of creativity he wrote a number of his major works including the *Tusculan Disputations*. Bacon had been writing about science and method since the 1590s, and in the years before his fall from office had been working at what he hoped would be his major contribution to the progress of thought. Now, with enforced leisure, he set himself to finish what would, had he succeeded, have been a vast encyclopaedic undertaking on the scale of Pliny's *Natural History* or the later *Encyclopédie* of Diderot and d'Alembert. In the event the work from this period that proved most influential was *The New Atlantis*, published posthumously in 1627, in which he sets out the concept of 'Solomon's House'. This was the idea of a research institute for collaborative scientific effort, an idea that directly inspired the founding of the Royal Society in London in 1662, as its founders themselves acknowledged.

Bacon's commitment to promoting science had the practical aim of improving humankind's lot through greater understanding and control of nature. Contrary to the usual view of him that he was only a theoretician of method rather than a practising scientist, he did indeed engage in scientific work, constructing a physical system and doing experiments. It was as a result of an experiment on refrigeration (stuffing a dead chicken with ice to see how long it could be preserved) that he caught pneumonia and died. His system of physics was not a great deal more speculative than Descartes' theory of the plenum and its vortices, though it was geocentric and in residual ways Aristotelian in character, despite his avowed opposition to Aristotelianism. But his really significant contributions lie, first, in his advocacy of the concept of science as a co-operative enterprise requiring an institutional basis for experiment and exchange of ideas, and secondly, in the idea of scientific method itself. He had already set out these ideas in *The Advancement of Learning* of 1605 and in the unfinished *Instauratio Magna*, of which one part, the *Novum Organum Scientiarum* published in 1620, was of particular significance.

Bacon was an empiricist, and argued that science must be based on observation of facts from which theory can be adduced by inference. This view is often caricatured as saying that enquirers are to gather observations at random, and then find a theory to explain them; but that is clearly the wrong way to proceed, and it is not what Bacon meant. The caricature of Baconian method was nevertheless widely held; even Newton and Darwin subscribed to it, and in both cases approved of it. In the second edition of the *Principia* Newton wrote, 'hypotheses . . . have no place in experimental philosophy. In this philosophy particular propositions are inferred from the phenomena and afterward rendered general by inductions.' Likewise Darwin, in his *Autobiography* where he describes the evolution of his views about natural selection, wrote, 'it appeared to me that . . . by collecting all facts which bore in any way on the variation of animals and plants under domestication and nature, some light might be thrown on the whole subject. My first notebook was opened in July 1837. I worked on true Baconian principles, and without any theory collected facts on a wholesale scale.'[2]

What Bacon himself meant by his method is much closer to the now standard view that observations are gathered to test an antecedently formulated hypothesis which specifies which of those observations would be relevant to refuting or supporting the hypothesis. What he thought is clearly set out in the 'Plan' of the *Instauratio Magna*, intended to be his *magnum opus* on the nature and procedures of science:

> hitherto the proceeding has been to fly at once from the sense and particulars up to the most general propositions, as certain fixed poles for the argument to turn upon, and from these to derive the rest by middle terms: a short way, no doubt, but precipitate; and one which will never lead to nature, though it offers an easy and ready way to disputation. Now my plan is to proceed regularly and gradually from one axiom to another, so that the most general are not reached till the last: but then when you do come to them you find them to be not empty notions, but well defined, and such as nature would really recognise as her first principles, and such as lie at the heart and marrow of things.
>
> But the greatest change I introduce is in the form itself of induction and the judgment made thereby. For the induction of which the logicians speak, which proceeds by simple enumeration, is a puerile thing; concludes at hazard; is always liable to be upset by a contradictory instance; takes into account only what is known and ordinary; and leads to no result.
>
> Now what the sciences stand in need of is a form of induction which shall analyse experience and take it to pieces, and by a due process of exclusion and rejection lead to an inevitable conclusion. And if that ordinary mode of judgment practised by the logicians was so laborious, and found exercise for such great wits, how much more labour must we be prepared to bestow upon this other, which is extracted not merely out of the depths of the mind, but out of the very bowels of nature.[3]

This method is explicitly empirical, with observation and experiment as the foundation. It somewhat anticipates what are now known as Mill's Methods, after John Stuart Mill's account of induction in his *System of Logic* (1843), in particular the methods of agreement and concomitant variation. Bacon was alert to sceptical considerations that can be used to undermine reliance on sense-experience, but he has a riposte: we are to:

> receive as conclusive the immediate informations of the sense, when well disposed . . . the information of the sense itself I sift and examine in many ways. For certain it is that the senses deceive; but then at the same time they supply the means of discovering their own errors; only the errors are here, the means of discovery are to seek . . . I have sought on all sides diligently and faithfully to provide helps for the sense – substitutes to supply its failures, rectifications to correct its errors; and this I endeavour to accomplish not so much by instruments as by experiments. For the subtlety of experiments is far greater than that of the sense itself, even when assisted by exquisite instruments; such experiments, I mean, as are skilfully and artificially devised for the express purpose of determining the point in question.[4]

A striking feature of Bacon's thinking about science is his insistence that it should be guided by the practical knowledge accumulated in crafts and trades, in the experience of builders, butchers and cabinet-makers, of farmers and sailors – of people who work with materials, with nature itself, who have hands-on experience of how things work and what can be done with them. There is no room for top-down *a priori* musing in Bacon's form of enquiry, but a strong current of empirical practicality from start to finish. In this way, he argued, we ensure that the foundation of scientific enquiry is how things actually are, not as we fancy them to be:

> Of this reconstruction the foundation must be laid in natural history, and that of a new kind and gathered on a new principle . . . For first, the object of the natural history which I propose is not so much to delight with variety of matter or to help with present use of experiments, as to give light to the discovery of causes and supply a suckling philosophy with its first food . . . I mean it to be a history not only of nature free and at large (when she is left to her own course and does her work her own way), – such as that of the heavenly bodies, meteors, earth and sea, minerals, plants, animals, – but much more of nature under constraint and vexed; that is to say, when by art and the hand of man she is forced out of her natural state, and squeezed and moulded. Therefore I set down at length all experiments of the mechanical arts, of the operative

> part of the liberal arts, of the many crafts which have not yet grown into arts properly so called, so far as I have been able to examine them and as they conduce to the end in view. Nay (to say the plain truth) I do in fact (low and vulgar as men may think it) count more upon this part both for helps and safeguards than upon the other; seeing that the nature of things betrays itself more readily under the vexations of art than in its natural freedom . . . And all depends on keeping the eye steadily fixed upon the facts of nature and so receiving their images simply as they are.[5]

In insisting on empirical method, and correlatively insisting that science should be a collaborative enterprise – not the secret endeavour of this individual alchemist or that magician, jealous of what he knows – and a practical one, both in what it draws upon and in what it aims to do, Bacon was urging something wholly new and indeed revolutionary. These are commonplaces now, which obscures the importance of what he was saying.

Of course practical people have always observed the world, learned from it, and on that basis invented and improved technologies in their farms, forges and shipwrights' yards. The concept of humanity as par excellence the tool-using animal reflects this fact. It is likely that throughout human history there has been no sharp division between theory and practice considered as two kinds of knowledge, one sought for its own sake while the other is applied and useful. Such a division had to wait until a leisured class in a wealthy society could detach itself from the necessities of making and mending so that it could pursue purely intellectual interests. Bacon urged a reconnection of the link, arguing that theory has a great deal to learn from practice, and perhaps – at that stage in the growth of knowledge – even more than practice had to learn from theory.

Bacon's writings helped to promote the change of perspective on the nature of knowledge that is distinctive of that pivotal period. The standard view had always been that the ancients were superior to all their successors in wisdom and knowledge, their time a golden age to which following times could only look back with wonder and, if possible, emulation – not always possible, given how much knowledge, not least practical knowledge, was lost in the 'Dark Ages' under the hegemony of the Church. Many centuries lay between the Roman engineers' knowledge of how to raise the domes on the Basilica of Maxentius in Rome's Forum and the Hagia Sophia in Byzantium, and Brunelleschi's Duomo in Florence. A symptom of this looking-back with admiration at the ancients is that Copernicus' heliocentric model was dubbed 'the Pythagorean system', to mark the opinion that his theory was merely a restatement of something that had already been known in antiquity. The clincher was that God had come down to earth to save mankind in those ancient times, yet a further reason for thinking that everything had since been a declension from all that was good and worthy.

Bacon did not think like this. His outlook was characteristic of that aspect of the Renaissance which did not think of itself as reviving the past only, but as a rebirth in the real sense of starting afresh. Science was forward looking; it was engaged in discovery, in finding out, in making new things, improving and advancing, aiming to place mankind on a higher plane of knowledge and ability.

It was of course of the essence, for such progress to be possible, that scientific enquiry should be genuinely free. Because at the time he wrote enquiry was not free, Bacon found it necessary to argue that it should be – and in particular to find a way of disentangling science and religion so that the latter would not hamper the former's progress. Part of this task was to combat superstition, religion's natural and constant corollary. Bacon wrote, 'it was a good answer that was made by one who, when they showed him hanging in a temple a picture of those who had paid their vows as having escaped shipwreck, and would have him say whether he did not acknowledge the power of the gods, "Aye" he answered again, "but where are they painted that were drowned after their vows?"'. The near relation of superstition is what Bacon called 'blind immoderate religious zeal' which he described as 'a troublesome and intractable enemy' to science. He remarked on the fact that in ancient times charges of blasphemy were laid against people who postulated that thunder was not caused by gods but had natural causes, how the same happened to geographers who said the earth is spherical and that the antipodes might be inhabited, and how 'in our own days discussions concerning nature have been subjected to even harsher constraint'.[6]

I consider science's escape from the requirements of religious orthodoxy in a later chapter. The present point concerns the insistence on method as a differentiator between science and occult philosophy. In line with the great debate about the relation of science and occultism in the period, it is natural to ask how far Bacon himself was one of those who felt the tension within himself, or how far his own views about method and the desirability of co-operation in enquiry either came from or were a reaction to occultism. In a significant contribution to debate about the intellectual history of the Renaissance, Paolo Rossi argued that Bacon was not merely the product of the antecedent occultist tradition, but a direct intellectual descendant of Cornelius Agrippa.[7] Rossi wrote, 'the metaphysical aspects of magic and alchemy had little or no influence on Bacon; but he did borrow from this tradition the idea of science as the servant of nature assisting its operations and, by stealth and cunning, forcing it to yield to man's domination; as well as the idea of knowledge as power'. This is especially so, Rossi argued, because of the aim they shared of 'dominating nature' in the interest of securing benefits for humankind – a view Agrippa had expressed by thinking of 'man as magus', wielder of the knowledge that gives control over things.

But it would be a mistake to see this as a vindication of the thesis that Bacon was an adherent of short-cut Dr Dee-style occultism. A key passage in Agrippa says: 'magicians are like careful explorers of nature, only directing what nature has formerly prepared, uniting actives to passives and often succeeding in anticipating results so that these things are popularly held to be miracles when they are really no more than anticipations of natural operations; as if someone made roses flower in March . . . therefore those who believe the operations of magic to be above or against nature are mistaken because they are only derived from nature and in harmony with it'.[8] Insofar as Bacon learned from Agrippa, this was the lesson. But it would appear to be about the only aspect of the preceding tradition Bacon could agree with.[9]

In fact, Bacon was expressly hostile to most of what was important in the occultist view. For one thing his commitment to the idea of science as a co-operative enterprise requiring public institutional backing was the opposite of what the occultists thought. Agrippa wrote to an aspirant magus, 'be sure you conceal so great a mystery in the secret, inmost room of your devout breast, and hide it in unfailing silence, for it would be the work of an impious spirit to divulge to the many words filled full of the majesty of divine power'. Likewise Girolamo Cardano wrote, 'Work has no need at all for partnership. So far as I am concerned not even twenty out of sixty discoveries owe anything to others . . . So what have I to share with my fellows?' It turns out that Cardano's knowledge of 'eternal secrets' and 'the Universe and everything contained in it' came to him 'entirely from a tutelary Spirit who simply demonstrates, revealing cause and essence by means of an infallible proof'.[10]

Bacon would have no truck either with the exclusivity of the magus keeping his knowledge and powers to himself, or with the supernaturalism of Cardano's or Dee's kind. He was sweeping in his dismissal of his forebears, including even those who might have been close, in at least some of their views, to him – such as Paracelsus and the Agrippa of the first quotation above. Rossi wrote:

> Bacon attacked pitilessly such attitudes and the ideals they implied. In the *Temporis partus masculus* he described Paracelsus as a monster and a fanatical breeder of phantasms whose inquiries are surrounded by the trumpets of ostentation, the subterfuge of darkness, and the connivance of religion. He describes Agrippa as a clown who turned everything into a futile joke, and Cardano as an untiring weaver of cobwebs . . . if magic, encompassed in a framework of lies, is put to any use, it is only for its novelty or to provoke admiration.[11]

(Elsewhere Bacon was a little kinder to Paracelsus, noting that he did at least try to encourage enquirers to experiment.) Rather aptly Bacon also remarked that science has the aim of making things seem less, not more, remarkable; to contrive to make them seem more remarkable is merely to practise deceit.

Perhaps the most luminous of all Bacon's remarks on this head is this: 'For my part I am emphatically of the opinion that man's wits require not the addition of feathers and wings, but of leaden weights. Men are very far from realising how strict and disciplined a thing is research into truth and nature, and how little it leaves to the judgment of men.'[12] He saw the occultists as claiming feathers and wings, and he objected vehemently to their obscurantism and secrecy. His objection to occultism went hand in hand with his rejection of Aristotelian Scholasticism and his insistence that enquiry must begin again, with a new logic and a new methodology.

If there was one earlier thinker Bacon might have quoted with approval it was Georgius Agricola (the by-name of Georg Bauer, 1494–1555), regarded as the founder of geology and by extension of mineralogy and metallurgy. In the preface to his most famous work, the *De Re Metallica*, published posthumously in 1556, Agricola wrote, 'I have omitted all those things which I have not myself seen, or have not read or heard of from persons upon whom I can rely. That which I have neither seen, nor carefully considered after reading or hearing of, I have not written about. The same rule must be understood with regard to all my instruction, whether I enjoin things which ought to be done, or describe things which are usual, or condemn things which are done.' Agricola stressed the need for clarity of language, detailed illustrations of equipment and the objects studied, avoidance of fabulous, supernatural or legendary accounts, and concentration on what is useful and familiar rather than on the marvellous, strange and rare, which is what distracted everyone else.[13] With all this Bacon would agree. But Agricola was a rare bird in this respect, and in any case his adjurations came at a time when occultism was in flood; Bacon's strictures were offered at a point where the time itself helped to make them audible.

The contest that gripped Europe, or at least its educated classes, in the 1620s and contributed greatly to the demise of occult philosophy was not the war then being fought by the armies of the European princes, but the war of words between Robert Fludd, Marin Mersenne and Pierre Gassendi.

Robert Fludd, who gave himself the by-name Robertus de Fluctibus, was an Englishman born in 1574 (he died in 1637) who was a Paracelsian physician, an astrologer, Cabalist and defender of Rosicrucian ideas. His father was a minister in Queen Elizabeth's government and a member of Parliament. Fludd himself was educated at Oxford, travelled in Europe to further his studies of medicine and Hermeticism, and made a reputation for himself as an apologist for occultist beliefs. In his medicinal practice he used procedures involving the ritual repetition of the name of Jesus, whom he identified with the Cabalistic angel Metatron, said to be the heavenly form of the Messiah and the 'world soul'.

Fludd's theory of the creation begins with an account of the macrocosm's emergence from the abyss, followed by the emergence in turn of man as microcosm. In his own turn man is the macrocosm to the microcosms of his body's cells, each of which is in turn a macrocosm to a yet smaller microcosm – and so on until the cycles of creation reach completeness.

It was not Fludd's way to keep his loyalties any more secret than his views. He dedicated his works to the Brothers of the Rosy Cross, and his closest associate, Michael Meier, explicitly claimed to be a Rosicrucian. It is no surprise that the writings of this notorious Hermetic master, viewed with awe and suspicion in his native land, therefore stirred excitement and anxiety in France, making Mersenne determined to refute them.

Fludd's chief work is the *Utriusque Cosmi*, the *History of the Two Worlds*, these being the macrocosm and the microcosm. He accepted the Paracelsian idea that salt, sulphur and mercury are the basic elements, and among other things he argued that the most important aspect of human health was the influence of 'aerial nitre', which was formed in the tabernacle of the aerial spirit, which is the sun. It could be harvested from wheat, which captured and distilled the sun's rays and thereby embodied the healing force of light. There is much more of this kind in his theories, but perhaps enough has been said to indicate their tenor.

When the Rosicrucian fever was growing in the years after 1612 Fludd published several defences of its claims, not as a professed Rosicrucian himself but to offer a rejoinder to charges that Rosicrucian ideas were heretical and diabolical.[14] As if it was not enough that he defended these ideas, he also engaged in controversy with Kepler and others on the emerging natural philosophy of the day, altogether making him a natural target for Mersenne, who spared him nothing in his *Quaestiones Celeberrimae in Genesim* of 1623.

Mersenne accused Fludd of heresy, atheism and the practice of magic. He called him an 'evil magician' and denounced his Cabalistic, Paracelsian and alchemical interests as an effort to offer salvation outside Christian doctrine. He thought Fludd's views implied a demotion of Christ to the angelic world, and he especially disliked Fludd's concept of the 'anima mundi', the world soul, and the notion that individual souls 'whether of man or brutes' are sparks struck from it.

Fludd replied to Mersenne in print, and there followed a debate between them that absorbed the attention of Europe for years.[15] At least two important points arise out of Mersenne's assault on Fludd. One is that his criticism of Fludd was at the same time a subtle defence of scientific enquiry itself, not just against the fanciful extremes of *magia*, *cabala*, *alchymia* but against the hostile attitude of the Church too. There was a danger that if *magia*, *cabala*, *alchymia* invited too much repression from the authorities, real science might be affected along with them, so it was necessary to protect the latter's credentials from being tainted by them. It was a delicate matter to fend off threats from religious orthodoxy on one side and false 'science' on the other, but Mersenne (along with Descartes and others) saw the task as a necessity.

Another point was that the fracas with Fludd prompted Mersenne to suggest that a public institution should be set up for the study of natural philosophy, which would have responsibility for policing the vocabulary of research in order to maintain focus on the investigation of nature, excluding discussion of religion and occult ideas, and keeping charlatans out. Pierre Gassendi joined Mersenne in attacking Fludd, arguing that the doctrines that Fludd and his like advanced were not susceptible of empirical demonstration or quantification. The atomism advocated by Gassendi – the idea that matter is composed of tiny particles interacting causally – was a response to the fanciful ideas advanced by Fludd and others. In their combined aversion to the type of thinking represented by Fludd, whose mind is that of the old world, Mersenne and Gassendi represent the mind of the new. The exchanges among the three are a distillation of what was at stake in the questions of method and outlook.

Although it is easy to see how *magia*, *cabala*, *alchymia* gets in the way of genuine scientific enquiry, it is readily forgotten how threats of punishment by the authorities would have a chilling effect, silencing or delaying enquiry. In the years in which Mersenne was combating Fludd and at the same time carefully defending scientific enquiry from censorship by orthodoxy, there was a lively memory of how science could be conflated with *magia* and the rest, dangerously for enquirers. Galileo was the last throw of the dice by the Church in this respect, but the chief example at the time was that of Giulio Cesare Vanini, who was burned at the stake in Toulouse in 1619 for 'atheism'.

Vanini became a symbol of hatred for opponents of science, who took the naturalistic approach of science to entail a rejection of religion – hence the 'atheism' that Vanini's naturalism was interpreted as. He was the subject of a vitriolic denunciation by a Jesuit called François Garasse, who described him as the very paradigm of a threat to religion and society. At the end of the seventeenth century Pierre Bayle defended Vanini as a martyr for the cause of science, but for most of the century 'Vanini' was a name of malediction.

Vanini started as a Carmelite monk. He studied theology and medicine in Naples, Rome and Padua, travelled extensively throughout Europe, and like many educated but impecunious young men served as a tutor and secretary in several aristocratic households. Hostile accounts say that he was perennially in trouble because he was a homosexual, and that he had to flee to England and live there for a while because he had killed a man in a fight. While in England he abjured his Catholicism. There is doubtless some truth in the claim that he was a wanted man, because when he returned to France he travelled under a pseudonym, 'Pompeio Usiglio', carefully stayed in the south of the country, and lived by private tutoring. He had the ill fortune to be denounced for heterodoxy by one of his pupils, who said that he 'mocked at sacred things, vilified the Incarnation, refused God, attributed everything to fate, adored nature as the bounteous mother and source of all being . . . he had fallen into impiety and sacrilege and disgraced his priest's habit by the publication of a book called *The Secrets of Nature*'.[16] The government of Toulouse chose to act against him because 'the unfailing attraction of novelty for the young brought him many disciples, especially from amongst the young men fresh from school'.[17] Among the views Vanini expressed were that men do not have souls but die as other animals do, and that because the Virgin Mary was a woman like any other she needed to have sexual relations to get pregnant. Such remarks were outrageous to the sensibilities of the time.

The chorus of vilification prompted by Vanini's name resulted from the violence of Garasse's assault on him. Garasse's criticisms did not address Vanini's views at all, but were purely *ad hominem*. Mersenne undertook a more considered criticism of Vanini in his *L'Impiété des déistes* (1624).[18]

The Vanini affair encapsulated the fears prompted in votaries of the old way of thinking by the challenge of the new ways. Vanini's execution was the prelude to more attacks on heterodoxy. One was the execution of Jean Fontanier in Paris in 1622; Fontanier was a mystic and occultist who claimed to have acquired secret knowledge while on travels in the East. In the following year a charge of atheism was brought against the poet and socialite Théophile de Viau. He was tortured and condemned to death, though his sentence was commuted to banishment, almost certainly because he had influential family connections and was a favourite in Parisian society. But the experience of his persecution had broken his health; he died in 1626, just a year later, at the age of thirty-six.

The trigger for de Viau's arrest was the 'obscenity' of poems he had published in *Le Parnasse satyrique*. He was also suspected of being homosexual. These considerations do not imply, as they might seem to, that charges of atheism were just concealed ways of clamping down on homosexuality and obscenity. Instead these latter were regarded as indications of atheism, if not positively identical with it. For how could anyone be homosexual or tolerate obscenities if he was orthodox in his beliefs?

This background explains why, in the summer of 1624, the *parlement* of Paris banned a debate about Aristotelianism. Three 'erudite sceptics' had announced their intention to hold a public debate about fourteen propositions in atomistic philosophy, in the course of which they would, they said, refute Aristotle not only by argument but by demonstrating chemical experiments. The three were Antoine Villon, Etienne de Claves and Jean Bitauld. Since the old thinking was Aristotelian and intimately associated with religious orthodoxy – think Aquinas, and the strictures of the Jesuits – the challenge was a serious one.

The debate was scheduled for a day in August 1624. It roused great interest, and Villon and his colleagues expected an audience of a thousand people. But the *parlement* banned the meeting and banished all three from Paris on pain of death. On 4 September, just a few weeks later, it then published a decree outlawing under penalty of death the teaching of any ideas 'contrary to the ancient approved authors, and from holding any public debates other than those approved by the Doctors of the Theology Faculty'. Unsurprisingly, the decree had been drafted in consultation with those selfsame Doctors of the Theology Faculty at the Sorbonne.[19]

Vanini, the arrest of de Viau, the banning of the debate about Aristotelianism, were of a piece with the Rosicrucian scare and the Fludd controversy. This was the stuff of the first half of the seventeenth century, as the old and new minds did battle.

Legend says that when Vanini was advised by the priests attending his execution to ask God's mercy, he replied that if there were a God he would ask him to blast the *parlement* of Toulouse with lightning, and if the devil existed he would ask him to drown the *parlement* in hell; but that since neither of these beings existed, he could not pray to either. As he was tied to the stake in Toulouse's Place du Salin he cried out in his native Italian, 'I die cheerfully as befits a philosopher!'

Descartes' philosophy is imbued throughout with the importance he attached to questions of methodology. There are two aspects to his conception of right method. One is that it consists in taking small, careful, systematic steps from one clear idea to the next, carefully reviewing each step until the chain of reasonings is complete. The other aspect consists in ensuring that the starting point of this chain of reasoning is indubitable, unquestionable, absolutely certain. To achieve certainty, the method to be employed is *the method of doubt.* Add together an indubitable starting point and scrupulously careful small steps onward, and you are guaranteed to reach the truth.

Descartes' first published work was therefore, inevitably, about method: *The Discourse on the Method of Rightly Conducting the Reason, and Seeking Truth in the Sciences* (1637). In its opening section he wrote:

> it has been my singular good fortune to have very early in life fallen in with certain tracks which have conducted me to considerations and maxims, of which I have formed a method that gives me the means, as I think, of gradually augmenting my knowledge, and of raising it by little and little to the highest point which the mediocrity of my talents and the brief duration of my life will permit me to reach. For I have already reaped from it such fruits that, although I have been accustomed to think lowly enough of myself, and although when I look with the eye of a philosopher at the varied courses and pursuits of mankind at large, I find scarcely one which does not appear in vain and useless, I nevertheless derive the highest satisfaction from the progress I conceive myself to have already made in the search after truth, and cannot help entertaining such expectations of the future as to believe that if, among the occupations of men as men, there is any one really excellent and important, it is that which I have chosen.[20]

The 'fruits' of which Descartes speaks were his discoveries in geometry and optics, and the physics which he was to expound fully in the later work, *The Principles of Philosophy.*

In the second part of the *Discourse* Descartes sets out the methodological steps themselves:

> The first was never to accept anything for true which I did not clearly know to be such; that is to say, carefully to avoid precipitancy and

prejudice, and to comprise nothing more in my judgement than what was presented to my mind so clearly and distinctly as to exclude all ground of doubt.

The second, to divide each of the difficulties under examination into as many parts as possible, and as might be necessary for its adequate solution.

The third, to conduct my thoughts in such order that, by commencing with objects the simplest and easiest to know, I might ascend by little and little, and, as it were, step by step, to the knowledge of the more complex; assigning in thought a certain order even to those objects which in their own nature do not stand in a relation of antecedence and sequence.

And the last, in every case to make enumerations so complete, and reviews so general, that I might be assured that nothing was omitted.

The long chains of simple and easy reasonings by means of which geometers are accustomed to reach the conclusions of their most difficult demonstrations, had led me to imagine that all things, to the knowledge of which man is competent, are mutually connected in the same way, and that there is nothing so far removed from us as to be beyond our reach, or so hidden that we cannot discover it, provided only we abstain from accepting the false for the true, and always preserve in our thoughts the order necessary for the deduction of one truth from another. And I had little difficulty in determining the objects with which it was necessary to commence, for I was already persuaded that it must be with the simplest and easiest to know, and, considering that of all those who have hitherto sought truth in the sciences, the mathematicians alone have been able to find any demonstrations, that is, any certain and evident reasons, I did not doubt but that such must have been the rule of their investigations. I resolved to commence, therefore, with the examination of the simplest objects, not anticipating, however, from this any other advantage than that to be found in accustoming my mind to the love and nourishment of truth, and to a distaste for all such reasonings as were unsound.[21]

Descartes applied his method to a set of four basic related questions. One was a question about the nature of knowledge, two were about the nature of the material universe, and the fourth was a fundamental question of metaphysics. The first question was: What can I know with certainty? The two physics questions were, What is the constitution of the universe, and What are the relationships between its fundamental constituents? The metaphysical question is whether there is a deity. As often happens in philosophy, Descartes' answer to the question about knowledge – the methodological question, again – defines the position he takes regarding the three others.

The answer to the knowledge question is: I know with certainty that I exist, and that 'I' am a mind or thinking thing, even if I do not have a body. Descartes then proceeds to argue that the existence of a deity – a *good* deity: the qualification turns out to be important – can be proved, and that error is the result of our fallen natures. From these considerations he concludes that responsible exercise of our mental abilities will get us to truth, largely because a *good* deity would not give us mental abilities which, even if used in accordance with the careful method outlined in the *Discourse*, would not get us to truth.

It happens that the path to knowledge thus described is not quite all primroses – left unclear, for example, is the vexed question of how mind and matter interact, but Descartes eventually concluded that as there is a good God the palpable fact that mind and matter do succeed in interacting can be left to his larger intellect to understand.

These central features of Descartes' philosophy are the subject of an entire industry of scholarship. There are however three worthwhile comments to make about Descartes' project, given how exemplary it is of the seventeenth-century intellectual revolution. One concerns its famous starting point, *I think therefore I am*, while the other two concern Descartes' method of exposition, itself a feature of his thinking about method.

The idea behind the proposition for which Descartes is known, even among those who know nothing else about him, *I think therefore I am* (in Latin *cogito ergo sum*, hence known as 'the cogito'), is that one cannot doubt one's own existence, which provides the foothold of absolute certainty that Descartes sought. This idea was not invented by Descartes. St Augustine in the early fifth century CE wrote that we can doubt everything except that we doubt, and probably did not think that he was saying anything novel. Neither presumably did Jean de

Silhon, whose *The Two Truths* was published in 1626 and contained the sentence, 'It is not possible for a man who has the ability, which many share, to look within himself and judge *that he exists*, to be deceived in this judgement, and *not exist*.'

Descartes knew Silhon's work, which predates his own version of the cogito by at least five years (he drafted the *Discourse* in about 1630, though it was not published until 1637), for he writes approvingly of it without quoting it. In fact Descartes owes more than the cogito to Silhon; in the passage where the latter states a version of the cogito, he also says that a proof of God's existence can be constructed from one's own existence – a vital step for Descartes' programme, because the authentication of beliefs acquired by responsible methods depends as we saw on the existence not just of a deity but of a *good* deity, the *goodness* of whom is the guarantee that responsible reasoning will take us to truth.

A striking feature of Descartes' method of presenting his views it that it takes a colloquially autobiographical form. It is a highly suitable method for his aims, in that he makes his views seem plausible by showing how he arrived at them. The reader is made to occupy the thinker's point of view – to become the reference of 'I', the first person pronoun used throughout – and in this way to feel the conclusions as convictions. This was important for Descartes because his philosophy requires that a mind must be convinced from within its own experience of the truth of what it thinks, because that is where thinking starts. But it therefore has to find grounds to rely on for what it believes to be the case in an external world.

Descartes is a repetitive writer – all three of his chief works, *Discourse on Method*, the *Meditations* and the *Principles of Philosophy*, iterate the same set of claims. One reason was that he was anxious to show that his views about physical reality – which were Copernican, materialist and mechanistic – do not challenge Christian doctrine, but are in fact consistent with it. In this respect Descartes was, in the end, a major factor in the liberation of science from the interference of religion, despite the fact that in his own day and for decades afterwards his wish to be believed was not granted by those he most wished to convince: namely, the Church and the Jesuits.

Descartes' 'method of doubt' involves setting aside any belief or claim to knowledge which admits of the least scruple, however improbable or absurd that scruple might be. The aim is to see what is left behind, if anything, once one has called everything possible into question. Whatever is left behind will be invulnerable to doubt: it will be a point of certainty. Since certainty was Descartes' aim, the method of doubt is crucial. It would take impossibly long to subject every individual belief one by one to scrutiny, so Descartes needed a wholly general method of setting aside what can be doubted. This he did by employing the arguments of the sceptic.

His use of sceptical arguments did not make him a sceptic; on the contrary, he used them as merely heuristic devices to set up his theory of knowledge. He therefore merits the label 'methodological sceptic' rather than 'problematic sceptic', by which latter term is meant anyone who thinks that scepticism poses a real threat to the acquisition of knowledge. Many philosophers who have considered Descartes' arguments conclude that he did not succeed in answering the sceptical challenges he used, and that accordingly scepticism is indeed a genuine problem. Descartes was emphatically not of that view.

The sceptical arguments Descartes used are familiar. One is a reminder that our senses sometimes lead us astray; perceptual mistakes, illusions and hallucinations can and occasionally do give rise in us to false beliefs. Another is that we sometimes sleep and dream, and do not know we are dreaming when we dream; how then can I rule out the possibility that I am not dreaming at this moment? A third is that we make mistakes in reasoning, even in something as elementary as doing an arithmetical sum. But the most swingeing doubt would be created if I allowed myself to imagine that an evil demon exists who fools me about everything that I can be fooled about – even that one plus one equals two. Is there anything such a being could not fool me about? Yes: that I exist.

Some critics of this method have argued that the sceptical arguments Descartes uses do not work. They are not themselves credible, for example; or, we would not know what we meant by talk of dreams or being deceived unless we understood the contrast with waking or being right, which would seem to require that we sometimes know we are awake or not deceived. But such efforts to show that Descartes' method of doubt cannot even get started do not work. There is no need for the sceptical arguments to be plausible. They are indeed vastly less plausible than what they challenge; but that is irrelevant. They are simply an heuristic which helps us see how saying 'I exist' must always be true.

The great weakness of Descartes' methodology as applied in his work is that it turns out not in fact to be sufficient in itself – that it is not enough just to go by careful steps from what is clear and evident – because it turns out that we need a guarantee for the reliability of the steps themselves. This guarantee, as we have seen, is the goodness of a deity. In the *Meditations* Descartes gives two arguments for the existence of a God, purporting to establish that there is a deity as conceived of in the tradition of revealed religion, viz. an omnipotent, omniscient and wholly good God. Neither work, and their failure to provide the epistemic bridge from the inner consciousness of experience to an independent reality beyond is fatal to his project.

Descartes' religious commitments were probably very sincere as well as epistemologically convenient. But even though most if not all of his contemporaries and successors shared his religious views, few of them appealed to a deity's properties as an essential feature of their thinking about method. The important point here, though, is that Descartes cared about method, and moreover method which was not that of mysticism and magic, but of reason. In that respect, a deity and its moral qualities aside, he is a seminal figure in the seventeenth-century revolution.

17

The Birth of Science

DESPITE THE ALTERNATIVE history of magic and the occult sciences which, once one looks into it, seems to absorb all the energy and endeavour of the sixteenth century, most histories of science take the year 1543 – right in the middle of that century – as their starting date for what is known, with perfect aptness, as 'the scientific revolution'. In that year appeared Nicolaus Copernicus' *On the Revolutions of the Heavenly Spheres* (*De Revolutionibus Orbium Coelestium*) and Andreas Vesalius' *On the Structure of the Human Body* (*De Humani Corporis Fabrica*). The first revived a heliocentric theory of the universe, but with better mathematics to support it than had been available to its first proponents in classical antiquity. The second put the study of human anatomy on to a firm observational basis for the first time. Prior to these two seminal works, most theorising about the natural world was derived from the frequently misleading authority of the ancients, found in Aristotle, Galen, Pliny the Elder's *Natural History* (*Historia Naturalis*), and elsewhere. Among the first serious challenges to the standing of these great past authorities was a little book published half a century before Copernicus' *On the Revolutions of the Heavenly Spheres*, in the year 1492 – a date more popularly associated with the transatlantic explorations of Christopher Colombus and the expulsion of the Jews from Spain. The little volume was called *On the Errors of Pliny and Other Medical Writers* (*De Plinii et Aliorum Medicorum Erroribus*) and it was written by one Nicolai Leonicini of Ferrara. It details the mistakes in Pliny's *Natural History*, which had hitherto been regarded as both encyclopaedic and authoritative. Leonicini's original aim had been to establish a correct text of Pliny's book, into which many textual errors had crept over the centuries as a result of the mistakes, weariness, inattention or other lapses of successive generations of copyists. He entered into correspondence with Angelo Poliziano to discuss the matter, and the correspondence served as the basis of his book. In the process of writing it he had to deal with the question whether the errors were scribal or the fault of Pliny himself. He concluded that what Pliny wrote 'was insufficiently researched and confirmed by him'.[1] That was both a comment on the fallibility of the ancient authorities and a statement of scientific principle, and both constituted a major step towards modern science and the modern world.

Ensuring 'sufficient research and confirmation' came into its own as a principle in the century after Copernicus. This was the distinctive departure that made the scientific revolution. Employment of an empirical methodology and quantitative mathematical techniques allowed the later Renaissance's enquirers to challenge the hegemony over thought not just of the ancient writers but – more importantly still – of religious orthodoxy; and as we have seen to disentangle science from the pseudo-sciences that aimed by quicker and easier means to achieve most of the same ends.

To accept the conventional dating of the beginning of modern science is not to withhold credit from the advances in science, mathematics and technology in the period from classical antiquity until the mid-sixteenth century, for there had most certainly been much of all three, mostly in India, the Middle East and (especially) China. Discoveries in these times and places were relevant to the rise of science in the sixteenth and seventeenth centuries. So too was the development of instruments, chief among them the telescope and magnifying lens, as already noted.

But the nature of progress in European scientific thinking from the mid-sixteenth century is of a different order from what had gone before, and fully deserves the name of 'revolution'. One has only to look around at the world today, the manifest product of that revolution, to see how true this is. The crucial point is how it was done. Science is the work of many hands – to the names in the seventeenth century of Gassendi, Galileo, Huygens, Boyle, Newton and more, we would continue by adding the later names of Priestley, Volta, Faraday, Maxwell, Einstein, Bohr, Heisenberg, Dirac and still others who are rarely mentioned in popular histories of science. Together they represent the collegial, mutually critical, peer-reviewing, competitive and collaborative community which built a new understanding of the world. This collaborative enterprise took its full shape in the seventeenth century.

To appreciate just how revolutionary the scientific revolution was, it is instructive to compare the world-views prevailing before it began and after it was properly under way. The fullest comparison would be between the world-view of a reasonably well-educated contemporary of Luther's in the early sixteenth century and that of a reasonably well-educated person today. But in fact the comparison can be made more tightly: between someone living when Henri IV of France came to the throne at the end of the sixteenth century, and someone living when Queen Anne sat on the throne of England at the beginning of the eighteenth century.

When Henri IV became King of France in 1589, what almost all Christian theologians, and certainly those of the Roman Catholic Church, regarded as an acceptable view of the universe – because it was conformable to scripture and sanctioned by the doctors of the faith – was a combination of Christian theology and Aristotelian philosophy. The principal author of this synthesis, magisterially achieved, was St Thomas Aquinas, in the system which has ever since been known as 'Thomism'. Aquinas brought together the material and the spiritual by joining Aristotle's science, Ptolemy's astronomy and Galen's medical theories – together offering a picture of the material aspect of man's existence – with the Church's teachings on the nature and destiny of the soul. He worked the thought of the ancients into a unified philosophy fit to be the servant of theology, not merely thereby constructing a system satisfactory for the faith, but protecting the faith from any apparent conflict with the more ancient (and philosophically much richer and deeper) traditions that preceded it.

This brilliant synthesis, highly elaborate and detailed, constituted the framework for thinking about the world for all denominations of Christian thinkers in the sixteenth century, not just the Catholics; and it provided ground-rules for what could count from a theological point of view as acceptable in philosophical (which meant also scientific) enquiry. It did this despite the fact that it had earlier left plenty of room for debate and dispute among the philosophers of the medieval schools. But in general design the theologically consistent outline of this world-view was what all protectors of orthodoxies regarded as acceptable.

In the sixteenth century as in all the centuries of the Christian era beforehand, revelation was the primary source for understanding God's purposes and the nature of the universe itself. The Roman Catholic Church had since its beginning taken it as a matter of doctrine that revelation is a continuing process; the Church had licence from the deity to exert its own authority as a source of teachings regarding all matters. It was exactly this view that the proponents of the Reformation rejected in matters of theology and morality.

But both the Roman and Reformation theologians were silently agreed on a different and very significant point: that revelation is to have the final say in all questions of science. For Protestants revelation resides in scripture; for the Roman Catholic Church it lies both in scripture and in the continuous relationship of the Church with God. Scripture by itself was regarded by both as sufficient on such matters as the nature of the universe and its origins; it unequivocally stated that God had created the heavens and the earth, and had populated them with vast numbers of creatures ('created beings'), including a host of angels, one-third of whom – if we follow the traditions adapted by Milton in his epic of the loss of Paradise – had rebelled and followed the archangel Lucifer, otherwise known as Satan, into hell, from whence they ceaselessly endeavour to upset God's plan for humankind.

A key point about the religious view of the universe is that the most important consideration in it is the moral purpose for which, in its opinion, the universe exists. That is why the doctrines of the faith subordinated the little said about the origin and nature of the material world to its incidental role as theatre for the supposed grand narrative of the moral story. This story is familiar enough, but bears restatement, because in its incidents and details lie religious, anti-scientific bias.

God's first human creatures were Adam and Eve, to whom he gave a beautiful garden as a home. Satan seduced them away from their obedience to God, with the result that the entire human race now suffers punishment for their fall. That was the first sin; 'sin' means 'disobedience'; the disobedience in question lay in eating the forbidden fruit of the tree of knowledge of good and evil. That the first crime was disobedience to an injunction not to seek knowledge in a central area of human concern is a speaking fact, and one that connects directly to the disobedience of humankind represented by the scientific revolution itself.

The rebel angels, now in the character of demons, traverse the world in search of souls to capture for eternal damnation, by tempting them into such wickedness as heresy, greed and lust – and false beliefs. In his efforts to rescue mankind from itself God tried various remedies – drowning in a flood all but a handful of human beings so that he could start the enterprise over; sending teachers and prophets, too many of whom were ignored, or driven away, or even killed. Finally – so (most) Christian doctrine has it – God resorted to assuming human form and sacrificing himself as an atonement between himself and humankind. How people respond to that sacrifice will be assessed on Judgment Day, an event confidently regarded as imminent by almost every generation of true believers in Christian history.

These views of course included a plethora of fine details and nuances – details that sent many to the stake who could not agree with (or sometimes perhaps did not understand) them. Doctrine on these matters only began to take established form several centuries after the legendary death of Jesus, and involved much conflict over 'heresy' – a word chiefly denoting the beliefs held by the losing side in the argument. But the theories of the natural world adopted by the Church were far older than its theological doctrines, and were still fundamentally Aristotelian in the sixteenth century.

In this Aristotelian theory the physical world consists of combinations of the four 'elements' – earth, air, fire and water. There is a fifth element, the 'quintessence', called aether, of which the heavenly spheres and their passenger bodies are made. The four non-aetherial elements can manifest any two of the four respectively associated properties dry, cold, hot and wet. Their combinations give rise to the characteristic nature of physical entities: earth is cold and dry, water is cold and wet; fire is hot and dry, air is hot and wet. Each of the four elements has its natural place. Earth, because it is heavy, tends towards the centre of the universe. Water is also heavy, but not quite as heavy as earth, so it lies on the earth's surface. Air occupies what would otherwise be the empty gap between water and fire, which latter is the lightest element. Fire is most at home above the earth; some later thinkers said it is what can be seen twinkling at night through the many little apertures in the spheres that surround the earth.

According to this theory we never encounter the elements in their pure and original form. They only ever come as alloys or mixtures. This is readily shown by experiments in chemistry, in which the elements are separated or rendered pure, chiefly by heating them. This is what gave rise to alchemy; if everything is a combination of the four elements, and if these mixtures can be separated out and then recombined in different ways, it must follow that precious metals such as gold can be formed from a base metal such as lead, and it must be possible to find the substance that would guarantee long life, perpetual youth or even immortality in the flesh. For example: gold is the most beautiful and desirable metal and – obviously – the most useful to own. This means that it must be a perfectly proportioned mixture of the four elements. Baser metals, consisting of unequal proportions of the elements, therefore need only to be reassembled into perfect proportions to become gold. It was further concluded that because gold is the perfect arrangement of the elements, it must likewise be the best possible medicine. This belief led to its being swallowed in liquid form as a cure for a wide variety of ailments.

Aristotle inferred from the 'nature' of each of the elements what their 'natural motion' is: earth and water have a naturally downward motion, while air and fire have a naturally upward motion. But this motion would occur only if something else applies a force to them, just as a person moves a pebble by throwing it. If the impulsive force ceased, so would the motion it produces. Accordingly there is no concept of inertia in Aristotle's science. This was a major reason why a God was needed, to get things moving in the first place – the spheres of the stars and planets, for example – and then either to keep them moving or to arrange for agencies to do the work for him.

The theories of astronomy developed in antiquity were also adopted, more or less unchanged, by Christian thinkers. The heavenly bodies were thought of as orbiting a stationary earth occupying the centre of the universe; they were carried along in 'crystalline spheres' that had been set going by God and which were kept moving in their orbits – so some authorities taught – by a superior kind of angels (called 'Intelligences') whose duty it was to keep the stars and planets in their allotted courses. The spheres were made of crystal because they had to be both transparent and solid, and the only then known natural material combining these two properties was crystal. The beauty of crystal was a further recommendation for this important office.

The moon is the lowest and nearest of the sky's residents, and the least refined; its sphere has the swiftest revolution around the earth. Then, in order of distance from the earth, come Mercury, Venus, the Sun, Mars, Jupiter and Saturn, each of them revolving more slowly than the one beneath it. They are composed not of earth, air, fire and water but of the fifth element – the 'quintessence' – and their orbits round the earth are perfect circles. They are themselves similarly perfect, and like Plato's Forms they are unchanging. As they circle round the earth they pour out divine music – rather as a string hums when a weight is attached to one end and is swung round – which we humans cannot hear because of the baseness of our material bodies. The faithful who make it to heaven will be able to hear the music of the spheres on arrival.

The theory has yet further elaborations, from the medico-psychological theory of 'humours' – which we still refer to in talking of someone as melancholy or bilious, sanguine or phlegmatic – to astrological theories of personality and fate, and from there to the idea that the human world is a divinely ordered hierarchy from the highest king to the lowest serf. Indeed the theory of 'degree' extends even further than the human social hierarchy, for it runs from God all the way down to the humble worm. Human beings are situated halfway between, the link between angels and beasts, sharing a bit of the nature of each – and therefore acting as the link between earth and heaven. This theory also had its subtleties; angels know more than humans do, but humans are better than angels at learning; humans have more intelligence than beasts, but beasts have more strength than humans; and so forth.[2]

Most of this constituted the world-view of the educated and (perhaps in more rudimentary form) of the uneducated for many centuries, right through the sixteenth century and into the seventeenth. It is difficult now to imagine what it was like to think in these terms. In many respects it was a satisfying and even comfortable view – despite the devil and his agents constantly prowling about to ensnare one into eternal torment: a ghastly thought – for it put humankind and its world at the centre of creation and made it God's chief interest and care; and it made man (here I use the masculine term advisedly) the lord of that world at least in temporal terms. To be confronted with a profoundly, even violently, different view of the universe; to be confronted with the highly unsettling idea that the earth is not stationary at the centre of things, but flies through immense tracts of empty space in a universe larger than imagination can grasp; that the universe is not actually about humankind or for humankind – this is not merely a blow to humanity's self-esteem (no longer to be a possible hero in a cosmic and eternal drama is quite a demotion), but it is in itself vertiginous at least and positively terrifying at worst.

Worse still, these new theories directly challenged, indeed impugned, scripture in particular and the authority of religion in general. The proposal that we should view the earth as flying round the sun through great arcs of space seemed to the Church to be worse than a lie – it was a blasphemy; remember Cardinal Bellarmino's warning to the Carmelite monk Foscarini: Psalm 104 verse 5 unequivocally states that God 'set the earth on its foundations; it can never be moved'. Bellarmino had further warningly reminded Foscarini that God made the sun stand still as a help to Joshua in massacring his enemies – was this not conclusive proof that it is the sun, not the earth, that moves through the sky? No wonder that the Church was prepared to put to death those who refused to accept the scriptures as the repository of scientific truth.

The stage was thus set for conflict between, on the one hand, a new world-view based on commitment to observation and reason unconfined by the requirement to square with religious doctrine, and, on the other hand, the authority of scripture and the Church. It was a direct confrontation. The Counter-Reformation's new shocktroops, the Jesuit order founded in 1534, which had astutely chosen education as its prime weapon in the war to recover Christendom's lost souls for Rome, described its curriculum in its *Ratio Studiorum* (schedule of study) in the following unequivocal terms: 'In logic, natural philosophy, ethics and metaphysics, Aristotle's doctrine is to be followed.' This instruction was issued by Francis Borgia – generally known as St Francis Borgia, General of the Jesuit order, in a memorandum which went on to state that no one is allowed to 'defend or teach anything opposed, detracting, or unfavourable to the faith, either in philosophy or theology. Let no one defend anything against the axioms received by the philosophers, such as: there are only four causes, there are only four elements, there are only three principles of natural things, fire is hot and dry, air is humid and hot. Let no one defend such propositions as that natural agents act at a distance without a medium, contrary to the most common opinion of the philosophers and theologians . . . This is not just an admonition, but a teaching that we impose.'[3]

'*This is a teaching that we impose.*' It is not surprising therefore that the new ideas advanced by science were greeted with vigorous opposition and sometimes persecution. And this was despite the fact that the first advocates of the new ways of thinking did not venture them as alternatives to Church doctrine. In the preface to his classic work, Copernicus said only that a heliocentric hypothesis made better sense of observation and the associated mathematics, but it must be regarded as an heuristic device merely, not a claim that he wished his readers to take literally.[4]

There is therefore a stark contrast between the pre-scientific world-view which constituted orthodoxy at the beginning of the seventeenth century and the world-view that science has developed since then. The real contrast, of course, is between the kinds of thinking that respectively give rise to these ways of looking at the world. As Bertrand Russell said, it is not what one believes but one's reasons for believing it that really matter; and what the seventeenth century put to work to its full and proper extent was a different way of acquiring beliefs about the natural realm. The repudiation of the obedience of faith in matters of enquiry was the clinching point; the contrast in the outlooks is most economically described as follows.

Religion in the ideal offers us the supposed word of a deity or deities. Its chief requirement is that we believe in the benevolent government of the deity or deities and respond accordingly – which means, to worship and obey, not to doubt and question, but to accept: that is the meaning of 'faith'. In two of the world's leading religions, Christianity and Islam, this is a cardinal virtue. 'Islam' indeed means 'submission'; in Christianity likewise submission to the authority of the deity is central – the prayer that all sects utter, the 'Our Father', includes the words 'not my will but yours be done' – and a trope of observance is 'dying to oneself' and 'handing oneself over to God'. One of the worst sins is 'pride', which means relying on one's own judgment and standing on one's own feet, in this way repudiating the doctrine that the frailty of mankind in every respect requires the support and salvation of the deity. Faith as acceptance even in the face of reason and contrary evidence is a great virtue, as witness the story of Doubting Thomas in the Gospel according to John (chapter 20 verses 24–9), and the teaching of Søren Kierkegaard about 'the leap of faith' (more accurately, the 'leap *to* faith') needed to cross what Gotthold Lessing had described as the 'ugly wide ditch' that he could not leap over in order to believe in a religion based on claims about miracles. In this Lessing was a true child of the Enlightenment, one of whose leading figures he was. Had he known the witticism of his near-contemporary David Hume that the age of miracles was not over because the fact that people still held religious beliefs was a miracle in itself, he would doubtless have appreciated it.

Science is a markedly different matter. In the ideal it is an objective and impersonal endeavour that seeks to be as intellectually responsible as possible in devising and testing hypotheses, and in going where the evidence leads. It does not have a conclusion in advance, for which it seeks support; that is the way of the dogmatist. On the contrary, it does everything it can to exclude bias, and to conduct itself in openly scrutable ways, with its results being subject to public challenge, independent verification, and replication of results. Reliance on observation, rigorous reasoning, careful design of experiments and constant review by independent scrutineers are the standard commitments of scientific procedure, and together are the least that is expected of anyone seriously engaged in scientific enquiry.

If evidence were required for the success of science's methods and norms, one need only say, *si monumentum requiris, circumspice*: look around at today's world. The results of scientific endeavour are overwhelmingly endorsed by outcome. The application of science by means of technology is testimony to its success and – arguably – its advance towards truths about the world; even if, as must always be acknowledged, the benefits are not unmixed with problems that science and technology also bring.[5]

The relevance of this to the intellectual revolution under consideration is of course a straightforward one: the seventeenth century is the moment when one world-view was displaced by another because the scientific version displaced that of faith. 'Displacement' is the appropriate word. The universe revealed by science is *toto caelo* different from the various universes portrayed by religions. These latter offer us a small human-centred creation having an expressly moral purpose – that of serving as a testing-ground for human beings, preparatory to their real existence after bodily death in either a paradisical or hellish eternal reality. Here human powers of imagination impose the limits on what nature can be, whereas in science far more can be envisioned, though only through the lens of mathematics – a conceptual tool of much greater range and accuracy than human fantasy – and experiment. Scanning the horizon of modern science's progress from Galileo and

Newton to relativity and quantum theory, and adding to these their accompanying advances in chemistry, biology and technology, we see that science reveals the impoverishment of pre-scientific views of the universe, and the limits of human imagination.

One distinctive characteristic of the scientific mind-set is scepticism, accompanied by readiness to adjust one's opinions when better evidence or more persuasive argument indicates that they are inaccurate, and to change them when they are shown to be wrong. For this reason science requires freedom both of expression and of enquiry; it cannot conform to a non-scientific agenda, no matter whether theological or political. If the effect of theological dogma on sixteenth-century science is not persuasive enough an example of this, consider 'Soviet biology' and in China the agricultural miracles of rice production in which yields were made to seem hugely increased – achieved, of course, by deceptively filling paddies with rice harvested from elsewhere, so that when top Party cadres drove by they could witness the miracle of agricultural fertility that Marxist-Leninist-Mao Zedong science made possible.

The Soviet and Maoist climate of pseudo-thought is closely analogous to what existed in the sixteenth century and beforehand, when the Church demanded, on threat of punishment, that scientific enquiry should not disagree with doctrinal orthodoxy. All too familiarly, the Church was prepared to persecute to guarantee observance of this requirement. The example always rightly cited is that of Galileo.[6]

The example of Galileo's trial matters because it marks the last major attempt by the Church to prevent or at least control the scientific revolution. Like the story of modern science itself, the story once again begins with the publication in 1543 of Copernicus' classic *De Revolutionibus*. The aim of that work, one recalls, in offering a heliocentric model of the universe, was to provide an easier way to characterise the movements of the stars and planets than had been provided by the geocentric model of Ptolemy. That model – formulated in the second century CE on the accumulated data of (literally) millennia of star-gazing – began from the assumption that the stars, sun, moon and the five planets then known all orbit the earth in perfect circles, the reason being that of all geometric figures the circle is most perfect.

But observations of stellar and especially planetary movements did not fit this assumption; too many anomalies and irregularities were observable. We now know that because the planets in our solar system follow elliptical orbits around the sun at different speeds and distances from it, some of them between earth and the sun and some far outside earth's circumsolar path, they will appear to an earth-bound observer sometimes to speed up and sometimes to slow down, and even to go back on themselves at times. They wander across the majestically wheeling backdrop of the 'fixed stars' with apparently purposeful whimsy. To cope with their perceived variabilities, adjustments to the perfectly circling system had to be made.

Ptolemy therefore proposed that, although the planets indeed move in perfect circles, they do not do so around the earth itself but instead around points which themselves travel in perfect circles around the earth. These local orbits within their larger earth-orbit are called 'epicycles'. The points themselves each sit in the plane of a crystal sphere, and these crystal spheres also move in perfect circles, but again not around the earth itself but around a set of points called 'equant' points which are situated just a little way from earth.

These refinements are obviously *ad hoc*, indicating that the model is jerry-built; all the adjustments and embellishments are invoked to square antecedent assumptions ('the heavenly bodies must of course move in perfect circles') with recalcitrant observations. They are like the extra Maoist rice in the paddy field. A much older idea, put forward by Aristarchus in the third century BCE (500 years before Ptolemy), that the sun sits at the centre of the universe with the earth and other bodies orbiting it, seemed simpler to Copernicus, and when he tried it he found that it fitted the observational data more accurately and effectively.

Copernicus was Polish (not German as Fontenelle had it), born in Toruń on the Vistula river. His father, who was a wealthy man, sent him to study in Italy where, in the early years of the sixteenth century, he absorbed humanist culture, learned Greek as well as Latin, and made translations of texts from one to the other. He had gone to Italy to study medicine and law, but appointment to a sinecure as a canon of Frombork Cathedral at home in Poland allowed him to dedicate his life to study instead.[7]

His interest in astronomy was sparked during his time in Italy, when he read a summary of Ptolemy's system published together with observations and questions by the German savant Regiomontanus (Johannes Müller; his scholarly name is a Latinised obeisance to the city of his birth, Königsberg). In his commentary Regiomontanus discussed a long-recognised problem with Ptolemy's geocentric model, which is that it does not accord with what we see of the moon, whose apparent size does not fluctuate as the Ptolemaic model says it should. That model would have the moon regularly seeming to get larger and smaller as it first approached and then withdrew from earth – which it would do if it were moving in a perfect circle round its equant point. Copernicus solved the problem by hypothesising that whereas the moon indeed orbits the earth, it and the other planets, together with the crystal sphere of the stars, all together orbit the sun. This gives the happy result that the universe has a single centre, this being the sun, rather than a rash of equants near the earth.

But it introduces problems of its own. If the earth is flying round the sun, why do we not feel the wind of its movement blowing in our faces? Why do the oceans not rise and flood over the land just as the water in a bucket spills over the edges when the bucket is swung round? If the sun is at the centre of everything, how is it that the earth and planets do not fall into it? If the crystal sphere of stars orbits the sun too, it must be extremely far away from the planets, leaving a yawning gap between themselves and the solar system. Why would God create such an oddly shaped universe?

There was too little knowledge in the sixteenth century to provide answers to these puzzles. But other aspects of Copernicus' model made it compelling. One is that it allowed Copernicus to answer a different awkward question, which is: Why can Venus and Mercury only be seen at dawn and dusk whereas Mars, Jupiter and Saturn are visible at any time? Ptolemy's answer had been that Venus and Mercury accompany the sun on its voyage round the earth, but Copernicus saw that the difference must imply that Mercury and Venus have orbits inside earth's orbit, placing them closer to the sun, while the other three have orbits outside the earth's orbit. Accordingly he was able to place the planets in their right order by inferring it from the pattern of their heliocentric orbits relative to the earth: outwards from the sun the order is Mercury, Venus, earth, Mars, Jupiter, Saturn. This simple result is beautiful science.

Although Copernicus arrived at these ideas as a young man he did not publish them, recognising their dangerous implications, until the very end of his life. Indeed it is said that a finished copy of his book reached him from the publisher as he lay on his deathbed. It is a touching but probably untrue tale. He was persuaded, against his inclinations, to publish by his friend Rheticus (Georg von Lauchen), the Professor of Mathematics at Wittenberg University. Rheticus had published an outline account of Copernicus' system years before, in 1540. A Lutheran minister named Andreas Osiander was hired to prepare Copernicus' full manuscript for the press, a task for which he became solely responsible when Copernicus fell into his last illness. The book appeared a quarter of a century after the Reformation began, and just a year after the Roman Catholic Church launched its eventually anti-science Counter-Reformation at the Council of Trent.

Osiander was the author of the much quoted preface stating that Copernicus' system is not to be taken as describing the true layout of the universe, but instead should be regarded merely as a model or hypothesis. He did not put his own name to the preface, so allowing it to be believed that Copernicus himself had written it. Osiander's motive is easy to understand: he knew that if the theory were claimed to be true it would invite condemnation. But despite the disclaimers he inserted in the preface, his fears were soon confirmed as justified.

An historical oddity attaching to this story is that when Copernicus first developed his ideas, more than thirty years earlier in 1510, he made a synopsis of them and circulated them to acquaintances in a manuscript entitled *Commentariolus* (*A Little Commentary*). The pamphlet excited admiration, even in the Vatican, where it was the topic of a talk given in the presence of Pope Clement VII by a papal secretary named Johann Widmanstadt. A cardinal present at the talk, Nicholas von Schönberg, wrote to Copernicus urging him to publish a more complete version of the theory. When Copernicus' book appeared in 1543 the cardinal's letter was printed at the beginning, a figleaf which proved inadequate to protect those who were later persecuted – even burned to death at the stake – for accepting the Copernican view.

The year in which Copernicus published the early sketch of his theory, 1510, lay in the lull between the end of the excesses of Torquemada's Spanish Inquisition and the nailing of Luther's *Theses* to the church door at Wittenberg. It was the era of Erasmus' influence, whose fame, and the irenic nature of whose humanism, had a positive although only temporarily calming effect on the European mind. It was not a time when zealous attention was paid to recondite works of natural philosophy in the hope of detecting heresy.

Just thirty years later matters were very different. Copernicus' hesitation about publishing is a speaking fact. So is Osiander's attempt to disguise the heliocentric theory as merely a mathematical heuristic. Osiander knew his Bible; he knew Psalm 104, he knew that in chapter 10 of the Book of Joshua it says that the sun stood still for an entire day, and the moon likewise. Copernicus and God were therefore authors of competing accounts, so unless Copernicus could be represented as saying that he did not seek to challenge the veracity of scripture, there would be trouble.

But of course there was trouble anyway. It was inevitable that the implications of Copernicus' model would attract the Church's notice. It is perhaps surprising that it did not happen earlier, but the second half of the sixteenth century was a time of much distraction and anguish arising especially from the wars of religion. It took a particular incident to obtrude the implications of Copernicus into the Church's awareness, and until then his views were ignored or overlooked. That incident was the trial for heresy of Giordano Bruno, and his execution in Rome in February 1600.

Bruno was not a discreet man. Like many of his contemporaries in the late sixteenth century he had a wide-ranging and miscellaneous set of interests in Hermeticism, mysticism and much besides, but he also openly stated his acceptance of the Copernican model as a correct description of the universe. He did this in full consciousness of the danger; but he did it anyway. When it became apparent during the two decades after Bruno's execution that increasingly many savants were persuaded by the literal truth of the heliocentric theory, Copernicus' *De Revolutionibus* was put on the Vatican's *Index of Forbidden Books* where – along with most of the rest of the world's greatest and most influential literature, which the *Index* has inadvertently raised to prominence – it shed its undimmed mathematical radiance on the scientific revolution that followed.

The event that precipitated this typically heroic act by the Church was the attempt by Foscarini, already described, to persuade the Church that scripture and Copernicus were not at odds. Bellarmino's response on behalf of the Vatican could have been written at any time in the preceding thousand years, but it could not have been written a mere fifty years later. It would be hard to believe that Bellarmino and his colleagues in the hierarchy of the Church were not conscious that the current of history was against them, were it not that the Church remained so obdurately wedded to its beliefs for centuries afterwards despite no longer being able to compel others to believe likewise. Although the Church was unwilling to tolerate theories that disagreed with scripture, it was even then increasingly reaching a position where it had little choice in the matter. Its silencing of Galileo on this point, by threatening him with death, was in effect its last throw of that die.

Galileo had been a problem for the Church for more than two decades when it finally indicted him before the Inquisition on the Copernican question. Trouble had begun early, in 1604, when he lectured on Kepler's supernova observations, demonstrating that it had to be as far away as the rest of the fixed stars, and that therefore it had to be one of the fixed stars undergoing change – which contradicted Aristotle's (and therefore the Church's) view that the stars never change. Galileo's lecture also therefore had troubling implications about the size of the universe.

Then Galileo constructed his own telescope and made astonishing discoveries by its means. He had heard that someone in the Netherlands had made a powerful 'spyglass', so, using his considerable gifts as both a craftsman and a mathematician, and putting what he knew of the laws of refraction to work, he made one for himself. This was in 1609. His first telescopes had a magnification of approximately four, but he was soon grinding lenses that yielded a magnification of eight or nine. He had entrepreneurial as well as scientific talents, and turned this work into cash by persuading the Venetian Senate that he was the inventor of the telescope and that it had great potential in military, commercial and maritime respects. The Senate gave him a generous sum for the right to manufacture his 'perspicullum'. He had to quit Venice very hastily when the Venetians learned that he was not the telescope's inventor, and had no rights to the patent they had bought from him.[8]

Although Galileo was alive to the commercial value of his version of the telescope, he was more acutely alive to its scientific promise. Through it in December 1609 he saw something that put the seal on humanity's changing conception of the universe. He saw mountains on the moon, sunspots, a vastly more numerous array of individual stars in the Milky Way, and several moons orbiting Jupiter. He immediately gave the name 'the Medicean stars' to these moons and sent news of their discovery and their names – along with a good telescope – to the Medici ruler of Florence, the Grand Duke of Tuscany, Cosimo II. As a reward the Duke appointed Galileo 'Ducal Mathematician and Philosopher' at a large salary.

Galileo published his telescopic discoveries in his *Sidereus Nuncius* (*The Starry Messenger*). This short book made him famous everywhere in Europe. Yet his most fascinating discoveries were yet to come. He continued to gaze through his telescope, making more accurate observations of Jupiter's moons. While pondering certain inconsistencies in the data he thus collected, he realised that he had to take account of variabilities in his own position relative to the motions of the planets and their satellites, variabilities which could be explained only if the earth was itself moving round the sun. This constituted powerful evidence that Copernicus' model was much more than a mere heuristic, but rather a literally correct description of the solar system.

Galileo had in fact been convinced of this since at least 1598; in that year he had written to Kepler saying that he was a Copernican. But he did not say anything publicly at this juncture, aware of the implications; he continued to enjoy plaudits and honours, including election to a fellowship of the prestigious Accademia dei Lincei in Rome.

But the Copernican theory would not lie quiet. One of Galileo's former pupils, Benedetto Castelli (1578–1643), a professor of mathematics at Pisa University, was invited by Cosimo II and his mother the Grand Duchess Christina of Lorraine to give a lecture on the contradictions between the Copernican model and scripture. In his lecture Castelli defended the Copernican model, and afterwards wrote to Galileo to tell him that he had done so. In reply Galileo said what he thought: that scripture should always be interpreted according to the discoveries of science, not, as the Church required, the other way round. Somehow copies of his letter got into the hands of the Inquisition. At that point the Inquisitors did nothing, most likely waiting for a better moment to make life difficult for Galileo.

Unwisely, Galileo was made bolder by their inaction, and himself wrote to the Grand Duchess Christina in 1616 saying,

> I hold that the Sun is located at the centre of the revolutions of the heavenly orbs and does not change place, and that the Earth rotates on itself and moves around it. I confirm this view not only by refuting Ptolemy's and Aristotle's arguments, but also by producing many on the other side, especially some pertaining to physical effects whose causes perhaps cannot be determined in any other way, and other astronomical discoveries; these discoveries clearly confute the Ptolemaic system, and they agree admirably with the Copernican position and confirm it.[9]

This letter in its turn also fell into hostile hands, and now the Church felt compelled to act. Pope Paul V ordered Cardinal Bellarmino to refer the question of Galileo to the Sacred Congregation of the Index (the Inquisition's official label). Its cardinals considered the matter in

February 1616. They took evidence only from theologians; neither Galileo nor any other scientist was invited to testify, nor was he or any other scientist asked to submit written evidence. Unsurprisingly the cardinals concluded that the Copernican theory must be condemned, pronouncing the heliocentric view not merely 'foolish and absurd' but heretical, adding that the idea that the earth flies through space is 'at very least erroneous in faith'.[10]

'Erroneous in faith': this phrase, offered in rebuttal of scientific observation, might have an alien ring now, no longer carrying the threatening weight of authority as it did then; but alas there are too many still for whom it retains significance. That this can still be so in the twenty-first century illustrates a problem to be solved. But in the seventeenth century it was the scientific view, not the concept of the trumping truth of doctrine, that seemed to the Church to be the problem.

Cardinal Bellarmino accordingly summoned Galileo to an interview, reported what the Sacred Congregation had concluded, and told him that he was therefore and thenceforth forbidden to hold, defend or teach the Copernican theory. Some historians suggest that neither Bellarmino nor Pope Paul V wished to see Galileo in trouble. They even (some go on to add) wished him to be free to continue teaching the Copernican theory, and for this reason their version of the ruling did not contain a prohibition against teaching it. But when Bellarmino informed Galileo of the Sacred Congregation's ruling, he did so in the presence of its members, who were eager for an opportunity to prosecute Galileo further. They had inserted the prohibition against teaching in order to see whether he would agree. Because they were present, therefore, Galileo had to agree, and Bellarmino's attempt to spare him the prohibition was foiled. This embellished story goes on to claim that Galileo was immediately afterwards invited to an audience with Paul V who assured him that while he, Paul, was on St Peter's throne, Galileo would be safe.

This pleasant story does not, alas, have much truth to it. If Bellarmino and Paul V were Galileo's allies, and by extension therefore friends to the Copernican theory, Foscarini would not have been admonished, and Galileo would not have kept so loudly silent for the remainder of Paul V's life. He would almost certainly not have waited to publish his next important work, *Il Saggiatore* (*The Assayer*), a disquisition on scientific method, until a new pope – a positively Galileo-friendly pope – was in the Vatican.

This was Pope Urban VIII, installed on St Peter's throne in 1623. Before then he was Cardinal Maffeo Barberini, and had been a friend to Galileo's work for a long time. Galileo now published his *Assayer* and dedicated it to Urban. It contained a passage that became and remains famous:

> Philosophy is written in this grand book, the universe, which stands continually open to our gaze. But the book cannot be understood unless one first learns to comprehend the language and read the characters in which it is written. It is written in the language of mathematics, and its characters are triangles, circles, and other geometric figures without which it is humanly impossible to understand a single word of it; without these one is wandering in a dark labyrinth.

Pope Urban laughed uproariously at Galileo's digs at the Jesuits in *The Assayer* when it was read to him. He invited Galileo to a total of six audiences, showing him favour and friendship, and thereby leading Galileo to believe that he could resume teaching the Copernican theory openly, not least in the *magnum opus* he was then busy writing, his *Dialogo sopra i due massimi sistemi del mondo* (*Dialogue Concerning the Two Chief World Systems*). His work on the book was slow because interrupted by bouts of recurring ill health, which delayed its completion until 1629. When it was finished he sought permission for its publication by the Accademia dei Lincei in Rome; but because it happened just then that the Academy was in turmoil following the death of the 'Chief Lynx' – its president – and even though he had the censor's approval, Galileo decided to publish in Florence, where after yet further delays – this time caused by outbreaks of the plague – it at last appeared in 1632.[11]

There was no trouble at first, but Galileo's enemies were waiting for their chance, and they soon spotted it. Galileo's principal enemy was a Jesuit named Christoph Scheiner – rather aptly because he had written about sunspots (aptly but, according to Galileo, ineptly – thus attracting Galileo's scorn, which had filled Scheiner with resentment. They each accused the other of plagiarism, and otherwise crossed swords; history has been unkind to Scheiner, who after all was quite an expert on the sun, and invented the pantograph). Scheiner and his allies found their chance in the fact that Galileo had printed the censor's preface to his book in a typeface different from the main text, thus distancing himself from it, and moreover had given the dialogue's defeated disputant a remark to the effect that the Copernican system was merely an hypothesis. This cautionary observation had been recommended to Galileo by Urban VIII himself, as a way of protecting the book. Galileo's opponents persuaded Urban that attribution of the words to the unsuccessful because less intelligent contender in the debate was an insult to Urban, who was accordingly angered.

The Jesuits now had their chance. They scoured Galileo's writings in search of further damning evidence, and there it was in the 1616 judgment forbidding Galileo to hold, defend or teach the Copernican system, which he was manifestly doing – doing all three – by giving the exposition and defence of it to the *Dialogue*'s winning party.

Galileo was again required to appear before the Inquisition. He delayed as long as possible, pleading illness. His former protector at Florence, Cosimo II, had died some time before, and the new young Grand Duke did not know how to play at politics with the Vatican. Galileo eventually had to give in and go to Rome.

He arrived in February 1633, and was immediately put on trial. The outcome was never in doubt; Galileo was sixty-nine years old – a grand age in those days – arthritic, almost blind, ill and weak. He recanted. He was obliged to say, 'I abjure, curse and detest my errors,' and to deny that the earth moved. He thereby saved himself from execution. Instead he was condemned to life imprisonment, and, as mentioned earlier, the sentence was commuted to house arrest at his home in Arcetri. He spent the closing decade of his life there, fruitfully engaged in writing his last book, the *Discorsi e dimostrazioni matematiche, intorno a due nuove scienze* (*Discourses and Mathematical Demonstrations Concerning*

Two New Sciences), which described and summed up his life's work. It included accounts of the pendulum, inertia and mechanics, and expanded his views on scientific method. He was visited in his retreat at Arcetri by many men of distinction, including Milton and Hobbes.[12]

Galileo undoubtedly knew that although he had lost a battle, science had won the war. His *Dialogue* and especially his *Two New Sciences* were immensely influential among learned men everywhere in Europe, and fuelled the scientific advances that followed. Italy, in contrast to the rest of Europe, was scientifically paralysed by the Inquisition's condemnation of Galileo, and became a backwater.

The history of seventeenth-century science moves seamlessly from Galileo to Harvey, Huygens, Boyle and the great achievement of Newton, taking the formation of the Royal Society in 1662 on the way. Theories that failed are left out of account because they are not signposts on the high road to the present. But it is of significance to note that there was for a time a competitor as a new physics: the system devised by Descartes.

In the second half of the seventeenth century and afterwards Descartes' scientific theories were much debated. What attracted attention was not his philosophical views as studied in universities today, but his physics, and specifically his theory of 'vortices'. Newton challenged Descartes' theory at the close of Book II of the *Principia* in preparation for setting out his own account of how the motion of bodies occurs 'in free space without vortices'.[13]

Descartes' theory was that the universe is a plenum – a solid continuum – of matter in different states. There is no vacuum; space and matter are the same thing. For objects to move they have to be moved by something other than themselves. Descartes argued that this entails that there must be indefinitely many local vortices or swirls of matter in different grades of coarseness or fluidity, the matter at the outer margins of each vortex moving more swiftly than the matter at the centre. Because of the nature of the matter at the centre of vortices, where it forms as fluid around bodies, the centres of vortices are suns, and their outward pressure on the universal fluid is what we experience as light when our eyes are turned towards them. The heavenly bodies are made of coarser particles of matter, and are transported by the vortices – the earth itself does not move, being without its own principle of motion, but it is carried round the sun by the fluid vortex encompassing and supporting it.

Descartes explained motion in the vortices according to his theory of mechanics, which uses only the concepts of size, speed and rest or motion. These latter two states of bodies depend upon the mechanical interactions between bodies, imparting motion or change. Vortices contain three types of matter: aether, consisting of very fine fast-moving particles of the kind that constitutes the sun and stars; tiny, smooth spherical particles which Descartes called 'celestial matter'; and lastly larger irregular particles that aggregate or stick together to form planets and comets.

Although Descartes' theory looks like an ingenious way of being Copernican without being theologically unorthodox – in his theory the earth indeed orbits the sun, but does not itself move, for it is carried passively along in its vortex – its main basis lay in adherence to the principle that there is no vacuum. The subsequent history of science shows that Descartes was wrong about this, but his mistake had two fruitful consequences. The first relates to his theory of vision, which is that vision is the result of pressure on the eyeball by the universal fluid. The sun, for example, is the centre of a vortex, and its outward pressure on the universal fluid translates into pressure on any eye directed towards it. (Newton offered a refutation of this by saying that if vision is caused by pressure in this way, anyone could see in the dark by running fast enough. Descartes has an answer: no one *can* run fast enough to see in the dark.)[14] Descartes' idea is an antecedent of thinking of light as waves emanating from a source, rather like the ripples caused by a stone thrown into a pool. This idea was explored later in the seventeenth century by Christiaan Huygens; Descartes was on to something right.

Secondly, the theory of vortices had a great negative utility in being what Newton rejected in the search for his own theory of gravitation. Newton's theory involves accepting 'action at a distance', in contrast to the seemingly more sensible theory of Descartes that there can be no such thing. The resulting controversy between the Cartesians and Newtonians was fierce. The Cartesians adhered to the common-sense idea that physical interactions must be the result either of collisions between particles describable in terms of mechanics, or (as in Descartes' theory) of the fact that everything is physically connected to everything else in the plenum, so that pressure and motion is transmitted by contiguity. The competing idea that there can be action at a distance without such contiguity led to the concept of the field, eventually of great importance in Maxwell's work on electromagnetism in the nineteenth century, and in the whole subsequent development of physics. But at the time Newton's claim that gravity acts instantaneously at any distance without a mediating physical link seemed like an invocation of 'occult powers', a notion that the Cartesians vigorously opposed.

Newton's rejection of the Cartesian vortex theory was, however, well founded. For one example, he showed that Descartes' view conflicts with Kepler's third law – the 'Harmonic Law' which relates two quantities, one being the time it takes for a planet to orbit the sun, the other being the planet's mean distance from the sun. In direct contrast to what is entailed by Descartes' theory, Kepler's third law states that the planets closest to the sun move at the greatest speeds and have the shortest orbital periods. According to Descartes it should be the planets furthest from the sun that move fastest. Further, Newton showed also that unless there is a constant input of energy at the centre of each vortex, vortices could not sustain themselves in being; Descartes had failed to consider this problem.

Descartes' foremost achievement was, arguably, to help solve a quite different problem, one that was every bit as important if not more so. It was the familiar and pressing problem of the relation between science and religion. As the case of Galileo demonstrated to anyone who thought about it, there was a serious need to separate, or find a way of separating, the spheres of religion and science, given the apparent impossibility of making them compatible, or otherwise achieving peaceful cohabitation between them. The alternative to finding a solution to this problem was the suffocation of scientific enquiry, as so vigorously attempted by the Church to that point. This was a separate problem, but it was every bit as urgent, from the methodological problem of separating science from the *magia*, *alchymia*, *cabala* entanglement that continually threatened to misdirect it.

An idea that attracted those eager for a solution was to argue that religion and science are not competitors for the truth in the same regions of enquiry. If religion could attend exclusively to matters of heaven and spirit, while science restricts itself to the sublunary world, there would be no need for the Church to be anxious about the hypotheses and discoveries of science, and science would be able to proceed without incurring the sometimes mortal danger of upsetting religious sensibility.

The challenge of arguing for a separation of the spheres of science and religion was accepted by the same two major figures who had argued for the disentanglement of science and occult philosophy: René Descartes and Francis Bacon. Precisely because Descartes had made significant contributions to mathematics and science, it mattered to him personally that his scientific work should not be seen to impugn the Church's teachings. This was based on his anxious desire to please the Jesuits, in particular, who he hoped would adopt his books as texts for their schools, for they were still teaching Aristotelianism and Thomism, which he emphatically opposed. Although Descartes had been a pupil of the Jesuits at La Flèche, and perhaps their servant in the espionage of the Thirty Years War, he was disappointed in this hope; his books were soon to find their way on to the Vatican's *Index of Forbidden Books* – like that of Copernicus, and just as much of an unintended honour.

The solution to the problem of the competing spheres of religion and science lay in a theory Descartes advanced in his *Meditations on First Philosophy*. In it he argued that mind and matter are essentially different substances – using these terms in their technical philosophical senses: *essential* denotes 'of the essence or defining nature' and *substance* denotes what is metaphysically basic and fundamental. He put the contrast by defining mind as thinking stuff, *res cogitans*, and matter as spatial stuff, *res extensans*. This division between mind and matter caused his philosophical successors serious problems, most especially with the question of how the two substances can interact. As Princess Elisabeth asked, how can mental events cause bodily events – how does the thought 'It is time to get up' result in my body rising from the bed? – and how do bodily occurrences result in events in consciousness such as feelings of pain and pleasure, emotions and memories?

Despite these problems, the theory nevertheless offers a solution to the problem of whether Church doctrine is threatened by treating the physical world exclusively in terms of scientific law. That solution is to treat the material realm as a mechanism which God had invented and set going, thereafter running in accordance with the laws – the laws of science – that he had laid down. The seventeenth century's dominant scientific analogy was clockwork, as described by Fontenelle in his *Conversations on the Plurality of Worlds*. Matter was visualised as composed of atoms or 'corpuscles' ('little bodies') interacting on mechanical principles. Descartes' separation of the realms was intended to serve as a licence not merely for the scientifically minded to get on with their investigations of the mechanism of nature, but for the devout to let them do it without anxiety. Scientific enquiries, he implied, would not touch the great spiritual truths; instead they are a celebration of the handiwork of the divine.

An even more robust line on the question of science's relation to religion was taken by Francis Bacon. He wished to specify techniques of enquiry that would yield truth and practicality, as described in an earlier chapter, but it is easy to overlook the significance of his achievement in this regard. He effectively unseated the antecedently prevailing view that was premised on two things: the belief that the ancients (not just the philosophers of classical times but the Cabalists, Hermeticists and magicians too) knew more than the moderns, and the alleged certainties of revelation and Church authority. Earlier enquirers and the Church were thus taken as the two fountains of truth, telling us how things are. As we saw, Bacon opposed this view by arguing that, through observation and experiment, enquiry should begin again on a different foundation with the aim of discovering how things are in themselves.

He also argued that the outcomes of scientific enquiry should be used to advance the practical interests of humankind. We now take it for granted that scientific research, technological invention and advances in the techniques of both have practical applications as their major aim; but we also take it for granted that pure research, the pursuit of knowledge for its own sake, can often turn out to have highly useful applications. When Bacon pointed this out it was by no means the commonplace it has since become. In his day knowledge, if the quest for it were permissible, was either conducted for its own sake entirely, or it was regarded as providing support for the orthodoxies of faith.

Practical people – the farmers, blacksmiths, shipbuilders, carpenters, masons and others mentioned earlier – had of course always observed and learned from the world, as a result inventing technologies and improving the ones they already possessed. Bacon wished to re-establish the connection between theory and practice; that is one underlying tenet of empiricism outside the ivory tower. And the point is that the practical endeavours of blacksmiths and carpenters had never been in conflict with dogma; indeed carpentry had a most respectable lineage in this regard.

Another significance of Bacon's contribution is that it helped to change thinking not just about the nature of knowledge but about the possibility of its acquisition. It was as if his immediate predecessors among thinkers lacked confidence in their capacity to make original advances in knowledge. Bacon changed this. He represented an aspect of the Renaissance mind which did not think it was confined only to rediscovering and copying, but was capable of discovering and making new advances.

Once again, the fundamental point was that all this is possible only if scientific enquiry can proceed in freedom. That meant drawing a clear line between the business of religion and the business of science. Bacon's emphatic view that it is always a mistake to 'commix together' science and religion played a major part in liberating enquiry from the demand for doctrinal conformity.

The argument between science and religion in the seventeenth century was an argument about *authority* – authority over minds and outlooks. At the beginning of the century the Church was prepared to kill in order to keep control of what can be thought; by the century's end this was no longer possible in Europe. Alas, it remains possible in a number of regions in today's world – a state of affairs which shows that those parts of the world still await their seventeenth century and its offspring, the following century's Enlightenment.

But the change of view about what is to have intellectual authority is central to the emergence of the modern mind itself, as witness how the idea that observation and reason are those authorities – rather than the Church's teachings or the supposed wisdom of the past – came to be an assumption of the Enlightenment. Note this: an *assumption*, not a hope or a claim, but something taken for granted, so far had minds been freed from the trammels of dogma. The scientific attitude – the attitude of rational enquiry controlled by the facts and dedicated to understanding the universe and relating it to practicalities – had come to displace the previous intellectual authorities as what must supervise thought and action.

This change is the key to understanding the Enlightenment of the following century, which at its core is shaped by the idea that the methods and concepts of science should be applied in all domains of enquiry, as far as is consistent with the subject matter in question. Newton was enough of a scientist, despite his occult interests and hopes, to close his *Optics* (published in 1704) with the words, 'if natural philosophy in all its parts, by pursuing this Method [i.e. scientific method], shall at length be perfected, the bounds of moral philosophy will be also enlarged'. By 'moral philosophy' he meant, as his contemporaries meant likewise, all of ethics, politics, economics, psychology and history. This is what makes the Enlightenment what it was: an extension of the scientific approach to wider domains of interest. It is the idea that underlies the *Encyclopédie* of Diderot and d'Alembert. Its consequences include among them the major political revolutions of the eighteenth century. Writing in the mid-eighteenth century David Hume noted that there had been 'a sudden and sensible change in the opinions of men within these last fifty years, by the progress of learning and liberty'.[15] At the time he wrote those words they were more true of England than most other parts of Europe, and of the British colonies in North America; but they were true enough everywhere to be an important part of the explanation for the great revolutions that transformed politics and society in those colonies and France, and eventually large parts of the world.

A point on which Bacon repeatedly insisted was that science should be a collegial affair, and that there should be institutions dedicated to co-operative scientific research. He decried the habit of the supposed cognoscenti who kept as close to their chests as possible whatever secrets they learned about nature. From the 1590s he broached the idea of an academy of science; when James I came to the throne he argued that the ancient universities should be encouraged to set up science research institutes, and when it became clear that this was unlikely to happen he resumed the case for a self-standing such institute. This is one of the chief reasons why he is cited by the founders of the Royal Society of London as an inspiration.

Attempts had been made to establish scientific societies as early as the sixteenth century, in imitation of the ancient academies of Plato and Aristotle, which had been closed after nearly a thousand years of existence by the Christian Emperor Justinian in 529 CE. Justinian's reasons were these:

> We wish to extend the law that we and our father, of blessed memory, formerly made against all still-remaining heresies – we call 'heresies' those beliefs which hold and assert anything other than the teaching of the catholic and apostolic orthodox church – in order that the law should also apply to Samaritans and pagans, so that, because they do so much harm, they should no longer have influence, or respect, or serve as teachers of any subject, in case they drag the minds of simple people into their own errors, and in this way take the more ignorant among them away from the pure true orthodox faith. Thus we permit only holders of the orthodox faith to teach and to be paid from public funds.[16]

The principal sixteenth-century effort to establish a specifically scientific academy – there were already literary and humanistic ones – fared no better. Founded by the polymath Giambattista della Porta in Naples under the name Academia Secretorum Naturae – the Academy of the Secrets of Nature – its membership was open to anyone who could present 'a new fact in natural science'.[17] The Inquisition investigated it in 1578, and as a result Pope Gregory XIII ordered its closure on suspicion of sorcery. The suspicion was doubtless deepened by the mere title of della Porta's book, *Magia Naturalis* (*Natural Magic*).

The next effort was the founding of the Accademia dei Lincei – the Academy of the Lynxes – by Federico Cesi, son of the Duke of Acquasparta. Cesi was a devotee of botany, but with his fellow founders he wished to extend enquiry into all forms of science. They named their academy after the picture on the front cover of della Porta's *Magia Naturalis*, which was of a lynx, together with a legend adverting to the lynx's legendarily sharp eyesight which enabled it to observe everything in the minutest detail – even through walls and stone – just as a scientist should.

The Lincean Academy effectively died when Cesi did, in 1630 (though while it was still engaged in publishing a monumental multi-volumed account of the flora, fauna and pharmacopoeia of Mexico it kept going, until 1651. The Academy was revived in the nineteenth century and now occupies the handsome Palazzo Corsini in Rome). But while it lasted it promoted the ideal of observation – Cesi's motto was *minima cura si maxima vis*, 'care of the little things yields maximum results' – and Galileo was proud to become a member of it.

Some of Galileo's students were among those who founded the Accademia del Cimento in Florence in 1657. Unlike other scientific societies the Cimento never organised itself on a formal basis, but remained a group of friends who, under the patronage of two sons of Cosimo II de' Medici, pursued their investigations independently and jointly. Nevertheless they had a significant impact on scientific procedure, stating adherence to the experimental method, making instruments for laboratory use, standardising systems of measurement, and insisting (as their motto had it) on *Provando e Riprovando* – 'try and try again' (or 'prove and again prove'). The group published a manual in which they described experiments, the highly accurate instruments they had made for the purpose of those experiments, and the carefully calibrated systems of measurements they had devised in order to record weights, times, temperatures and pressures. The book – *Saggi di naturali esperienze fatte nell'Accademia del Cimento* – took more than five years to write and is handsomely illustrated with drawings of instruments along with instructions for their use.[18] Members of the Cimento corresponded with members of other societies around Europe, but because it never put itself on to an institutional footing it eventually disbanded as the individual members grew old, drifted away or died.

Matters were otherwise with the Academia Naturae Curiosorum, founded in Schweinfurt in 1652, and better known as the 'Leopoldina'. It still exists as Germany's national scientific academy, until recently known as the Deutsche Akademie der Naturforscher Leopoldina. It therefore lays claim to be the oldest continuously existing scientific academy in the world, and the first to publish a journal, the *Ephemeriden* or *Miscellanea Curiosa*. From the outset the society had a primary interest in medicine and physiology. It was only after the First World War that it acquired a permanent home, until then being located wherever its current president happened to live. (It is now based in Halle.) The blot on its copybook is its expulsion of Jewish members in the Nazi period, among them Einstein. There is no doubt that this is something most of its extraordinarily distinguished roll-call of members would regret: in addition to Einstein it includes Goethe, Darwin, Max Planck, Ernest Rutherford and Otto Hahn.

In France an informal academy of science sprang up around Henri Louis Habert de Montmor, writer and polymath, who was one of the founding members of the Académie Française in 1634. He wished to set up a parallel academy for science, and invited friends to join him. He was a serious scientist; he edited the complete works of Gassendi after the latter's death, and in imitation of Lucretius wrote a poem called *De Rerum Naturae* on Cartesian physics. Some of the men who joined his informal Montmor Academy were very distinguished – they included Pierre Daniel Huet, Adrien Auzout, Girard Desargues,

Samuel Sorbière, Claude Clerselier (the associate of Descartes), Jacques Rohault, Gilles Roberval and Christiaan Huygens.

The society lasted until 1664, dispersing as a result of quarrels among some of its members, but one of them, Auzout, persuaded Louis XIV – or more accurately, his chief minister Jean-Baptiste Colbert – of the need for a publicly funded observatory and associated academy. In 1666 the Académie des Sciences came into existence as a result. At the outset it had, like the Cimento, no formal constitution and no rules apart from a prohibition on discussing religion and politics. It met informally in the King's library. In 1699 Louis XIV at last gave it the equivalent of a Royal Charter: a set of rules, the right to call itself the Académie Royale des Sciences, and a home in the Louvre.

In the vicissitudes and changes of France's always interesting political life, the adjective 'Royale' came and went several times, as did the academy itself when the Revolution incorporated it into a new structure of academies. Its membership was not always exclusively scientific; Napoleon was elected to it, and indeed became its president (on the strength of having been to Egypt). Its own worst blot is that it did not admit women to membership until 1979 – which meant that Marie Curie, twice winner of a Nobel Prize, was excluded.

The Royal Society of London is often regarded as paradigmatic of what an academy of science should be. It grew out of the so-called Invisible College of the 1640s in England, the period of the Civil War, and came into more formal existence in 1660 when Sir Christopher Wren, then Professor of Astronomy at Gresham College in London, together with a group of friends, decided to set up 'a Colledge for the Promoting of Physico-Mathematicall Experimentall Learning'. Besides Wren the early members included Robert Boyle, John Wilkins and Sir Robert Moray. The members employed Robert Hooke as their first Curator of Experiments, and met weekly to witness experiments and discuss ideas.

Sir Robert Moray told King Charles II about the society, and the King took an interest. In 1662 he granted it a Royal Charter incorporating it as 'The President, Council, and Fellows of the Royal Society of London for Improving Natural Knowledge'. The Society adopted the motto *Nullius in Verba* which in effect means 'don't take anyone's word for it' – that is: look and think for yourself, go to the facts, test and examine. Among its first publications was Hooke's *Micrographia*.

The idea of a 'Colledge' specifically for the pursuit of scientific enquiry was not derived from the idea of an Oxford or Cambridge college – though the members of the Invisible College of the 1640s had largely been based in Oxford – but instead came from Bacon's idea for 'Solomon's House' in his *New Atlantis*, published in 1627. A character in the book says, 'Ye shall understand (my dear friends) that amongst the excellent acts of that king, one above all hath the pre-eminence. It was the erection and institution of an Order or Society, which we call *Salomon's House*; the noblest foundation (as we think) that ever was upon the earth; and the lanthorn of this kingdom. It is dedicated to the study of the works and creatures of God.' Among the duties of the 'Fellowes, or Brethren' of this institution is that of venturing abroad to learn everything about the knowledge and productions of other societies: 'there should be a mission of three of the Fellowes or Brethren of Salomon's House; whose errand was only to give us knowledge of the affairs and state of those countries to which they were designed, and especially of the sciences, arts, manufactures, and inventions of all the world; and withal to bring unto us books, instruments, and patterns in every kind'.

Developments in military technology and in scientific discovery were often closely connected. Studies of the movement of planets and the movement of cannon balls were related, the telescope brought moons and opposing armies equally into focus, new engineering principles were applied in fortification building. The access of power and technique brought by these advances is well illustrated by the difference between the Ottoman sieges of Vienna in 1529 and 1683 respectively. In the first, the Turks were only just beaten back, and they remained in possession of a large slice of central Europe and the Balkans after it. Centuries later residents of these regions would still refer to a journey across the old frontier as 'going to Europe'.[19] The Ottoman invasion of 1683 was a very different affair. One hundred and fifty thousand Ottoman troops were met by a Polish–German force of 68,000, and were comprehensively defeated by them. The clinching Battle of Zenta fourteen years later saw over 20,000 Ottoman troops killed for the loss of 300 in the Imperial Austro-Hungarian army, with all the Turkish artillery and supplies lost (along with ten members of Sultan Mustafa II's harem). The Battle of Zenta was a significant moment: it ended the ambition of the Ottoman Empire to increase its possessions in Europe. The date of the battle is resonant: 11 September 1697. Moreover it was on 11 September that the siege of Vienna was lifted in 1683, at the beginning of the final war waged by the Turks to conquer Europe. Those who find significance in such things – and there are plenty who over-emphasise coincidences – naturally take it that those who flew the fateful aircraft into New York's Twin Towers and Washington's Pentagon on 11 September 2001 chose that date for this reason, as presaging the return to power of their view of the world.

The superiority of weapons that at last drove off the Ottoman threat is part of a larger story about the relation of science and war in the seventeenth century. It is told in the next chapter.

18

War and Science

THE SEVENTEENTH CENTURY saw only three years in which there was no fighting: 1669 to 1671. The year 1610 was almost war-free, except that several large armies were on the march and shots were exchanged, though without turning into general conflict. In 1680–2 open war was confined to the far east of Europe, where Russia fought the Ottomans. But in every other year of the century there was warfare, and all the major European powers were at war with either one or more other powers, typically as part of an alliance, or with themselves in civil strife, for over half the century. War was therefore the normal condition of the time; war was the wallpaper. The scale of financial, human and material commitment involved was huge.

The measure of the period's investment in war is not represented by crude estimates of the size of the armies deployed. Until the middle of the seventeenth century few armies were as large as 50,000 men. Today this number represents just two divisions of a modern army. The forces mobilised by the main combatants in the First World War dwarf these numbers: Russia put 12 million men into uniform, Germany 11 million, Britain 8.9 million, France 8.4 million, Austro-Hungary 7.8 million, Italy 5.6 million, the US 4.4 million, Turkey 2.8 million. These are vast forces. Not all of these men carried weapons, of course, or fought in the trenches; the logistics of that war required the bulk of enlisted personnel to be working behind the lines to supply their comrades at the front.[1] But of course everything is relative: the populations of European countries in the seventeenth century were small in comparison. England had a population of about 4 million in 1600, France about 20 million, and the total population of Europe was about 78 million. It did not rise by much thereafter, at the end of the century standing under 83 million.

The main factor keeping armies relatively small in the seventeenth century's conflicts was the logistical one of arming, clothing, housing, feeding, training, transporting and commanding them. When armies were on the move, feeding and transporting them was done at the expense of the places they moved through: the effect was that of swarms of locusts descending on towns and rural areas, the impact not restricted to damage to local economies, but physical damage to the fabric of the communities and their farmlands, and to the people themselves – rape and rapine were commonplace, and in enemy territory the actions of soldiery could be brutal beyond description.[2] One of the worst events of the Thirty Years War was the Sack of Magdeburg in 1631, already described.

The size of national armies in the seventeenth century is a telling representation of the fate of the states they served. In the year 1600 Spain had 200,000 men under arms across its empire, which then stretched from central and south America to Italy and the Netherlands. A century later its army was less than a quarter of that size at its largest extent, and indeed in the interim had fallen much lower; some accounts say that at the time of the Portuguese revolt in 1640 it had trouble mustering 15,000 men in the Iberian Peninsula itself. In the same period between the years 1600 and 1700 the free states of the Netherlands went from an army of 20,000 to one of 100,000, France from 80,000 to 400,000 under Louis XIV at the height of his power, England from 30,000 to 90,000 (but it relied on its powerful navy even more than the Dutch relied on theirs), Russia from 30,000 to 170,000.

The increase in France's army under Louis XIV was the principal reason why almost all the armies of Europe grew so much in the period. Some historians cite France's burgeoning military power as the reason that England became a military nation too, but it is more likely that the experience of the Civil War, in which a total of 140,000 men on both sides became soldiers, had an influence in this respect. England's Dutch king William III fielded an army of 90,000 in his campaigns in the 1690s. At the time it was thought that if a country were well organised and wealthy it could field as much as 1 per cent of its population as a military force. This was a reflection of the way national finances were harvested and applied by central governments, for of course finance is one of the key factors beside available manpower and national willingness. Greater efficiency in taxation, and the wealth to generate tax income, underlay the increase in size of armies as much as the need to have larger armies to deal with the international situation of the time. And a tax regime requires an administrative machine to manage it, a machine whose nature and efficiency is therefore comparable to the one required to raise and manage a large army.

Another great change was the art of war itself, and the weaponry available. In the year 1600 the only state with a standing army was the Ottoman state. It was the menace of the Ottoman threat that made European powers see the necessity for organised forces. Gradually traditional militias and feudal arrangements were replaced by new arrangements. In England from medieval times every man was liable for military service and had to practise archery, but the demands of the new world order made this an inefficient way of being militarily prepared. In the Holy Roman Empire, with its disparate populations and territories, armies consisted largely of mercenaries, who in earlier times were engaged at the beginning of the summer fighting season and paid off in the autumn. By the seventeenth century it was recognised as more expensive and less efficient to do this; the realisation was that it was better to pay a wage through the winter and maintain troops under training, than to incur the large expense of levying and discharging troops each year.

Training troops required discipline; discipline and loyalty to a state or a king brought uniforms into existence; uniforms in fact represented a saving on the costs of fielding an army because they could be mass-produced to a pattern. Weapons too had to be standardised for the same reason. States became major purchasers of clothing, machinery, weapons, provender, horses, carts, canvas and much besides, fuelling the change in commerce, industry and trade in the economies of Europe.

One outstanding example of changes in the ways armies were trained, equipped and managed will suffice to indicate the enormous difference that the war-torn seventeenth century made in these respects. The example is that of Maurice of Nassau, Stadthouder of Holland, at the beginning of the seventeenth century. The reforms he introduced into the army of the United Provinces, aided by his cousin William-Louis, Stadthouder of Friesland, were instrumental in their eventual victory over the Spanish Habsburgs and the permanent separation of the two halves of the Netherlands.

Maurice and William-Louis took to heart a revival of interest in Roman military methods that was then in train, and applied these to their own forces. Some of their experiments failed, such as requiring footsoldiers to carry shields. Others were very successful: training troops to dig, as the Romans had done, not only proved useful in providing defences on the battlefield, but was excellent for discipline and *esprit de corps*, aided also by rigorous drill. They thought about tactics and strategy, making use of armies of lead soldiers to lay out dispositions for discussion. They standardised equipment and in particular weaponry, reducing infantry weaponry to just two items, the pike and the matchlock firearm. Infantry companies were grouped into regiments, and in winter quarters they continued with their training and in the process staged mock battles.

Most importantly of all, Maurice and William-Louis were quick to introduce any technical innovations they thought would be of material use. An important one was the telescope. Maurice is said to have been the first commander to climb a church tower to view the enemy through a telescope. His troops had the first practical time-fuse for delaying the detonation of explosives, and therefore had the first hand-grenades. He made his cavalry employ the recently invented curb-bit, which provides greater control over a horse because of the bit's lever-action principle, which works the bit on several different parts of a horse's mouth and, via the shanks and chain, simultaneously on its head. As a youth Maurice was tutored by Simon Stevin, the mathematician and engineer, and when he came into office he employed Stevin on the design of fortifications, asked him to found a new department of engineering at the University of Leiden, and made him quartermaster-general of the army.

The Dutch army did not keep either its technological or its organisational lead for long. Others were quick to follow, and the seventeenth century saw many advances. The Swedes gained ascendancy in the techniques of artillery, the French under Louis XIV adopted the bayonet, in particular the socket-bayonet, and as these developments occurred so tactics and fortifications came under constant review in response, with much resulting development. Some states lagged behind; as late as the first decade of the eighteenth century Saxon troops were still armed with the pike. But the urgencies of warfare did not allow many militaries to remain ignorant of advances in technology and technique in other militaries; arms races have always been a feature of dangerous times.

A consequence of these developments in Europe was that when the imperialistic European powers encountered peoples across the seas, their great superiority in equipment, firepower and military organisation made conquest a much easier matter than if resistance had been offered on equal terms. That was a lesson long before learned by the Spanish in the New World.

Perhaps the greatest revolution in warfare took place at sea. In Chapter 11 above the significance for subsequent history of the seventeenth century's Anglo-Dutch naval wars was emphasised; they were fought on, and their victories and defeats were predicated upon, the basis of developments in marine engineering that had been accelerating in the previous hundred years.

Until the seventeenth century there had been slow progress from the Mediterranean-confined sea battles which had begun in classical times with oared galleys and remained that way for centuries, right up to the Battle of Lepanto in 1571, the last galley-fought war, which saw the end of Ottoman efforts at expansion along the northern side of the Mediterranean. The ships that sailed the Atlantic and round the world in the first great age of navigation were small and inefficient; in naval conflicts at the end of the sixteenth century the few purpose-built men-of-war were accompanied by a gaggle of merchantmen pressed into service for the occasion and rigged with temporary fighting equipment. Such was the great Spanish Armada of 1588, defeated by a combination of English and Dutch sailors and the weather round the coasts of Britain. Most fighting at sea was done by privateers raiding merchant ships, there being little difference between privateering and pure piracy, even though much of the former was officially sanctioned.

The effectiveness of the English ships involved in defeating the Armada has been attributed to superior craftsmanship and design in the capital ships of Queen Elizabeth's navy. They were faster and more nimble than the Spanish galleons, yet at the same time could carry heavier guns. The pattern was the first pair of 'race-built' ships, the *Foresight* launched in 1570 and especially the *Dreadnought*, launched in 1573. The high forecastles and aftercastles distinctive of the galleon design were dispensed with – they were 'razed', hence the description 'race-built' – making them sleek and streamlined not just in appearance but in actuality, with less 'windage' and less top-weight, enhancing their speed and manoeuvrability. This counted in the actions against the Armada in 1588 when the English fleet was able first to break up the Spanish fleet – 'running rings around them' one naval historian writes – and then harried its dispersed elements into the North Sea, as they tried to escape around the northern reaches of the British isles. There they met with severe storms that drove many of the Spanish ships on to the coasts of Scotland and Ireland.[3]

These innovations, and the evolution of the galleon-design into the frigates of the seventeenth century, were inevitable concomitants of the spread of national interests across the oceans. But what really changed the face of maritime warfare occurred in the second half of the seventeenth century. These were the three wars fought between the English and Dutch, described in more detail in an earlier chapter. The war which took place between 1652 and 1654 was fought entirely at sea and consisted of a number of major battles, which demonstrated to both sides that they needed fleets that were entirely purpose-built and with crews trained for the task. From then on there was no place for merchantmen either hired or pressed – often unwillingly – into service. In England a regular naval officer corps was created. Big battleships were built, capable of fighting only in the summer months but so effective that smaller vessels disappeared from the line. The logistical requirements of navies were even more demanding than those for armies, in that the personnel, equipment and provender could not be resupplied while the navy was at sea, so an efficient land-based infrastructure had to be organised to ensure that the navy was fully operational once it set sail.

The consequences of this were far-reaching. In England carpentry, shipbuilding, the manufacture of canvas, nails, pitch, the protection and management of oak woodlands, and much besides, already established in the previous century, now advanced by bounds. A long list of services and industries flourished in specific response to the needs of the navy that England maintained from the mid-seventeenth century onwards, under the management of Robert Blake during the Commonwealth and Samuel Pepys after the Restoration. By the closing decade of the century, when the Dutch fleet was put under Royal Navy command by William III, the British navy was the largest in the world.

From the Revolution in England of 1688 until the end of the Napoleonic Wars in 1815 there was a constantly recurring state of hostilities between England and France, in which the Royal Navy played a central role. What presaged the nature of the conflict was the fact that when William III came to England to take the throne, it was in a fleet of 100 warships and 400 transport ships carrying 11,000 infantrymen and 4,000 cavalrymen with their mounts. A few days later Louis XIV declared war on England in support of James II's claims, and there followed a succession of naval battles, ending in English victory at the Battle of La Hougue four years later. The naval opposition of the states facing each other across the Channel was thus set for the succeeding century and more.

In the case of the growth of armies and navies required by the seventeenth century's constant state of war, two factors were crucial:

the growing wealth of the major states of Europe apart from Spain, and the increasing power and efficiency of state bureaucracies. The latter was necessitated by the task of raising revenues to fund the forces required to fight the wars, while the logistics of being at war improved the effectiveness of state administrations required to manage the complexities involved. The point of noting this is a very particular one: it shows how the emergence of modern state institutions was fostered by military exigencies, or at very least that these played a major part in the emergence of the modern state. Wars and emergencies make demands on the creativity of individuals caught up in them, not just in direct and obvious ways relating to weaponry and tactics, but in the more remote-seeming reaches of offices and workshops far behind front lines. The idea that the growth of modern forms of administration resulted from these military developments was first put forward by Michael Roberts in his study of Sweden in the period between 1560 and 1650; although controversial, the thesis has much to recommend it, as another element in understanding how the modern outlook was forged.[4]

And this was a matter not only of bureaucracy, but of the political order which it served. In this respect the century saw as great a change as in epistemology and the understanding of nature.

PART V

THE SOCIAL ORDER

19

Society and Politics

In the year of the Treaty of Westphalia, 1648, Paris and indeed the whole of France was in turmoil because of the Fronde, a civil insurrection against the government of the infant King Louis XIV and his chief minister, Cardinal Mazarin. It was prompted by the burden of taxes that had been raised to pay for the military expenses of France's participation in the Thirty Years War and war with Spain. The Fronde was a dangerous affair, because the aristocracy sided with the *parlements* (especially of Paris) in defending the feudal liberties of the latter, which meant in effect that the country had risen against the Crown, in what was a straightforward rebellion. Cardinal Mazarin, a much hated figure, triggered the uprising by arresting the leaders of the *parlement* of Paris when they refused to pay a new tax. Their arrest brought the citizens of Paris on to the streets; there were barricades, and as turmoil spread through the country it became increasingly violent, turning into a civil war. The troubles continued until the early months of 1653, making nearly five years of unrest and uncertainty in all.

The sequence of events constituting the Fronde (the word means 'sling'; the *frondeurs* used slings to hurl stones as did the Old Testament's David) need not be recounted; the important point is its outcome, namely, an eventual victory for the monarchy in the person of Louis XIV, and his determination – highly successful as it proved – to assert absolute rule over France.

In this respect France and the way it was governed in the second half of the seventeenth century represents a step backwards, moving against the current of progress in both political theory and practice that was running elsewhere, notably in England. The absolute monarchy of Louis XIV brought great prestige and power to France; it became the leading country in succession to Spain, by then much enfeebled, and it so far impressed its culture and language on the world that all the ruling classes of Europe from the Atlantic to the Urals spoke French, and French remained the language of international diplomacy into our own era. But of course the eventual cost of absolutism was the French Revolution, and Louis XIV might be regarded as the last great despot ruling by a supposed divine right.

To illustrate how different matters were elsewhere, and at the same time to get a sense of how the mind of the seventeenth century was changing, it is instructive to look at the evolution of political circumstances in just one notable country – England – between the death of Elizabeth I in 1603 and the accession of Queen Anne in 1702. In that hundred years the world shed the last hints of medievalism. Take the single example of kingship: the distance from the horror of King Duncan's murder in *Macbeth*, staged in 1606, to the execution of King Charles I in 1649, to Parliament's placing a crown on the head of William of Orange in 1688, is immense. After this last event Parliament had the ultimate say on the royal succession, and on the powers – as time went by, increasingly limited – that monarchs could wield. This achievement was the proximate outcome of the Civil War a quarter of a century before.

Histories of the English Civil War call it 'the English revolution'. So it was; but it denotes a larger event, of more extended duration than the years of actual fighting between supporters of Crown and Parliament in the 1640s. This is because it is also the forerunner to the 'Glorious Revolution' of 1688, which chased James II from the throne and replaced him with the joint monarchs William (of Orange) and Mary, daughter of James II. Mary was a Protestant, crucially unlike her father. James II had invited trouble by attempting to reinsinuate Catholics into English institutions and Catholicism into English life. In choosing William and Mary to replace James II, Parliament significantly diminished the Crown's powers by the Bill of Rights – a document specifying the rights of Parliament vis-à-vis the Crown, not the rights of individuals, as later Bills of Rights in the Western political canon did.[1] The history of events in England in the sixty years between 1630 and 1690 have their very different theoretical justifications in the writings of Thomas Hobbes and John Locke.[2] The latter's contribution, in particular, in giving a rationalisation of the aims and outcome of the 'Glorious Revolution', establishes much of the foundation for the political liberalism of the following centuries.

The dramatic change in the politics and government of England in this period was not replicated anything like so dramatically in the rest of Europe. As already noted, France moved in the opposite direction in becoming an even more centralised and autocratic state. Louis XIV's position was ultimately strengthened by the Fronde not least because of his sense of outrage at having been subjected to profound indignities by it; he and his mother, Anne of Austria, had experienced hunger, fear and cold while in hiding during the worst of the uprising. As soon as he could he established his court at Versailles, away from the Parisian mob, and he weakened the aristocracy by making it waste its time, energy and money in pointless attendance at Court. He also diluted the aristocracy by creating thousands of new nobles, much to the old nobles' disdain. In the event, his doing so only provided extra food for Madame Guillotine during the Terror which followed the Revolution of 1789, itself the long-term consequence of the absolutism that Louis practised.

If Louis XIV is the paradigm of an absolute monarch, the political philosophy of Locke is the period's most significant theoretical rejection of absolutism. Locke was not a maker of the bloodless middle-class revolution of 1688, but rather its explainer and justifier. He wrote to describe the principles exemplified by the event, and to support them. This is why his writings proved of such importance for the political upheavals in North America and France a century after his time.

Locke was both physician and secretary to Lord Shaftesbury, opponent of James II and proponent of the idea of a new constitutional settlement. Being in opposition to the Crown was dangerous, and necessitated a period of exile in the Netherlands for Shaftesbury and Locke both before and during James II's reign. This direct involvement at the heart of events that resulted in England becoming a constitutional monarchy informed all of Locke's political writings. It is no surprise therefore that he is quoted, and at considerable length, in the documents of the American and French revolutions. To the *philosophes* of the French Enlightenment he was a hero.

To get a measure of Locke's task in propounding the idea of political liberalism it is educative to look at the embodiment of what he was arguing against – namely, the absolute rule of Louis XIV and the ideas that were invoked in justification of it.

An absolute monarch is a ruler who is above the law – or more accurately, who *is* the law – and over whom there is no higher authority (some had enough respect for the consequences of hubris to say 'other than God' – but of course some thought they *were* God, e.g. Caligula; and officially some *are* God, e.g. the Japanese Emperor). An absolute monarch is therefore one who, at least theoretically, acts without any restrictions other than those he accepts from his own conscience and what he is willing to accept from his forebears', country's or people's traditions. Of course, even absolute rulers are rarely without *some* constraint, whether it is the opinion of the people, the fear of an avenging deity, or his own ethics or sense of humanity. But being above the law and without equal, he has no otherwise recognised restraints; he has unlimited power over his subjects. There are of course qualifications to this definition – an absolute ruler is 'theoretically' and 'technically' without restraint – but these terms express the reality that rulers always have some term to their power, even if only in being assassinated or in provoking rebellion because of (say) the cruel and arbitrary exercise of that power.

Absolute monarchy of Louis XIV's paradigmatic kind was the long-term outcome of the death of feudalism. Feudal kings were far from absolute; they were *primus inter pares*, the leading member of a group of leaders who worked together to keep control, mainly by force. The word 'peer' to denote a nobleman captures the near-equal status of barons with monarchs to whom they were anyway closely related, by blood as well as political necessity and convenience. In this dispensation kings relied on the loyalty of their barons and a complex structure of customs, traditions, rights and dues, together with the power to grant land, titles and privileges, that supported the Crown's authority but at the same time imposed checks on it. With the evolution of more centralised government necessitated by taxation and the organisation of armies and navies, the power of kings grew while that of nobles diminished.

The central question in political theory is: from what source comes a governing agency's right to govern? What confers authority on a ruler? We must suppose that in earlier phases of history the source of power was sheer strength. In feudal times this strength was jointly exercised by a self-interested cartel of nobles among whom the king was the senior member. In democracies the ultimate source of authority is the people's will as expressed at the ballot box. But what was it in the period between the end of feudalism and the beginning of democracy?

For the increasingly centralised states that evolved from the fifteenth century onwards a new account of government authority was needed. Strength or might could no longer be a justification even if it were a possibility; peers were no longer genuinely equals; the monarch both reigned and ruled – but what conferred his right to do so? The answer was: 'divine right'.

This answer was derived from a practice that the Church had eagerly promoted during the time of its greatest influence and power, which was in the high medieval period. It lay in the practice of the Pope giving his blessing – his seal of approval; his imprimatur – to a new king. From the Vatican's point of view this was a direct expression of the principle that the throne of St Peter is first among all thrones, that Christendom is as it were a single kingdom to which more local kingdoms are subordinate. Even if the various kings of the 'subordinate' kingdoms were not particularly happy with this way of seeing things, they went along with it because of its utility when there were disputed successions or armed challenges to the tenure of their crowns.

There was an evolution at work in the process described here. Originally, getting hold of the symbols of power – the sceptre, the crown – mattered because power resided in possession of the symbols: symbolism and actuality were intimately connected. But then the imprimatur of divine choice or approval came to be necessary. Shakespeare's way of writing about kingship is educative in this connection: in his account of it, regality is a mixture of the holy and the magical, something extraordinary and inviolable (and if violated then at great danger to the order of things), where everything otherwise normal to human life and experience is magnified into epic proportions.

But history was not kind to the useful doctrine that God was the author of the rights of kingship, as ratified by the liturgical nature of coronation ceremonies. For no sooner had the ordination of monarchs become the ground on which kings claimed their authority than Christendom began fragmenting into a variety of Protestant and one Catholic version of itself. In each of the political fragments resulting from this disruption, rulers demanded that their subjects follow their choice of religion – this being the Augsburg principle of *cuius regio, eius religio*: the religion of the ruler is the religion of the people. In Protestant countries there was no successor to the Pope to lay on hands and serve as the conduit of divine sanction; it now had to be thought of as coming directly and unmediatedly from the deity. Hence the idea remained that a king was divinely appointed and that allegiance was accordingly a religious duty.

Jacques-Bénigne Bossuet, in his *Politics Taken from the Very Word of Scripture* (*Politique tirée des propres paroles de l'Ecriture sainte*) (1679), was the theoretician who justified Louis XIV's style of monarchy, rather as Locke had provided justification and theoretical underpinning for the 'Glorious Revolution' – but of course to quite opposite effect.[3] Bossuet did not develop original ideas on the matter; he was influenced by the sixteenth-century lawyer and philosopher Jean Bodin, who was strongly in favour of independent centralised monarchical power, not so much as an instrument of authority over a populace but as a bulwark against papal power. Louis' assumption of absolute power is famously captured in his claim that *l'état, c'est moi*.

Bossuet made full use of the scriptural passages which unequivocally support a divine-right theory. Proverbs chapter 8 verses 15–16 says, 'By me kings reign, and princes decree justice. By me princes rule, and nobles, even all the judges of the earth.' In Romans chapter 13 verses 1–2 St Paul says, 'Let every soul be subject unto the higher powers. For there is no power but of God. Whosoever therefore resisteth the power, resisteth the ordinance of God: and they that resist shall receive to themselves damnation.' Commenting on these passages, Bossuet wrote,

> We have already seen that all power is of God. The ruler, adds St Paul, 'is the minister of God to thee for good. But if thou do that which is evil, be afraid; for he beareth not the sword in vain; for he is the minister of God, a revenger to execute wrath upon him that doeth evil.' Rulers then act as the ministers of God and as his lieutenants on earth. It is through them that God exercises his empire. Think you to withstand the kingdom of the lord in the hand of the sons of David? Consequently, as we have seen, the royal throne is not the throne of a man but the throne of God himself. The Lord 'hath chosen Solomon my son to sit upon the throne of the kingdom of Israel.' And again, 'Solomon sat on the throne of the Lord.' . . . It appears from all this that the person of the king is sacred, and that to attack him in any way is sacrilege. God has the kings anointed by his prophets with the holy unction in like manner as he has his bishops and altars anointed . . . Kings should be guarded as holy things, and whosoever neglects to protect them is worthy of death . . . The royal power is absolute . . . The prince need render account of his acts to no one.

Bossuet was not however an unintelligent apologist for absolute monarchy; he did not confuse the two different ideas of *absolute* and *arbitrary* power.

> But kings, although their power comes from on high, should not regard themselves as masters of that power to use it at their pleasure . . . they

> must use it with fear and self-restraint, as a thing coming from God and of which God will demand an account . . . Kings should tremble then as they use the power God has granted them; and let them think how horrible is the sacrilege if they use for evil a power which comes from God. We behold kings seated upon the throne of the Lord, bearing in their hands the swords which God himself has given them. What profanation, what arrogance, for the unjust king to sit on God's throne to render decrees contrary to his laws and to use the sword which God has put in his hand for deeds of violence and to slay his children![4]

The intriguing contradiction in Bossuet's account is that although the king is absolute in power, there is a limit: if he misuses his authority he violates God's law, and if he violates God's law, does he not thereby forfeit the right to rule? Can the Church oblige him to abdicate in such a case? Can the people – all the estates of the people: nobility, clergy, general populace – resist him? The question was intriguing because of a parallel consideration: in Church doctrine it is laid down that once a priest has been ordained it does not matter what sins he commits, he can still administer the sacraments because the powers conferred on him exist independently of him. Does this apply also to kings? Louis XIV embodies an answer to these questions, in regarding his right to rule as inalienable. This was not the majority view among Protestant theologians, however, which was a source of trouble for rulers who subscribed to their views.

Louis perfectly understood everything implied by his divine right to rule. In his childhood a book called *Educatio Regia* was read aloud to him, urging him to remember every morning that he had to play the part of God in his kingdom, and every evening to ask himself whether he had succeeded: *Hodie mihi gerenda est persona Dei . . . Deusne hodie an homo fui?* In a memoir he wrote for his son the Dauphin he said, 'holding as it were the place of God we seem to participate in his wisdom as in his authority; for instance, in what concerns discernment of human character, allocation of employments and distribution of rewards'.[5]

The jury is out as to whether Louis manifested any divine wisdom. The ministers he appointed were not as good as those in place when he attained his majority, which calls his judgment into question regarding the characters and abilities of men; but he was a 'quick study' when it came to mastering information and seeing how it might best be applied. What he certainly disliked was the labyrinth of traditions and customs that encumbered the throne, and he set about ridding himself of them as soon as he could. He took away from the *parlement* of Paris its role in the government of France. In less than three years from attaining his majority and beginning personal rule (in 1662) the Paris *parlement* was no longer a sovereign court. Louis did not summon the States-General until near the end of his reign, during the War of Spanish Succession (1701–14). Clergymen and nobles had only ceremonial positions at his Court, not government responsibilities. He ruled personally, helped by four ministerial councils and a small number of Secretaries of State.[6]

These Secretaries of State were drawn from two bourgeois families of professional civil servants, the Louvois and Colbert families, each of whom were personally loyal to Louis. They were not invariably good at their work. Among the worst judgments of Louis' long reign was the revocation of the Edict of Nantes, removing protection from France's Protestants. This maladroit decision, coupled with persistent mishandling of the nation's finances and Louis' frequent and costly wars, damaged France's economy so badly that it took more than a hundred years to recover.

Yet Louis kept his firm hold by ensuring two things: that the nobility were powerless and distracted, and that the populace loved him. He achieved the first of these aims very simply. Because he never forgot the nobles' treacherous part in the Fronde, he carefully arranged that they would be in no position to do it again. Nobles by birth – the *noblesse d'épée* – were required to attend him at Versailles almost permanently, performing the elaborate rituals and observing the elaborate protocol that required the filling of scores of nominal offices. An apartment at Versailles went with such appointments, and nobles competed for them fiercely, devoting endless time and money to keeping up appearances and performing trivial tasks. Louis kept something coming into his always emptying coffers by selling peerages by the hundred, creating scores of new merely decorative offices with patents of nobility attached, and making the newly created *noblesse de robe* hereditary and thus closer in status to the *noblesse d'épée*.[7]

The love that the French people felt for Louis is in fact rather puzzling. Somehow they were in a mood to idolise their King, perhaps star-struck by the pomp and splendour of Versailles – which they knew about only at second hand, through illustrations and gossip. They did not know that Louis chose to build his palace at Versailles precisely in order to be as far from them as possible. He was a tall man, always emotionless in expression, which gave him an appearance of distinction and self-command. He imposed wars and taxes on his people – the taxes necessitated by the wars – but otherwise did nothing to improve or ameliorate their lot, or indeed do anything else that could explain their adulation of him.

Louis' absolutism manifested itself in a variety of ways. He claimed ownership of all land in France; he said that what was considered to be private property in fact belonged to him, the titular owners merely having the usufruct. This was the logical conclusion of the doctrine that absolute sovereignty is equivalent to 'dominium' or ownership, in a king's case of the entire kingdom. One of Louis' few contemporary critics among Frenchmen, the Calvinist Pierre Jurieu, claimed that early in the King's reign there had been a plan to take all private property into the Crown's possession and then rent it back to its previous owners as a means of raising revenue. No such thing was done, but it is clear that having such a principle in place was useful in case of necessity. But it is a telling illustration of the principle of absolute monarchy, which entails it.

Another implication of the absolutist principle is that because the king answers only to God, he is not bound by promises or agreements with mortals, including other monarchs – which to Louis meant that he was not obliged to observe international treaties. He regarded them as temporary conveniences, and when they ceased to be convenient he had no hesitation in breaching them. In his memoir to the Dauphin there is a frank statement of this view; protestations of eternal friendship and permanent alliance are nothing more than diplomatic courtesies, Louis wrote, and have no meaning beyond the treaty's usefulness.

Absolutism has it, thirdly, that the king is above the law, and with this idea Louis certainly agreed. It led him to invoke or ignore laws at whim, again depending on convenience. It was the tradition in France as elsewhere that succession to the throne descended through the legitimate male line only. Louis appealed to this ancient principle in supporting the claim of Philip V of Spain, thereby triggering the War of Spanish Succession; but he ignored the principle in saying that his bastards could stand in line to the succession if there were no legitimate heir. Everything to Louis was expediency; that seemed to be the only law he obeyed.

England's 'Glorious Revolution' of 1688 was a complete and unequivocal rejection of the divine-right doctrine, and in its place were put the principles of parliamentary government. This is the great change that Locke set out to justify. Someone had to provide an argument defending this new basis for political authority, and Locke accepted the task. The new basis was established in practice when James II fled and Parliament announced on its own authority that the throne was vacant. It then invited William of Orange to sit on that throne, but only after long negotiations about what he could and could not do while he did so.

The legitimacy of these actions lay in the upheavals of the Civil War, when those on the Parliamentary side saw themselves as doing far more than resolving a quarrel between the Crown and Parliament. Independents and Levellers who demanded adult suffrage and annual parliaments were seeking a real change, notably the institution of a form of democracy. There were other campaigners too: the Diggers argued for common ownership of land so that all could be sure of eating; they were the victims of the heartless enclosures that had begun more than a century before, in which landowners drove many people from the land. Many of these many died of starvation.

The Diggers' radical demands show how far the change in mind-set had gone. Their demands were not met, and what transpired was far too conservative and incremental to help them. Still, the trend of history was such as to aid a shift in the sources of political authority, though only from the Crown to Parliament. The events of 1688 gave the great Whig families, and in due time their Tory opponents, the levers of government; but the transfer of power thus begun was eventually to result, 250 years later, in full adult suffrage and periodic parliaments.

A striking example of the maturity of thinking in the radical political atmosphere of the mid-seventeenth century is *An Agreement of the People for a Firme and Present Peace, upon the Grounds of Common-right and Freedome* (November 1647). This document was produced by the Army Council in response to what the soldiers of the Parliamentary army demanded. It says,

> Having by our late labours and hazards made it appear to the world at how high a rate we value our just freedom, and God having so far owned our cause as to deliver the enemies thereof into our hands, we do now hold ourselves as bound in mutual duty to each other to take the best care we can for the future to avoid both the danger of returning into a slavish condition and the chargeable remedy of another war; for, as it cannot be imagined that so many of our countrymen would have opposed us in this quarrel if they had understood their own good, so may we safely promise to ourselves that when our common rights and liberties shall be cleared, their endeavours will be disappointed that seek to make themselves our masters.

The *Agreement* then demands that Parliament be reformed, with a proper distribution of seats by population, elections every two years, and universal adult male suffrage.

To this eloquent demand for parliamentary democracy – at fault only in one but very important respect, namely the exclusion of women from the franchise – is then added others: religious toleration, no military conscription, equality in application of the law to all, and with all this the aim of promoting the safety and well-being of the people. The *Agreement* continued,

> These things we declare to be our native rights and therefore are agreed and resolved to maintain them with our utmost possibilities against all opposition whatever, being compelled thereunto by the examples of our

> ancestors, whose blood was often spent in vain for the recovery of their freedoms, [and] also by our own woeful experience who, having long expected, and dearly earned, the establishment of these certain rules of government, are yet made to depend for the settlement of our peace and freedom upon him [i.e. Charles I] that intended our bondage and brought a cruel war upon us.

It took several centuries more for these demands to be met – and it is debatable whether they have indeed all been met yet. Reforms were made in small steps, just enough each time to deflect revolt – the protesting crowds in London's streets smashed windows in support of their demand for Parliamentary reform in 1832, yet were pacified by a very small extension of the franchise. This fact is significant in understanding Locke's justification of Parliament's assumption of increased power in 1688.

The 'Glorious Revolution' established two linked points – more accurately, the reverse and obverse of the same point – the sovereignty of Parliament and the rejection of the divine-right doctrine. By putting a crown on William's head on its own terms, Parliament had achieved effective constitutional sovereignty. Control of national finances and the armed forces lay with Parliament, and with those two things lay everything. The settlement also and crucially secured the independence of the judiciary and a right of petition, two bulwarks of a free society.

Locke described his aim, in his political writings, as justifying William's possession of the throne 'to make good his title in the consent of the people' – by 'people' meaning Parliament, though the generalising ambiguity, in seeming to denote the whole nation, is doubtless intentional. Today his statement would be called 'spin'. The spinning was necessary; not everyone in England was happy with the arrangements. Quite a few Tories were deeply uneasy about the legality of what had happened, and were inclined to uphold James II's claim to be rightful king. Louis XIV helped Locke's side of the argument – he could do no other than support 'legitimacy' and thus James II's rightful possession of the throne, but his insistence on recognising James as the

King of England kept not just Whigs but the English populace on the side of the new arrangements.

The text – it became an instant classic – in which Locke sets out the justification for the 'Glorious Revolution' is his *Second Treatise of Government*. The *First Treatise* consists in a fully worked-out refutation of Sir Robert Filmer's defence of the doctrine of divine right in his *Patriarchia*. Monarchical absolutism is derived by Filmer (with commendable completeness and thoroughness, one has to say) from the authority given to Adam in the Garden of Eden. There the deity had conferred sovereignty over everything on Adam and his heirs for ever, Filmer pointed out, thus instituting absolute monarchy as the only correct political arrangement. With great patience Locke traced Filmer through the twists and turns of history to prove him wrong. If one asks why Locke devoted such attention to Filmer's thesis, it is because a far bigger prey lurked behind the argument of the *Patriarchia*, namely, Hobbes.

Filmer's book bears the subtitle 'A defence of the Natural Power of Kings against the Unnatural Liberty of the People'. It had been written during the reign of Charles I, but it was published only in 1680, when it was being suggested that James should not be allowed to succeed Charles II because of his – James' – Roman Catholicism. Like Bossuet, Filmer relied on the scriptures and the precedents provided by history, and he stated that he agreed with Hobbes on the question of 'the Right of exercising government' though not on how that right is acquired. For Filmer the right is endowed by God, transmitted through legitimate succession to the throne, while for Hobbes it is acquired from the consensual yielding up of each person's liberty.

Locke did not write directly about Hobbes because Hobbes' name was off limits – he was believed to be an atheist, and atheism was regarded with horror at that time. Moreover Hobbes' views were equally applicable to monarchical and republican regimes. If anyone tried to defend William's entitlement to the throne by citing Hobbes, William's opponents could just as easily cite Hobbes on the other side of the case.

Hobbes regarded membership of political society as the only guarantee of individual safety. Without such insurance against the depredations of each on each in the unpredictable and violent conditions of a 'state of nature', life would be – as he memorably put it – 'solitary, poor, nasty, brutish and short'. In the absence of an authority capable of keeping everyone safe, there can be no security; not even self-defence pacts formed by individuals in combination with each other would be sufficient: 'be there never so great a multitude; yet if their actions be directed according to their particular judgements, and particular appetites, they can expect thereby no defence, no protection, neither against a common enemy, nor against the injuries of another'.[8]

The only sure source of safety, Hobbes argued, is a 'common power', a central authority which Hobbes named 'Leviathan'. The Leviathan's authority is endowed on it by the agreement of each member of society to accept its unlimited sovereignty over them. The Leviathan could be an individual person, such as an absolute monarch, or a group or oligarchy, or indeed any other entity, so long as it possesses plenary powers:

> For by this authority, given him by every particular man in the commonwealth, he hath the use of so much power and strength conferred on him, that by terror thereof, he is enabled to form the wills of them all, to peace at home, and mutual aid against their enemies abroad. And in him consisteth the essence of the commonwealth which is, to define it, *one person, of whose acts a great multitude, by mutual covenant one with another, have made themselves every one the author, to the end he may use the strength and means of them all, as he shall think expedient, for their peace and common defence.*[9]

The sovereign power, thus constituted by the agreement of those over whom it has complete sway, is under no obligation to the people once it is constituted, beyond ensuring their safety. Hobbes accords the sovereign two inalienable and unlimitable 'rights' which it must have in order to fulfil its function properly: it cannot have its power taken away or compromised by its subjects, and it can never be charged with treating any of its subjects unjustly. Hobbes' justification for attributing these 'rights' to the sovereign is that it embodies the will of the people, having been created by the mutual contract they entered for their own safety. Therefore to seek to overthrow the sovereign or oppose its decisions would be self-contradictory, because the people would thus be challenging their own reason for constituting that sovereignty in the first place: 'by this institution of a commonwealth, every particular man is author of all that the sovereign doth; and consequently he that complaineth of injury from his sovereign, complaineth of that whereof he himself is author; and therefore ought not to accuse any man but himself; no nor himself of injury; because to do injury to one's self is impossible'.[10]

The two unlimitable and inalienable 'rights' in question are what make the sovereign's power absolute. Only the sovereign can decide on matters of war and peace, on relations with other states, on what can be published or practised in the commonwealth, on property, punishments, official appointments, the distribution of honours, and all final matters at law. Hobbes says that these powers are the 'essence of sovereignty'; they are 'the marks whereby a man may discern in what man, or assembly of men, the sovereign power is placed and resideth'.[11]

Although by its nature the sovereign is above the law and in almost every respect unchallengeable, there is after all one great constraint on it. This constraint arises from the very reason for its existence, which is to ensure the safety of its subjects. Its 'office consisteth in the end, for which he was trusted with the sovereign power, namely the procuration of *the safety of the people*; to which he is obliged by the law of nature, and to render an account thereof to God, the author of that law, and to none but him'.[12] If the sovereign fails in this duty, the overriding concern of the subjects for their own self-preservation gives them the right to disobey the sovereign and even to rebel against him. Self-preservation is a need and a duty that is not cancelled when all other freedoms are yielded to the absolute control of the sovereign. At first blush this concession seems to lodge a contradiction at the very centre of Hobbes' thesis: for if the people possess an ultimate right to overthrow the sovereign should the latter fail to protect their safety, then they indeed have the ultimate say in the commonwealth.[13]

In the passage just cited we see Hobbes invoke the idea of a 'law of nature' which binds the sovereign to his duty of guaranteeing the people's safety. The concept of a 'law of nature' is ill defined, and as what provides the place for a regress to end – the regress to what ultimate authority is the ground for the authority of the sovereign itself – it is *ad hoc*. If there are natural laws providing an ultimate justification for claiming that the safety of individuals is paramount, why can they not be operative in the state of nature, perhaps by the light of something else equally supposed to be natural, viz. 'the light of reason'? Why can each individual not be 'obliged by the law of nature, and to render an account thereof to God, the author of that law, and to none but him', to ensure the safety of others as well as himself?

A compelling criticism of Hobbes is offered by Quentin Skinner.[14] The charge laid by Skinner is that Hobbes' account of the nature of liberty undermined the better notion of 'republican liberty' (sometimes called by Skinner 'Roman liberty') which sees liberty as the absence of dependence. Free people are those who do not live under any form of arbitrary power, whether or not it is exercised. The view that liberty is lack of interference or restraint – or in Hobbes' even more reductive view, that liberty is absence of impediment to motion – is insufficient to render people free; however benign the existence of power, its mere presence changes free people into slaves. And free people can only exist in a free state.

Skinner traces the history of the idea of republican liberty from ancient Rome to the Renaissance, and argues that it was at work during the Civil War in England in the 1640s, as the Parliamentary side fought against the Crown's claim to hold discretionary prerogative rights – which means, arbitrary rights – superior to those of Parliament or individuals. As examples of defenders of the republican view of liberty Skinner cites James Harrington, Algernon Sydney and John Milton.

It is in the earliest of his works, *The Elements of Law*, that Hobbes argued that the authority residing in an absolute sovereign is derived from the voluntary surrender to it of the power that individuals otherwise hold over themselves, and that they do this in the interests of their own welfare. In his next book *De Cive* Hobbes countered the idea that the mere fact of government, by its very existence, makes people slaves – this being the republican view – by arguing that liberty is 'absence of impediments to motion' and that this is consistent with there being an absolute sovereign. In *Leviathan* this definition of liberty was finally further refined to say 'absence of *external* constraints' – and this is what Skinner focuses upon as a signal moment in the history of political thought, because it introduces a distinction between *liberty* and *power*. Skinner says that this makes Hobbes 'the first to answer the republican theorists by proffering an alternative definition in which the presence of freedom is construed entirely as absence of impediments rather than absence of dependence'. From this has stemmed all subsequent thinking about liberty, which as a result misses the point about the many ways in which true liberty is rendered unattainable.

Liberty as 'absence of restraint' is described as 'negative liberty', following Isaiah Berlin's distinction between negative and positive liberty.[15] It is the idea of liberty which – whether or not as a result of Hobbes' influence – most people would now understand as the basic kind. Skinner's 'republican liberty' is a concept less easy to find compelling, if only because the sheer facts of history and geography, of society and human relationships, make the idea of a wholly independent individual a very implausible one; and it is not much helped by the idea that a free individual is one who is a citizen of a free state. It is true that the idea of a free state is one of the deepest sources of thinking about freedom itself, as exemplified (for a salient historical example) by the Greek city states in their opposition to the Persian invasion, as Herodotus tells us. But a city state might be free of dependence on or control by another city state or neighbouring empire, yet the inhabitants of it might not themselves be free of the internal constraints imposed by the manner of government of the city state itself. This was certainly true of the Greek city states in which most of the population were in any case disenfranchised: women, slaves, 'foreigners' and those who had lost citizenship rights in punishment for a wrongdoing of some kind.

Skinner means to focus principally on the idea of independence from the domination of a ruler or master, in this sense asserting a broader conception than a purely political one: but if one were constrained even in the most usual ways by the circumstances of one's life (the historical, geographical, societal webs in which one is enmeshed) the idea of there being no authority on whose say-so one's rights and actions are dependent, makes of liberty something all but notional. And in any case, it can be argued that the idea of 'having no master' – no arbitrary power over one, even if unexercised – is no different *in effect* from being free of restraints on choices and actions. The distinction between 'non-domination' and 'non-interference' is a real distinction, this argument says, but an abstract one, a distinction without a functional difference. Still, Skinner's point is a sharp and interesting one, and the conception of 'republican liberty' as an ideal is especially attractive.

The notions of natural law and natural rights figure centrally also in Locke's views, but for him they led to quite different conclusions from those reached by Filmer and Hobbes. He also employs the idea of a 'state of nature' as existing before the creation of civil society, but for Locke it was not an arena of dire and unending strife between people, but instead a place where individuals enjoyed freedom. Most of that freedom had to be yielded up to get the benefits of living in society, but Locke held that certain of those rights, chief among them rights to life, liberty and property, cannot be given up in a social contract. This fact by itself makes it impossible that there should be such a thing as absolute sovereignty; by its very nature absolutism is inconsistent with the natural rights that people bring into society when they engage in the mutual contract that brings that society into existence.

The ideas of natural law and natural rights are closely connected. In Locke's view, natural rights rest on the fact that in the state of nature individuals can freely use whatever nature offers in the way of shelter, comfort and sustenance. Natural law is what says what is allowed and forbidden to people given how things stand in nature: 'all men are naturally in . . . a *state of perfect Freedom* to order their actions, and dispose of their Possessions, and Persons as they think fit, within the bounds of the Law of Nature, without asking leave, or depending on the Will of any Man'. (Locke's alternative way of describing this state of affairs is to say 'In the beginning all the World was *America*.')[16] This is because everyone is equal in the state of nature; no one has greater status or more right than anyone else, and no one is in a position to dictate to others how they should live. Because all men, Locke says, are 'furnished with like Faculties, sharing all in one Community of Nature, there cannot be supposed any such *Subordination* among us, that may authorise us to destroy one another, as if we were made for one another's uses, as the inferior ranks of Creatures are made for ours'.[17] In this way Locke rejects Filmer's claim that a hierarchy of higher and lower among men was introduced in Eden by God's grant of lordship to Adam, first over his companion Eve and then his sons, and thence to all humankind.

The importance of Locke's argument on this point is that it asserts that each person has a right to self-preservation, and therefore a correlative obligation to each other person to respect his or her right to self-preservation – and indeed to be actively concerned for the welfare of others in this respect. The obligation thus entailed goes beyond refraining from doing harm to others, but requires acting to protect them from harm and punishing those who do harm.

Locke points out that in the state of nature it is difficult to ensure the proper protection of these rights and the exercise of these correlative obligations; he calls this the 'inconvenience' of the state of nature. But to set up a Hobbesian sovereign to enforce both would, he says, be worse than this inconvenience, because nothing could stop an all-powerful sovereign from preying on its subjects and even going to war against them. It is therefore wrong in principle for people to yield their rights to an absolute ruler; to do so not only forfeits the right to self-preservation but makes them unable to carry out their associated duties to others.

> Freedom from Absolute, Arbitrary power is so necessary to, and closely joyned with a Man's Preservation, that he cannot part with it, but by what he forfeits his Preservation and Life together. For a Man, not having the Power of his own Life, cannot, by Compact, or his own Consent, *enslave himself* to any one, nor put himself under the Absolute, Arbitrary power

> of another, to take away his life, when he pleases. No body can give more Power than he has himself; and he that cannot take away his own Life, cannot give another power over it.[18]

In answering Hobbes in this way, and in the process offering an argument against any form of absolutism, Locke is working with an assumption that might be independently questionable. In the quoted passage he is implying that the reason people cannot give up their right to self-preservation is that they are not owners of themselves – suggesting rather that they are owned by God; so they are not entitled to give away their freedom. This prompts the independently interesting question whether one can enslave oneself to another; could anyone be said to have the right to do that voluntarily? Locke says No. Hobbes' view is that the very foundation of society is that people have not only the right but the positive need to alienate their freedom.

Locke's point is the more persuasive. Civil society offers protection to individuals' lives, liberty and property. It is based on laws that everyone can know, with independent judges to apply them, and agreed structures to enforce them. An arrangement of this kind resolves difficulties about how such rights and obligations are to be exercised properly. 'Having in the State of Nature no Arbitrary Power over the Life, Liberty, or Possession of another,' Locke wrote, 'but only so much as the Law of Nature gave him for the preservation of himself, and the rest of Mankind; this is all he doth, or can give up to the Common-wealth, and by it to the *Legislative Power*, so that the Legislative can have no more than this. Their Power in the utmost Bounds of it, is *limited to the publick good* of the Society.'[19] If a government behaves in ways that run contrary to the 'publick good' of society it thereby 'dissolves' itself – Locke's term – because it makes itself illegitimate. This is what happened in the case of James II; his legitimacy 'dissolved' itself when he acted in ways contrary to the interests of his subjects. Locke's point is stronger yet: if an illegitimate government tries to stay in power, the people have not merely the right but the duty to overthrow it, and to put a better in its place.

Locke set out these points in the final chapter of his *Second Treatise of Government*, aiming by their means to justify what the English Parliament had done in deposing James II and putting William and Mary on the throne. They profoundly influenced the thinking of the eighteenth century, and as noted above are quoted verbatim and *in extenso* in the documents of the American and French revolutions. One major reason for their influence is that Locke introduced the idea that power is a trusteeship, and is held by the consent of those on whose behalf it is exercised. '*Who shall be Judge* whether the Prince or the Legislative act contrary to their trust?' Locke asked, and he answered, in a passage which has been key to the subsequent development of democratic ideas, '*The people shall be Judge*; for who shall be Judge whether his Trustee or Deputy acts well, and according to the Trust reposed in him, but he who deputes him, and must, by having deputed him have still a Power to discard him, when he fails in his Trust?'[20]

Which view of the state of nature is more plausible, Locke's or Hobbes'? The dangerous anarchy envisioned by the latter retains a trace in Locke's concession that without civil society and government the rights and obligations of natural law are more difficult to exercise. There is agreement that, therefore, civil society confers advantages once individuals have agreed to constitute it. But these are the only respects in which there is a measure of overlap. In all other respects their premises and views are *toto caelo* different. Set aside the fact that the same state of affairs – life without civil society or government – is given a malign cast by one thinker, a benign cast by the other. The key difference lies in their respective views about what individuals give up in order to enter the social contract. Hobbes says they give up everything apart from the right to self-preservation; Locke says they retain their naturally conferred rights not just to self-preservation but to liberty and property also. For Hobbes the state of nature is a lawless one, for Locke it is a realm of natural law. For Hobbes civil society introduces law – the sovereign's law – for Locke civil society makes the pre-existing natural law effective.

There is a very significant difference in the respective views of human nature at work in these conceptions. For Hobbes people are by nature violent, greedy, exploitative and adversarial. For Locke they are reasonable, interested in others, essentially social. For Hobbes civil society is an artificial restraint on the horrors that the natural state involves. For Locke civil society is the natural outcome of what human nature and the natural law jointly aspire to make of human life.

It was natural for Locke to focus on life, liberty and property as the fundamental rights to be protected by civil society, given that these were the demands made by the Independents in England's Civil War. Each notion had a clear sense for him as for them. 'Liberty' meant the right of an individual to make his or her own choices and to live by them, the only constraint being that they should be consistent with the requirements of natural law. Liberty and natural law are consistent because the latter exist to protect and enhance the former: they are – to take a prosaic example – like traffic regulations, compliance with which makes it possible for everyone to benefit.

The right to property is a less obvious choice as a fundamental in Locke's scheme. Locke derives this right from the assumption that although land and all that it provides is commonly owned in the state of nature, when individuals mix their labour with parts of it those parts thereby come to be privately owned by them.

In Locke's view the contract that creates civil society includes provisions that specify, and thereby limit, the power vested in the sovereign. Where Hobbes had it that the contract places all power in the hands of the sovereign, in Locke power remains with the contracting parties, and they delegate it to the governing authority, and can recall it if they are not satisfied with the exercise of it. For Locke, what the contract creates is the *state*; he never anywhere uses the term 'sovereign'. 'State' and 'government' are not the same thing; the state is the community created by the contract, the government is the entity deputed by the community to carry out the range of functions required for protecting the rights and interests of individuals in the community.

It was essential, in Locke's view, that the functions of legislature and executive should be separate. A legislature might convene in order to pass laws, and having done so, dissolve again. But the laws thus passed need to be applied and if necessary enforced. This is the task of the executive. Locke held that it was desirable not merely that the two arms of the state should be separate, but the people involved should be distinct also. Failure in this respect could have untoward consequences: if legislators and executives were not different people, they 'may exempt themselves from the obedience to the Laws they make, and suit the Law, both in its making and its execution, to their own private Wish, and thereby come to have a distinct Interest from the rest of the Community, contrary to the end of Society and Government'.[21] This is a further argument against the absolute sovereign, who of course is legislature and executive rolled into one all-powerful entity.

The question that immediately arises is: when can it be said that the government has overreached its authority? It is necessary to allow that a government might err or make unfortunate choices occasionally, so there can be no question of recalling a government just because of minor misjudgments. It would be wrong if there were rebellions on inadequate or unjustified grounds. Locke distinguished the case of James II: there it had been right to deprive him of the throne because he had bypassed Parliament, made arbitrary laws, sought to reintroduce Roman Catholicism, and made secret treaties with foreign governments, all in the interests of extending the reach of his powers. This constituted a breach of faith with the people, whose only remedy was to rise in insurrection against him.[22]

Because of his views Locke is regarded as the starting point for liberalism as we understand it in the English (not American) sense.[23] He articulates a view – a mind-set – which is distinctively modern. It would not have been possible to write at the end of the sixteenth century as he wrote at the end of the seventeenth. This does not mean that he was the first to formulate such ideas; the debate about constitutional matters during the Civil War in England had advanced and canvassed similar ideas, sometimes considerably more radical. Indeed his views incorporate much older traces, such as the Renaissance view that things were vastly better in olden times, and history has been a long declension from more perfect arrangements in antiquity. The very idea of a 'state of nature' in which people had lived in 'perfect freedom' (Locke's own words) is a residue of this attitude. But the manner in which he articulates his views has given them their enduring status in political theory since, and explains why they are quoted in the documents of the Enlightenment's revolutions.

Of course, Locke did not vanquish absolutism. Louis XIV, Frederick the Great in Prussia, Catherine the Great in Russia and her successors right up to the Menshevik and Bolshevik revolutions of 1917, Stalin, the Nazis, the Maoists in China, Pol Pot, Pinochet, the absolute rulers of today's Middle Eastern states, any number of pocket tyrants in various corners of the world, all testify that absolutism has flourished and continues to flourish. Theocracy by its very nature is a form of Hobbesian absolutism.

Moreover, simulacra of democracies as implied (not envisaged: he was not for universal adult suffrage) by Locke did not begin to appear until well after his own day. The United States and France are the two polities which first gave real momentum to his ideas in application. In Europe for much of the nineteenth century there was still a conflation of the idea of democracy with ochlocracy – rule by the mob – and Plato's disdain for the latter under the name of democracy was what kept ruling elites, educated by their reading of his *Republic*, leery about extending the vote too far too fast. Hobbes was particularly scathing about the Long Parliament in England in his own day; his description of it as 'democratical' was anything but a compliment, for he saw it as threatening a return to the raw and bloody conditions of the state of nature as he envisioned it. For him as so many before and since, democracy meant anarchy at the hands of ignorant, greedy and violent people.[24]

Britain in the nineteenth century is a prime example of the eking out of the suffrage in successive reforms separated by decades, as the pressure from larger sections of the community made it necessary, to avoid revolution, to hand out more in the way of a sop. Universal adult suffrage arrived in Britain only in 1929, two and a quarter centuries after an English philosopher set out the principles of liberal democracy. That is quite an achievement on behalf of the ruling elites who kept their hands on the levers of power so long.

In the seventeenth century and for a long while afterwards the philosopher Baruch Spinoza was regarded with suspicion because, in his unfinished masterpiece the *Tractatus Theologico-Politicus*, he championed the ideas of democracy and equality and defended freedom of expression. This latter was of particular interest to him; he said it was a high duty of any form of government to secure it. Indeed he said he would support any type of government that would ensure freedom of expression, though he was persuaded that a democratic and egalitarian dispensation would be most likely to do so. He also – not therefore putting himself into quite the same camp as Locke – held that all forms of government are in fact democratic because all forms ultimately rest on the consent of the people, which is the case even in the Hobbesian dispensation because the initial consent of the people was required in setting up absolute sovereignty. Spinoza accordingly held that democracy in this somewhat attenuated sense is the most fundamental and most natural basis of political authority.[25]

The reputations of both Spinoza and Hobbes were occluded for the next two centuries by the fact that they were both recognised as atheists. The influence of these thinkers on the formation of the modern mind is significant, for their arguments did not rest on biblical doctrine, revelation, religious tradition or authority – in short, their views are secular. But the phrase 'these thinkers' also in fact includes Locke, for although he was not himself an atheist, neither did he – *pace* some formulaic references – rely on doctrine, revelation, tradition and the rest; indeed, in explicitly rejecting the concept of the divine right of kings, he was disconnecting questions of the source of political authority from that of religious authority, and this is par excellence the point of secularism. As in so many other respects, therefore, the making of the modern mind is a function of the transition from theocentric attitudes to the reasonings of the secular intellect.

20

Language and Belief

As the foregoing repeatedly shows, the seventeenth century falls into two distinct halves. In the first half, scientific endeavour was an individual matter, with informal exchanges between enquirers mediated through correspondence. In the century's second half the enterprise of scientific enquiry had come to be more organised and formally collegial, no longer a matter only for self-financing individuals but, in the most developed cases, backed by state patronage. The Royal Society of London is the paradigm.

Other changes are as marked. At the beginning of the century the forms and styles of literature were still Renaissance in character, in the case of Marlowe and Shakespeare achieving a peak, but in too many other cases – even in Ben Jonson and John Donne – evidencing the beginnings of decay into over-elaboration. In prose the English language was written in a florid extravagance of manner, with deliberate obfuscation of reference, and erudite allusion taken as the mark of excellence. By the second half of the century a plainer, more direct style dominated. The same was true in French and Dutch, as demonstrated by the admiration with which François de Malherbe's restrained classical style was viewed in France, and by the influence of the *Muiderkring* in the Netherlands, this being the group that gathered round the poet Pieter Hooft and included Constantijn Huygens, the distinguished Golden Age poet Joost van den Vondel, the Visscher sisters and others.[1]

Examples of the baroque affectation of English in the early seventeenth century are afforded by John Florio's translation of Montaigne, and Sir Thomas Browne's ornate meditations. Florio is well anatomised in the following magisterial comment on his flourishes and neologisms: 'Turn where you will in his translation, and you will find flowers of speech, which grow not in the garden of the original. "*Je n'y vauls rien*," says Montaigne, and Florio interprets: "I am nothing worth, and I can never fadge well." For *soufflet* Florio can find nothing simpler than "a whirret in the ear"; for *finesses verbales* he gives us "verbal wily-beguilies",' nor could he resist neologising out of the French original: 'tintamare', 'entrecuidance', 'friandize' and 'mignardize' are among the more exotic and obscure – none of them made a permanent lodging in English.[2]

Likewise Sir Thomas Browne could not be content with one word if several will do, or with a plain word when a more ornamental coining can be found. 'Had not almost every man suffered by the press,' so Browne writes in his 'To the Reader' in the *Religio Medici*,

> or were not the tyranny of it become universall; I had not wanted reason for complaint: but in times wherein I have lived to behold the highest perversion of that excellent invention, the name of his Majesty defamed, the honour of Parliament depraved, the writings of both depravedly, anticipatively, counterfeitly imprinted; complaints may seem ridiculous in private persons, and men of my condition may be as incapable of affronts as hopeless of their reparations.

Count the syllables while you work out what he means.

Compare this with the plainer style of English prose in the later seventeenth century and the century following. The principal cleanser of style was the growing tendency of scientific and philosophical thought, and with it, naturally enough, the need for clear means of expression. In his history of the Royal Society, written just a few years after its founding, Thomas Sprat wrote that it was an express obligation for members to adopt 'a close, naked, natural way of speaking; positive expressions; clear senses; a native easiness; bringing all things as near the Mathematicall plainness as they can'. Likewise their written style was to avoid 'amplifications, digressions, and swellings of style: to return back to the primitive purity, and shortness, when men delivered so many *things* almost in an equal number of *words*'.[3]

These principles quickly spread to all forms of polite writing. Locke and not long after him Swift and Addison are not just examples but – especially in the two latter cases – exemplars of the modern English prose thus emerging. Addison wrote that he championed 'the essential and inherent perfection of simplicity of thought above that which I call the Gothic manner in writing'.[4] References to 'Gothic' and 'amplifications, digressions, and swellings of style' are apt descriptions of the Florio–Browne approach.

It was not just the scientific revolution that was responsible for this revolution in thought and its expression. Science might have rejected the ideas of the ancients, but it retained and indeed promoted the style in which the ancients stated their ideas. The direct, economical prose of the Latin authors, in which the manner lucidly and snugly fitted the matter being conveyed, was rightly admired. The effect on the seventeenth century was salutary – as regards prose; though the same cannot be said for poetry. Nicolas Boileau in France and Alexander Pope in England were influenced by Horace's strictures in the *Ars Poetica,* leading Pope to write:

> Words are like leaves; and where they most abound
> Much fruit of sense beneath is rarely found.

That speaks well to the condition of prose, and perhaps to some poetry too; but in the latter case it is questionable whether it relates to literary quality as much as it does to the 'fruit of sense'. This couplet occurs in Pope's *Essay on Criticism* (lines 311–12), an imitation of Boileau's *L'Art poétique*, itself based on Horace. Boileau's rules on all forms of poetry – ode, lyric, epic, elegy, satire, pastoral, tragedy – were highly influential, but like all rules attempting to dictate how a creative art-form should conduct itself, too limiting and formulaic. As a follower of the same principles one can say that Pope's verses – can one really call them poetry? – exemplify some of them too far.

Classicism denotes harmony and purity, dignity and measure. It denotes these characteristics not just in matters of style but in the sentiments that the style serves to convey. Later admirers of the Greeks were most drawn by the directness of their gaze at reality, and the hard tussle they were prepared to fight between reason and irrationality. In the seventeenth century what was even more admired was the Latin authors' clarifying plainness of manner, characterised by order in presentation, and an economy that verged on the pithy and aphoristic. Those who took the 'pointed' or epigrammatic style of Seneca as a model were on the road to Pope's overuse of that manner – or mannerism – which even in antiquity had been assaulted by critics, who argued that it took the form itself too far – not its clarity and directness, note, but because it so readily collapsed into nothing more than a relentless iteration of epigrams.

Where Shakespeare had been the outstanding literary genius of the early seventeenth century, that palm passed to the French dramatists of the century's second half. This was the Parnassian point of classicism in theatre, which observed the Aristotelian unities of time, place and action, and demanded of the subject matter that it be realistic, instructive and elevating – this last being the demand that it promote *les bienséances* or moral good taste. In practice of course these strict rules were often broken, usually to achieve some dramatic effect; but the writing for theatre at the end of the seventeenth century in France conformed more than otherwise to these powerful constraints.

Jean Racine is the leading figure of this period and style. Molière and Corneille are great names of theatre, but Racine outpaces even them. In the language of his *Phèdre* and *Andromaque* there is the elegance, purity and pace of the alexandrine metre as he wrote it, while in the conception there is an electrifying fury and tension that his handling of language creates. He is often said to be untranslatable, because the effects produced by his verse defy even the best efforts of poets who have tried, as did Robert Lowell and Ted Hughes – in the German case Schiller – to render the effect of his lines.

OENONE:
Hélas! Seigneur, quel trouble au mien peut être égal?
La Reine touche presque à son terme fatal.

En vain à l'observer jour et nuit je m'attache:
Elle meurt dans mes bras d'un mal qu'elle me cache.
Un désordre éternel règne dans son esprit.
Son chagrin inquiet l'arrache de son lit.
Elle veut voir le jour; et sa douleur profonde
M'ordonne toutefois d'écarter tout le monde.

(Alas my lord! What trouble could equal mine?
The queen is close to ending her life;
In vain I've watched over her, day and night.
She'll die in my arms of the illness she keeps secret;
An eternal disorder rules in her soul,
Sorrowful disquiet tears her from her bed;
She wishes to see daylight, yet with profound sadness
Orders me to shut out all the world.)[5]

The high drama of classical themes was not irrelevant to the times, because human nature is a perennial, and the greatest stories from all ages are those which, every time they are told, investigate and illuminate its concerns afresh. But the literature of the time also addressed its own concerns. In Marlowe's *Doctor Faustus* the hunger for knowledge and power, gained by the short-cut of *alchymia*, *cabala*, *magia*, is at the heart of the tragedy. The play opens with Dr Faustus dismissing logic, medicine, law and divinity in preference for the 'metaphysics of magicians and necromantic books':

These metaphysics of magicians,
And necromantic books are heavenly;
Lines, circles, scenes, letters, and characters;
Ay, these are those that Faustus most desires.
O, what a world of profit and delight,
Of power, of honour, of omnipotence,
Is promis'd to the studious artizan!
All things that move between the quiet poles
Shall be at my command: emperors and kings
Are but obeyed in their several provinces,

Nor can they raise the wind, or rend the clouds;
But his dominion that exceeds in this,
Stretcheth as far as doth the mind of man;
A sound magician is a mighty god:
Here, Faustus, tire thy brains to gain a deity.[6]

In Shakespeare's *The Tempest* Prospero does just what Faustus wishes to do: raises the wind and rends the clouds. Miranda, pitying those she sees aboard the storm-endangered ship, pleads with him:

If by your art, my dearest father, you have
Put the wild waters in this roar, allay them.
The sky, it seems, would pour down stinking pitch,
But that the sea, mounting to the welkin's cheek,
Dashes the fire out.[7]

Both playwrights wrote as the high point of hopes in *alchymia*, *cabala*, *magia* was passing and science proper was emerging. Yet not everyone was convinced enough, or perhaps brave enough, to accept and apply the new vision of the world when they still found the old so compelling. Milton, one recalls, had visited Galileo while on his Italian travels, and in *Paradise Lost* twice referred to the latter's observations of the moon. But when he has Adam question the archangel Raphael on the movements of the heavenly bodies, the archangel seems quite behind the times:

This to attain, whether heav'n move or Earth,
Imports not, if thou reck'n right; the rest
From man or angel the great Architect
Did wisely to conceal, and not divulge
His secrets to be scann'd by them who ought
Rather admire.[8]

The first version of *Paradise Lost* was published in 1667, after the founding of the Royal Society and therefore long after the triumph of the world-view which Galileo unwillingly had to disclaim to save his life. Perhaps when the poet met the scientist the latter did not add *eppur si muove* at the last moment. On the other hand, there is something doubtful about what Milton puts in the archangel's mouth; for the 'great Architect' did indeed divulge the answer several times – in Genesis, in Psalm 104 and in the Book of Joshua, among other passages, we are told quite clearly that earth *non si muove*. Perhaps Raphael in the courts of heaven was in the same quandary as Galileo in the courts of the Vatican, and had to equivocate likewise. But his journeys between the crystal spheres and the Garden of Eden would have given him empirical grounds for making up his own mind; and in that way he would have been a true seventeenth-century archangel after all.

But what of religion? As the Thirty Years War attests, the seventeenth century was as tumultuously and violently at war with itself over matters of religion as the preceding century had been, and the great argument of the century's first half – that selfsame war – was directly the result of the wide and bloody divisions that had opened in the preceding century. In the seventeenth century's first half Calvinists and Puritans exerted a quelling influence on social life as great as the Roman Church's attempt to stifle 'libertinage of the mind', that is, freedom in intellectual life. In the second half of the century 'libertinage' became not just an intellectual style – the style in which anything can be questioned and discussed – but a life-style, as in the courts of Versailles and London where monarchs had official mistresses and the likes of John Wilmot, second Earl of Rochester, could riot in the streets and successfully set themselves to die young from debauchery.

The word 'libertine' plays an illuminating role in the changes of the seventeenth century. The period of the 1620s and 1630s saw the first 'libertine era' in the free-thought sense of the term, denoting no-holds-barred discussion of new and radical ideas. Scepticism and open-ended enquiry were the first fruits of the new era's liberty of enquiry. The 'liberty' in 'libertinage' then meant freedom from two species of constraint: the constraint of religious orthodoxy, and the constraint imposed by the authority of the ancients.

But 'libertine' did not keep this sense for long. An interesting history lies behind the term. It was used first as the label for a Protestant sect in the Low Countries and Picardy which, on the basis of unimpeachable logic, had come to the conclusion that since everything had been created and ordained by God, nothing is sinful. They acted on this view, to the great disapproval of everyone else. As a result the term 'libertine' came to suggest sensuality, debauchery and depravity.[9] This is the origin of the now familiar sense of 'libertine'. But in the first half of the century the word denoted scientists and philosophers, not debauchees. Then, by association with the reference to advanced philosophical and scientific views, the idea arose that anyone who held such views must therefore be likely to reject the principles of religion. 'Libertine' was accordingly a misleading term, because not all of the scientists and philosophers of the time were atheists or anti-theists. Some were sincere Christians, or at very least took the view that religious orthopraxis – outward observance – was necessary, not only for their personal safety but for the good of society.

The developing use, later in the seventeenth century, of 'libertine' to denote debauched people rather than just those with intellectual interests rested not only on the assumption that advanced thinking implies rejection of religious beliefs, but on the further assumption that rejection of religious beliefs implied a decay of morals. This of course is nonsense. But so firmly established in the public's mind was this view that by the eighteenth century a distinction had expressly to be drawn between immoralists and intellectuals. Accordingly the term 'libertine' was kept as a label for the former while the latter came to be described as 'free thinkers' or *philosophes*. While the term was still in transition, authors such as Pierre Bayle had to mark the difference between intellectual and moral libertinage by describing adherents of the former as 'libertines of the mind' (*libertins d'esprit*) and of the latter 'libertines of the body'.

In the age of Louis XIV in France morals and language were equally liberated – moralists would say: degraded – so that 'libertines of the mind' in Bayle's sense might well have been libertines of the body also, maintaining a number of mistresses, frequenting brothels and larding their speech with profanities, all quite acceptable to everyone but the most straitlaced of puritans. Morals are things of fashion; laxity and puritanism come and go in cycles, independently of the long progress of thought; but it is natural to make a connection between the liberation of thought and the loosening of moral straitjackets as the seventeenth century progressed. The connection is unlikely to be a simple causal one, but rather a non-accidental covariance, doubtlessly predicated on the fact that a dispassionate scrutiny of straitlaced moralities finds most of what they enjoin illogical and absurd.

The 1620s and 1630s are labelled 'the libertine crisis' by some historians because they were a particularly significant moment in the separation of the new thought from the old. These years saw the last major effort by guardians of the old way of thinking to repress the new; the stories of Vanini and Galileo illustrate this fact.

The difference made by mere decades is striking. In the 1640s in England Puritans at last got their way and closed the theatres of London, criminalising theatrical performances and declaring actors 'rogues and vagabonds'. By the laws then passed anyone caught watching a play was to be fined five shillings, and those acting in it were to be whipped and imprisoned. For three-quarters of a century beforehand the more zealous among Reformed believers were splenetically hostile to theatre, and efforts had been made to prevent plays being performed even before Shakespeare arrived in London as a youth. The Civil War gave Puritans their chance, and they took it. It is astonishing therefore to think that not much more than twenty years after those anti-theatrical ordinances had been passed, the wild Earl of Rochester could be entertaining his friends with squibs like this:

Rouse stately Tarse
And lett thy Bollocks grind
For seed.

Heave up, faire Arse,
And lett thy Cunt be kind
To th' Deed.

Thrust Pintle with a force,
Strong as a horse:
Spend till my Cunt overflow . . .

If it be thought that Rochester was merely an example of the foul-mouthed swaggerer one finds among graceless young men in any age and clime, his own poetry suggests something different; namely, that he was of his time, not out of it:

Much wine had passed, with grave discourse
Of who fucks who, and who does worse
(Such as you usually do hear
From those that diet at the Bear),
When I, who still take care to see
Drunkenness relieved by lechery,
Went out into St. James's Park
To cool my head and fire my heart.
But though St. James has th' honor on 't,
'Tis consecrate to prick and cunt.
There, by a most incestuous birth,
Strange woods spring from the teeming earth;
For they relate how heretofore,
When ancient Pict began to whore,
Deluded of his assignation
(Jilting, it seems, was then in fashion),
Poor pensive lover, in this place
Would frig upon his mother's face;
Whence rows of mandrakes tall did rise
Whose lewd tops fucked the very skies.
Each imitative branch does twine
In some loved fold of Aretine,
And nightly now beneath their shade
Are buggeries, rapes, and incests made.
Unto this all-sin-sheltering grove
Whores of the bulk and the alcove,
Great ladies, chambermaids, and drudges,
The ragpicker, and heiress trudges.

> Carmen, divines, great lords, and tailors,
> Prentices, poets, pimps, and jailers,
> Footmen, fine fops, do here arrive,
> And here promiscuously they swive.

Samuel Pepys was Rochester's contemporary and his *Diaries* give no different impression of the London which had succeeded the Puritans' London of two decades earlier. This was almost certainly a reaction to Puritanical zeal, but it was a big reaction: not until the Victorian era did anything like a similar repressive moralism arise from religious sentiment.

The thought these considerations prompt is that the immense struggle of religion had not made the kind of impact its fiercest votaries, on whatever side of the argument they lay, most desired. By the end of the century weariness with religious disputes had set in, and expressed itself in the partial retirement of belief – though not of religious organisations as such – from the front lines of debate. It is in fact noticeable how far apart both the personnel and the discourses of religion and science had drifted as the century progressed. In England the preparedness to forgo quarrels to the death over details of doctrine, just so long as everyone would pay polite lip-service to the forms – the attitude known as 'latitudinarianism' – sums up the development well.

The only figure who made noticeable contributions in both the spheres of religion and science was Blaise Pascal (1623–62). He was a prodigy, a brilliant mathematician whose work on probability is lasting, and a scientist who demonstrated the existence of the vacuum. He was also an amateur theologian, whose *Pensées*, published after his death, are a minor classic for some devotees, though far more admired for the beauty of their prose than the convincingness of their arguments. They are fragments of what was to have been a much longer defence of Christianity. Note this fact: a *defence* of Christianity; it is of interest that Pascal felt it necessary to defend Christianity against the growing unbelief of the age. In the early history of the Church, apologetical literature – works explaining and defending the doctrines of the faith – were written by Origen, Augustine, Tertullian and others, in an effort to convince a sceptical age. By the high medieval period apologetics had ceased to be necessary, because by then it was a criminal offence not to believe those doctrines.[10] But the success of the revolution in mind-set of the seventeenth century made a return to apologetics necessary. In the century after Pascal's own there appeared numerous books on the 'evidences of Christianity' – William Paley's *Evidences* is one of the most famous – and in more recent times G. K. Chesterton, C. S. Lewis and numerous lesser figures have attempted the same.

One of the arguments of the *Pensées* has become well known. It is that even if there is only a tiny probability that there is a God – and Pascal took it that there has to be at least *some* probability that there is[11] – it is in one's interests to believe and act accordingly, because the benefit of doing so is infinitely great, whereas if one is wrong the loss is merely finite. (Voltaire acidly remarked that if there is a deity and one's reason for belief in it is this profit-and-loss calculation, the deity would not be impressed.) Another way of putting the argument is to say that philosophical scepticism of the kind practised by Montaigne, and employed by Descartes to clear the way for a positive epistemology, shows the finitude and impotence of the human mind; this, contrasted with the promise embodied in the idea of an infinite and omnipotent deity, makes it rational to believe in the latter and act on that belief. Pascal took the very existence of scepticism to be proof of the fallen state of man and his need for a God, and on this basis he accepted the whole raft of doctrines in which Christianity consists. We should, he wrote, submit ourselves completely to the Church, adopt a life of self-renunciation (of 'dying to the self') that turns its back even on personal affections and attachments, and accept that the natural state of man is sickness, weakness, affliction and suffering. Living to die, but in such a way as to attain eternal felicity, is the whole aim of life in this dispensation.

For all the charms of Pascal's prose, his views had little effect. 'Many of those who were able to appreciate his arguments', wrote G. N. Clark, 'were steadily drifting into rationalism, whether of the deistic or some other type, and ceasing to regard faith as co-ordinate with reason, let alone superior to it.'[12] Instead, as always happens when mainstream religious influence is in decline – relative decline, in the case of the seventeenth century – various minority movements appeared, such as the Quietism promoted by Miguel de Molinos, the Pietism that developed as a more austere and unworldly side-branch of Lutheranism, and – at the end of a different spectrum – a form of ecstatic mysticism with erotic overtones, as portrayed by Bernini's *Ecstasy of St Teresa* (carved between 1647 and 1652), to be seen in Santa Maria della Vittoria in Rome. St Teresa of Avila (1515–82) had written of visions in which she was repeatedly pierced by the arrows of Christ while in a 'devotion of union', experiencing 'sweet happy pain' from the piercings, accompanied by a 'fiery glow' and feelings of suffocation; when she recovered from her rapturous states she would be exhausted and in tears. Rapturous union in prayer with Christ or God as a form of sexual sublimation is further evidenced in some late seventeenth-century religious figures such as Marie Alacoque and the devotees of the Sacred Heart.[13] How close opposite extremes approach each other is well exemplified by the substance of St Teresa's and Rochester's respective experiences.

For Protestants the Bible gave shape and colour to the way they expressed themselves, even if its contents were increasingly taken metaphorically rather than literally. For Catholics it was the legends and teachings of the Church that provided a frame of reference at the personal level. In their respective ways these were the unquestioned backdrop of the lives of people at the time, even though the disconnection between them and the radically different world-view formulated by the sciences, and especially by astronomy, meant that the book and the traditions were shifting from the realm of information to a realm more like that of mythology. In this way the old mind could live on alongside the new, in a less central way and in a different key. Those who still fully *lived* the old mind, however, whatever their numbers, were now in the margins of things: the new mind was developing the technologies and social structures that were transforming the world.

There were obvious concrete results of this. For one thing, as already noted, politics was no longer as influenced by religion as it had been. Theology went one way, science and philosophy another; the place of theological considerations in the two latter were drawn from 'natural theology' as the residuum of explanation that, until Darwin two centuries later, and physics-based cosmology three centuries later, showed how life, and before it the universe itself, did not require a creator. Popular works like Bunyan's *Pilgrim's Progress* struck a chord with people who did not know science and who needed to hold on to the allegories that gave explanations and hope. Bunyan's readers and the Pietists of German Lutheranism despised learning and science, even feared it; in this they represent one trend that has always accompanied the growth of knowledge, a trend that attaches itself ever more firmly to knowledge's opposite – namely, the absolute certainties of faith, as a bulwark against the vertiginous alternatives revealed by enquiry.

PART VI

CONCLUSION

21

Is It a Myth?

THE CLAIM IN the foregoing pages is that the seventeenth century in Europe redirected the course of human history by changing humankind's perspective on the universe and itself. And I asked a question in Chapter 2 about this change, there writing, 'It is or should be a puzzle that this explosion of genius occurred in a century so tumultuous – a time of wars, civil strife and the continuation of post-Reformation religious agonies disruptive and destructive to an unparalleled degree in Europe's history to that point. How does one account for the coexistence of the flowering of genius alongside the attrition of such conflict? Does the tumult of the century in some way explain its genius and those changes, or cause them, or might there have been even greater innovation if it had been a time of peace?'

The answer in my view is that the wars and tumults of the century helped to make the change possible because of the failure of authority in both theoretical and practical respects during the chaos they caused. In the breakdown of systems of control over the movements of people and their ideas, exchanges especially of the latter were able to occur with much greater freedom than hitherto. The comparison is with the way border posts might be abandoned in a time of war, so that people can cross into neighbouring territories unhindered and unobserved. In effect, this is what happened in the seventeenth century, particularly its first half. With armies tracking destructively, like swarms of locusts, back and forth across Europe and for a time the British isles, with demographic upheavals and the breakdown of order, and with the distraction of authorities on matters mortal to their own concerns, gaps and holes opened for new and once death-inviting ideas to circulate and mutually potentiate each other.

'The distracted authorities' – I think there is a major clue in this. People were indeed distracted, busy with the problems that strife and change bring, unable to step back enough to notice that the scenery of the theatre of life was grinding round to something different. It is entirely plausible to think that there might have been some people living between 1620 and 1690 who woke one day to the amazed reflection that how things seemed to them in their adolescent years in the 1630s now belonged to an utterly lost era.

Others of course were all too conscious of the distresses of their time. Why would Hobbes think that in the state of nature human experience is of war of all against all, in a nasty, brutish and short existence, if he were not himself a deeply troubled witness to precisely such circumstances in the time's struggles, when order and authority collapsed, leaving individuals prey to those stronger than themselves? In the British isles the evaporation of central government resulted in an estimated 84,000 military deaths and a further 100,000 deaths from war-related disease and famine; his conception of a Leviathan of power before whom all must submit was motivated by the intense desire to find a guarantee of peace. Around him in the flames, screams, corpses and devastations of decade after decade of chaos in Europe was the motive for his argument.

A fractured and fractious time, therefore, helps change to happen, even if inadvertently; it has to be an ill wind indeed that does not allow anything good to come of it. But it is also the case that times of emergency make change happen faster anyway. The obvious example is military technique and technology; one never forgets – to take a much later but very speaking example – that the RAF still had Gloucester Gladiator biplanes in service in 1939, yet by 1945 had the Whittle jet fighter in flight; that Germany attacked the UK with guided missiles, the V1 and V2 rockets, and the US dropped atomic bombs on Japan. The world of 1945 was a remarkably different place from the world of

1939 because of the speeding up of history in those years. Transpose to the key of world-view, science, theory and belief, and the seventeenth century comes into view as a time when everything went into fast-forward in these respects, leaving one era behind and rushing towards a new one.

But! – this is not a view that everyone agrees with. Is the argument of this book the iteration of a myth, a new myth to replace all the old myths, a new myth about the recent history of the mind of humankind and the world it dominates? Some emphatically think it is.[1] They criticise all the Whiggish, progressivist, secularist accounts of the seventeenth and eighteenth centuries (the Long Enlightenment let us call it) – of which this book is one – as rationalisations, *parti pris* accounts rather than records of a great moment (as I put it, *the* epoch) in human history.

Let us see. The foregoing chapters claim this: that the revolution in thought in the seventeenth century produced the mind that recognises human beings as a species of animal on a small planet in an outer arm of a galaxy which is one among trillions of galaxies; *and* (and this is the equally important point) that the same knowledge which revealed this has also enabled the development of technologies (including medical technologies) which have transformed the existence of that species of animal and the small planet it inhabits – not always for the better, but largely so, and in many ways.

This transformation of world-view was not complete until after Darwin, of course, and its application via technology to the transformation of life in the world required the wider spread of literacy and education in the nineteenth and twentieth centuries. Moreover it is not by far the world-view of everyone even today – perhaps not even a majority of people today – but it is the world-view that drives almost everything of significance that happens in our world, from technologies to economies, with the resulting impact on the social and political organisation of *almost* all societies, even the ones where the majority of people still hold to a version of the pre-seventeenth-century mind-set.

I say *almost* all societies, because religious fundamentalism in its political and socially influential forms in some parts of the world keeps the pre-seventeenth-century mind actively in control of people's lives. That world-view is one that says our world is at the centre of the universe and we humans are at its summit, and that all lies under the government of a deity whose requirements are meant to shape most aspects of human lives – which means their choices and behaviour and their attitudes to each other The mental totalitarianism of Islam is the paradigm.

The power of societies in which the modern world-view has become the driver means that even though most people in the world, for most of the time since the seventeenth century, have in some sense remained pre-modern in mind-set, they are holders of what is in fact a functionally marginal view. In the few countries, and in a few places in some other countries, where this otherwise functionally marginal mind-set remains dominant, most are – if one indulges the requisite sombre survey – places of religious strife and backwardness.

Now: in asking whether there is something mythical about this picture, one is not asking whether it is untrue that science has had a major impact on world history since the seventeenth century. That of course is undeniable, even by those who most ardently wish it were not so. Rather, the mythical aspect of the story would instead be this: that the story is one in which heroes and martyrs (scientists, philosophers) struggled against the forces of darkness (superstition, ignorance), and eventually triumphed; that whereas the efforts of the heroes and martyrs displaced humankind from the centre of the physical universe, they firmly placed humankind at a new and better centre: the centre of the universe of thought and knowledge. Thus scientific salvation has come to a benighted world, where lives were short, diseased, constrained by false beliefs, and full of petty struggle – and liberated it, at least for those able to take advantage of the liberation.

This story appears to have all the lineaments of any narrative in which a battle against the odds is eventually crowned with victory, though with tragic losses on the way – with setbacks and lucky strokes, with its Odysseus and the Sirens, its Perseus and Medusa, its Harry Potter and Voldemort, its Siegfried and the dragon's blood, its holy grail or precious ring – its Manichean conflict between light and dark.

In this mythopoeic version of the revolution in thought, the heroes are the serious enquirers, some of them martyred for the cause; the villains are the occultists, Aristotelians and priests; the enemy is ignorance; the prize is truth and progress. And the prize was won, through the flames of the Inquisition pyre, in a battle against the mighty weight of history and its army of ghosts.

Well, think what you like: the story indeed has the lineaments of an epic myth. But it is nevertheless true. There are two twists in the tale, however, either of which could have a strangulating effect on a putative happy outcome. They are or can be related twists.

One is that as the scientific world-view becomes more remote, in its technicality, difficulty, mathematicity, and distance from the understanding of most people – who encounter it only in the most user-friendly ways by touching a screen (or, less frequently but more dreadfully, by being on the receiving end of a drone strike) – it leaves an ever widening gap to be filled by the old stories and beliefs. The old stories are so much easier to understand, and provide the neat narrative structure – beginning, middle, end and purpose – that human psychology loves. The basic story and requirements of any of the world's major religions can be explained in less than half an hour, which is within the attention span of most humans. By striking contrast, it takes years to master physics. It takes applied study to unfold the history of human thought as it moved from the shadows inside Plato's cave to the sunlight of knowledge based on evidence and reason. It takes intellectual maturity to see things as they are rather than as how so many wish they would be.

The second twist is that the active reassertion of the old stories and beliefs is under way in parts of the world where they never fully or even partially lost their hold. The reasserters are happy to use the technologies that the new mind has created in order to reassert the old mind's dominion: terrorists use anti-aircraft missiles and mobile phones to communicate with each other, inventions from a world that repudiated their vision of the world four centuries ago. Thus humanity is in a bottleneck of contradictions, a moment of peril, as the new mind outstrips the old mind so far that the old mind is trying to pull the new mind back, even trying to extirpate it, yet using its discoveries in a severity of self-contradiction that approaches madness.

The solution? It is what it has always been, though it has never been as successfully applied as it might be. The solution is education. What a cliché that seems; yet like most clichés it is so deeply true that we cease to see its truth. Scarcely anywhere do we really educate. The time, technique, cost and commitment it would take *really to educate* are applied in very few places – only in the most elite and expensive schools, and in the graduate departments of the world's top universities, hardly scratching the surface in world-population terms. It is not the fault of dedicated teachers at schools around the world – teachers are among the most important people on the planet, given what they can do in the way of inspiring and enlightening when they are really good at it, and are given the tools and opportunities to do it – but they rarely have enough of either. As the world moves forward in some respects, dragged sideways or back by the conflicts between the old mind and the new in other respects, a type and quantity of education scarcely different from fifty or a hundred years ago continues to let the majority slip further behind.

A new mythic adventure is therefore required: to make the world fully capable of using the mind that the seventeenth-century revolution brought to birth.

Notes

1. *Seeing the Universe*

1 Review by Laura Sangher of Paul Kléber, *Solomon's Secret Arts: The Occult in the Age of Enlightenment* (New Haven and London, 2013) in *English Historical Review* 129:541 (December 2014), p. 1508.
2 A. C. Grayling, *Berkeley: The Central Arguments* (London, 1986); 'Modern Philosophy: Locke, Berkeley and Hume', in *Philosophy: A Guide through the Subject* (London, 1998); *Descartes: The Life and Times of a Genius* (London, 2005); *Towards the Light* (London, 2007); 'The Enlightenment', in *Ideas That Made the Modern World* (London, 2008); etc.
3 The question of philosophers' interest in history is not to be understood as a quest for a Hegelian theory of its supposed meaning or unfolding of purpose – there are no ghosts of time working towards a goal, there are only people trying to make sense of things, formerly by means of traditions of belief, then from the early modern period with renewed emphasis on empirical enquiry and the application of logic. Bertrand Russell was drawn to history for the same reason that prompts the present book's fascination with the unfolding of ideas and their influence. Russell demonstrated this not only in his *History of Western Philosophy* (London, 1945) but also in *Freedom and Organisation 1814–1914* (London, 1934), *Authority and the Individual* (London, 1949), *Understanding History* (New York, 1958), and elsewhere. As in the pages that follow here, Russell's writings on these subjects consist in observations and reflections on what history offers; in this sense philosophical history has a part to play in the conversation about how – to the repeat the phrase used above – we are to make sense of things.

2. *The Epoch in Human History*

1 It is more correct to say 'Empirical *support* for theory'; later results might weaken or remove the support.
2 Greek *asteres planetai* 'wandering stars' from *planasthai* 'to wander'.
3 There is (as one would expect!) some controversy over the dating of this eclipse. The date given here is the accepted one, but there is a possibility that Thales' prediction related to an eclipse visible in the same region twenty-five years earlier, in 610 BCE. Both eclipses have been worked out from the data we have available to us now, by running the clock backwards

on the relative positions of sun, moon and earth over time, giving an accurate retrospective on all eclipses visible from different regions of earth throughout history.

4 It is not known how Thales managed to make his prediction. The Greeks after him did not repeat the achievement, for good reason: whereas a lunar eclipse (which happens when the earth is between the sun and moon, so that the moon is in the earth's shadow) can be seen from the whole of night-time earth for over an hour, matters are far otherwise with a solar eclipse. For when the moon is between the sun and earth, its shadow makes a tiny strip along the earth's surface, and at any one place is visible for only about 7.5 minutes. To predict a solar eclipse, therefore, you need to know the orbit of the moon with great accuracy – in fact, to a tiny fraction of one degree of arc. The Greeks did not have this kind of information.

5 This is an example of the 'genetic fallacy', the view that something is supported or discredited merely because of its origins. There is however much to be said about this point, which involves more complexity and sometimes less fallacy than at first appears. In my view it sometimes is, and sometimes is not, fallacious to base a judgment on facts about origins and development; it depends on subject matter.

6 One candidate for a circumbinary exoplanet is PSR B-1620–26 in the globular cluster M4. It is thought to be a huge object, two and a half times the mass of Jupiter, orbiting a binary system consisting of a pulsar and a white dwarf.

7 Carol Pal, *Republic of Women* (Cambridge, 2012), p. 6.

8 Debates about Descartes' views in the Netherlands in the 1640s resulted in riots: see A. C. Grayling, *Descartes: The Life and Times of a Genius* (London, 2005).

9 Kant, *Was ist Aufklärung, Berlinische Monatsschrift 1784*; T. Mommsen, 'Petrarch's Conception of the Dark Ages', *Speculum* 17, 1942, pp. 226–42.

3. *The Origins of the Wars*

1 The following account is culled from a variety of sources, chief among them Geoffrey Parker, *The Thirty Years War* (New York, 2nd edn, 1997); Norman Davies, *Europe* (London, 2014); Richard Dunn, *The Age of Religious Wars 1559–1715* (New York, 1979); C. V. Wedgwood, *The Thirty Years War* (London, 1938); and with great admiration P. H. Wilson, *The Thirty Years War: Europe's Tragedy* (London, 2009).

2 C. V. Wedgwood, *The Thirty Years War*, p. 506.

3 Wilson, *The Thirty Years War*, p. 9.

5. *The Mercenary Captains*

1 All eventually fell to the Imperial and Spanish forces, though Frankenthal, garrisoned by English mercenary troops, held out longest.

6. *The Edict of Restitution, 1629*

1 D. Power, *William Harvey* (London, 1897), pp. 85–6.

2 J. K. Jue, *Heaven Upon Earth: Joseph Mede (1586–1638) and the Legacy of Millenarianism* (Dordrecht, 2006), p. 69. See also Bodo Nischan, 'John Bergius: Irenicism and the Beginnings of Official Religious Toleration in Brandenburg-Prussia', *Church History* 51 (1982), pp. 389–404.

3 This was the struggle between France and the Habsburgs over control of northern Italy following the death without a direct male heir of the Duke of Mantua, Vincenzo Gonzaga. In

the complex tangle of family and dynastic relationships among the aristocracy and ruling houses of Europe – Ferdinand II was married to the sister of all the last three Gonzaga dukes, and he supported the claims of Ferrante II Duke of Guastalla and Charles-Emmanuel I Duke of Savoy, while the French supported the Duke of Nevers.

4 K. Cramer, *The Thirty Years War and German Memory in the Nineteenth Century* (Lincoln, NE, 2007), p. 149.

7. The Swedish Apogee

1 G. Parker, *The Thirty Years War* (London, 2006), p. 83.

2 M. Roberts, *Gustavus Adolphus and the Rise of Sweden* (London, 1973).

3 The complexities of these events are greater than any of the sketches here suggest: P. H. Wilson's *The Thirty Years War: Europe's Tragedy* (London, 2009) shows by its sheer bulk what a properly detailed account would offer.

4 I must confess to puzzlement at why churches are built by the survivors of plagues (and earthquakes and other natural disasters) to give thanks for surviving, rather than to express anger at the being supposed to be the author of all things and therefore of the plague (and other natural evils) itself. But then, the mind-set involved is not a rational one.

5 M. Sharratt, *Galileo: Decisive Innovator* (Cambridge, 1994).

8. From Wallenstein to Breisach

1 See R. Bireley, 'The Peace of Prague (1635) and the Counterreformation in Germany', *Journal of Modern History* 48:1 (March 1976), pp. 31–70.

2 The Académie Française has a good official website detailing its foundation and subsequent history. Not all the controversies that some of its pronouncements have caused are mentioned there. http://www.academie-francaise.fr/linstitution/lhistoire.

3 R. Bireley, *Ferdinand II* (Cambridge, 2014).

9. Towards Westphalia

1 Friedrich-Wilhelm is known as 'the Great' because of his astute political mind. The most influential of the Hohenzollern dynasty to that point, he recouped the fortunes of Brandenburg through his recognition of the importance of trade and commerce, and his support therefore of the rising middle class in his territories. As a staunch Calvinist the idea of material success as a sign of election for salvation came naturally. It was his achievement that saw the Duchy of Brandenburg become the Kingdom of Prussia under his son Frederick, who accordingly was elevated from Duke Frederick III of Brandenburg to Frederick I King of Prussia.

2 C. Hill, *The Century of Revolution 1603–1714* (London, 1961, 2nd edn, 1980).

3 J. N. Hays, *Epidemics and Pandemics: Their Impacts on Human History* (Santa Barbara, 2005), pp. 113–14.

4 L. Auchincloss, *Richelieu* (London, 1972).

5 D. Croxton and A. Tischer, *The Peace of Westphalia* (Westport, CT, 2002).

6 Pope Innocent X, *Zelo Domus Dei* (1648).

7 G. Evans and J. Newnham, *The Dictionary of World Politics: A Reference Guide to Concepts, Ideas and Institutions* (Hemel Hempstead, 1990), p. 501.

8 A. Osiander, 'Sovereignty, International Relations, and the Westphalian Myth', *International Organization* 55:2 (2001), pp. 251–87.

10. *In the Ruins of Europe*

1 The website Necrometrics cites a variety of sources on the mortality numbers: see necrometrics.com/pre1700a.htm#30YrW.
2 See D. Onnekink (ed.), *War and Religion after Westphalia* (London, 2013), passim.

11. *The Maritime Conflicts*

1 J. R. Jones, *The Anglo-Dutch Wars of the Seventeenth Century* (London and New York, 1996).
2 Glen O'Hara, *Britain and the Sea since 1600* (Basingstoke and New York, 2010), p. 107.

12. *The Intelligencers*

1 P. Dear, *Mersenne and the Learning of the Schools* (Ithaca, NY, 1988).
2 For tentative speculation on the reasons why, see A. C. Grayling, *Descartes: The Life and Times of a Genius* (London, 2005), Introduction passim.
3 Remarks like this greatly annoy historians of the Middle Ages, who wish to overlook the devastating reduction of literacy, culture and general knowledge that followed the collapse of the Roman Empire in the West and the rise to hegemony of Christianity both there and in what became Byzantium. Between the building of the Basilica of Maxentius at the beginning of the fourth century CE and the Hagia Sophia in the sixth century CE, on the one hand, and Brunelleschi's dome on Florence's cathedral in the fifteenth century CE on the other, the mathematical and engineering skills for work of the required kind were lost. That single fact – just one of very many – speaks volumes.
4 The Stanford University Humanities Center's 'Mapping the Republic of Letters' project is a rich resource for studying the networks of learning and communication in the seventeenth century and afterwards: see republicofletters.stanford.edu.
5 Daniel Garber and Michael Ayers (eds), *The Cambridge History of Seventeenth Century Philosophy*, vol. I (Cambridge, 2003), p. 23.
6 Ibid.
7 The following account is drawn largely from Laurin Zilliacus, *From Pillar to Post: The Troubled History of the Mail* (London, 1956), ch. V passim.
8 Ibid., p. 49.
9 Ibid., p. 50.
10 Ibid., p. 51.
11 Ibid., p. 57.
12 C. Adam and P. Tannery (eds), *Oeuvres de Descartes* (Paris, 1974–86, 2nd edn) Volume V, p. 72. Henceforth cited AT with volume and page; thus AT V 72 here.
13 The account of Hartlib here given draws on G. H. Turnbull, *Samuel Hartlib: A Sketch of his Life and his Relation to J. A. Comenius* (Oxford, 1920). The best account of Hartlib's educational, promotional and scientific contributions is R. H. Syfret, 'The Origins of the Royal Society', *Notes and Records. Royal Society of London* 5 (1947–8), pp. 75–137.
14 John Evelyn, *Diaries*, 17 November 1655, ed. E. S. de Beer (Oxford, 1955).
15 See G. H. Turnbull, *Hartlib, Dury and Comenius: Gleanings from Hartlib's Papers* (London, 1947), p. 167.
16 hridigital.shef.ac.uk/hartlib.
17 See Elizabeth Godfrey, *A Sister of Prince Rupert: Elizabeth Princess Palatine and Abbess of Herford* (London and New York, 1909).
18 Rodis-Lewis quoting the physician Samuel de; G. Rodis-Lewis, *Descartes* (Cornell, 1995), p. 151.

19 A. Nye, *The Princess and the Philosopher: Letters of Elisabeth of the Palatine to René Descartes* (Lanham, MD, 1909).
20 Léon Petit, *Descartes et la Princesse Elisabeth: roman d'amour vécu* (Paris, 1969).
21 AT VIIIA 1–2, 4.
22 AT XI 323–4.
23 R. Watson, *Cogito Ergo Sum: The Life of Rene Descartes* (Boston, 2002). Watson's idiosyncrasies make his account of the Descartes–Elisabeth story one of the best things in his book.
24 Z. Cope, *William Harvey: His Life and Times: His Discoveries: His Methods* (London, 1957).

13. The Short Ways to Knowledge

1 Roger Bacon was nearly prevented from studying and publishing the results of his work by the requirements of his religious order, the Franciscans: it makes one wonder how many mute inglorious Galileos lie in the graveyards of monasteries. Or, because of the effect on anyone's thought of the requirements of orthodoxy, in any graveyard.
2 Naturally enough the story of the development of both microscopes and telescopes, in both of which the Janssens figure, is a lot more complicated than one would wish. Take the case of telescopes: efforts by different people to patent early versions of telescopes in the Netherlands in the first decade of the seventeenth century were turned down on the grounds that there were competing claims about who had invented them.
3 Thomas Crump, *A Brief History of Science: As Seen through the Development of Scientific Instruments* (London, 2001).
4 See Frances Yates, *The Occult Philosophy in the Elizabethan Age* (London, 1979); Deborah Harkness, *John Dee's Conversations with Angels: Cabala, Alchemy, and the End of Nature* (Cambridge, 1999); Paolo Rossi, *Francis Bacon: From Magic to Science*, trans. from the Italian by Sacha Rabinovitch (London, 1968); Brian Vickers (ed.), *Occult and Scientific Mentalities in the Renaissance* (Cambridge, 1984), especially Vickers' Introduction, pp. 1–55.
5 Histories of science in particular and thought in general do indeed pay attention to the point, as a result among other major contributions of Keith Thomas, *Religion and the Decline of Magic* (London, 1997) and Paolo Rossi, *Francis Bacon: From Magic to Science*. As Rossi well puts it, at the beginning of the seventeenth century the 'intellectual was more than half medieval and around 1660 he was more than half modern' (p. x).
6 Richard S. Westfall, *Never At Rest: A Biography of Isaac Newton* (Cambridge, 1983).
7 The tercentenary of Newton's birth fell in 1942, but because of the war the celebrations were delayed until 1946. Keynes died before the celebrations were held, so his essay on Newton was read out to the audience by his brother Geoffrey Keynes.
8 Mark Rogers, 'Isaac Newton's Occult Studies', in *The Esoteric Codex: Alchemy I* (lulu.com, 2013), p. 138.
9 M. Boas, *The Scientific Renaissance 1450–1630* (New York, 1962), passim.
10 See M. Hunter (ed.), *Robert Boyle by Himself and his Friends* (London, 1994), pp. 29–30.
11 Rogers, *The Esoteric Codex*, p. 134.
12 Quoted ibid., p. 137.
13 Westfall, *Never At Rest: A Biography of Isaac Newton* tells the full story of Newton's life and extraordinary, brilliant, puzzling mind.
14 Isaac Newton, *Philosophiae Naturalis Principia Mathematica* (1687), Book III.
15 In the view of Brian Vickers and others, Neoplatonism was the trunk of the tree on which Cabala and (to an even lesser extent) Hermeticism were merely branches. In Vickers' own view, Hermeticism was even more merely a twig. Study of the magical and occult traditions lead back, to a considerable degree, to various syncretisms in later antiquity, but the most important and enduring of them was the thought of Plotinus and others. See Vickers, *Occult and Scientific Mentalities in the Renaissance*.

16 That the texts were written by Moses himself is said to have been confirmed by his wife after his death: Joseph Jacobs and Isaac Broydé, 'Zohar', *The Jewish Encyclopedia* (New York, 1901–6).
17 For details of this, as a contemporary application of Cabalistic play on the Hebrew alphabet and numbers, see the instructive (in an unintended sense) article at torahscience.org/communicat/hebrew_language.html. Near the end its author writes, 'Another method of calculating the triangle of an odd number is by multiplying it by its mid-point. In this case, 55x28=1,540. Editor's note: to get some idea of what this means physically, try building tetrahedrons from disposable cups. (By amazing divine providence, this is exactly what my 12 year old son just "happened" to be doing the week before I started working on this article!)' But the entire performance is evidence that credulity is a permanent human possession.
18 The distinction between astrology and astral medicine of the kind believed in by Ramón Lull and many others throughout the late medieval and Renaissance periods is well made in Yates, *The Occult Philosophy in the Elizabethan Age*, pp. 12–13.
19 This number resonates: Douglas Adams in *The Hitchhiker's Guide to the Galaxy* could not have quoted latter-day Hermeticists more aptly if he tried. It will be remembered that the great computer Deep Thought, after 7.5 million years of computation, came up with an answer to 'life the universe and everything' and it was: 42. (The problem was that the question to which this was the answer was unknown, and Deep Thought said it would have to create a bigger computer than itself with a 10-million-year run to find it. This computer was – humankind; 8 million years in, it was threatened with destruction to make way for an intergalactic bypass.) Despite persistent efforts to attach significance to Adams' choice of that number – in binary code 42 is 101010, it is the number of degrees at which light refracts from water to create a rainbow, light takes 10^{-42} seconds to traverse the diameter of a proton, and so on – Adams said that he chose it only because it is an amusing number, no hidden references involved.
20 F. Yates, *Giordano Bruno and the Hermetic Tradition* (Chicago, 1964).
21 Anthony Grafton, *Defenders of the Text: The Traditions of Scholarship in an Age of Science 1450–1800* (Cambridge, MA, 1991), pp. 145 et seq.
22 Ibid., pp. 147–8.
23 Quoted ibid., p. 152.
24 Ibid., p. 153.
25 Trithemius had become a Benedictine monk by accident, having taken refuge in a monastery of the order during a snowstorm, and staying on, eventually becoming its abbot and historian (though he was caught out inventing things). Neither his reputation as a magician nor his playing fast and loose with history prevented his becoming abbot of Schottenkloster in Würzburg.
26 Even as this second edition was being printed it was condemned by the Inquisition, which made Agrippa hastily add an appendix to Book III by way of disclaimer and retraction.
27 Cornelius Agrippa, *The Occult Philosophy in Three Books*, Book I, translated by 'J.F.' (John French? Some say J. Freake) (London, 1651). For the translation and other details see John Ferguson, *Bibliotheca Chemica: A Catalogue of the Alchemical, Chemical and Pharmaceutical Books in the Collection of the Late James Young of Kelly and Durris* (2010), vol. 1.
28 Philip Ball, *The Devil's Doctor: Paracelsus and the World of Renaissance Magic and Science* (London, 2006).
29 Ibid.

14. Dr Dee and the Potent Art

1 Victoria County History, 'The University of Cambridge: The Sixteenth Century', *A History of the County of Cambridgeshire and the Isle of Ely*, vol. 3 (London, 1959).

2 J. Peter Zetterberg, 'The Mistaking of "the Mathematics" for Magic in Tudor and Stuart England', *Sixteenth Century Journal* 11 (1980), p. 85. See J. Aubrey, *Brief Lives* ed. O.L. Dick (London, 1949), p. xxix.
3 Numerology is another quack survivor from this period; go online and you can see how to calculate your 'Life Path number' and your 'Birth Day number' and your 'First Challenge number' and your 'Pinnacle cycle' and your 'Heart's Desire number' – and so forth.
4 Descartes was so struck by the talking and moving statues of Saint-Germain that they convinced him that animals could seem to have souls (feelings, perceptions) as humans do, but without having them; they are in his view automata. He once threw a cat out of an upstairs window in Leiden to prove this point, though I do not see what the proof lies in. (Pope Francis, occupying St Peter's Throne at the time of this writing, takes a different view about animal souls, saying that they too can go to heaven.) The theatre built by Queen Christina of Sweden in the mid-seventeenth century was a mechanical marvel. Coincidentally, the only play Descartes ever wrote – a very poor one, but then: he wrote it reluctantly at Christina's request – was staged in that theatre.
5 This feature of mid-sixteenth-century England is discussed by Keith Thomas in *Religion and the Decline of Magic* (London, 1997).
6 Brahe made a detailed examination of the supernova in his *De nova et nullius aevi memoria prius visa stella* ('Concerning the Star, new and never before seen in anyone's life or memory') (1573) in which he recorded his own observations and analyses of the observations of many others. It was reprinted twice by Kepler in the early seventeenth century.
7 This was Thomas Digges; see Francis R. Johnson and Sanford V. Larkey, 'Thomas Digges, the Copernican System, and the idea of the Infinity of the Universe in 1576', *Huntington Library Bulletin* (1934), p. 111.
8 Another is not expected until 2383, which gives us a breather.
9 Deborah Harkness, *John Dee's Conversations with Angels: Cabala, Alchemy, and the End of Nature* (Cambridge, 1999) is a thorough examination of the motivations and content of Dee's endeavours in this regard.
10 Ibid., ch. 3 passim.
11 The saga of the angelic conversations is told in ibid. Dee's diaries are held in the British Library.
12 Benjamin Woolley, *The Queen's Conjuror: The Life and Magic of Dr Dee* (London, 2001), pp. 253–4. This is a highly readable account of Dee's adventures and vicissitudes, of great use here.
13 Ibid., pp. 268–70.
14 See A. C. Grayling, *Descartes: The Life and Times of a Genius* (London, 2005).

15. The Rosicrucian Scare

1 Frances Yates, *The Rosicrucian Enlightenment* (London, 1972). This invaluable study is my guide in what follows.
2 Elizabeth I called Duke Frederick 'cousin Mumpellgart', this being his family name, and he presumably provides the original for 'cosen garmombles' in Shakespeare's *Merry Wives of Windsor*, 'Garmombles' being the German Duke who hires horses at the Garter Inn – an allusion to the Duke's visit to Elizabeth in the 1590s to be, among other things, invested with the Order of the Garter. See Yates, *The Rosicrucian Enlightenment*, p. 44.
3 Yates, *The Rosicrucian Enlightenment*, p. 49.
4 Ibid., p. 51.
5 Ibid., p. 56.
6 Both the *Fama* and the *Confessio* are translated in the appendices to ibid. For this passage see pp. 297–8.

7 Yates, *The Rosicrucian Enlightenment*, pp. 73–81.
8 Ibid., p. 132.
9 See Berkeley's *Notebooks*; he deleted the phrase from his manuscript of *The Principles of Human Knowledge*. See relevant discussion in A. C. Grayling, *Berkeley: The Central Arguments* (London, 1986).
10 Yates, *The Rosicrucian Enlightenment*, p. 137.
11 Bacon's *Novum Organon* had appeared in 1620, promoting the use of inductive inference in empirical science, and his *Advancement of Learning* had just appeared in 1623. In the latter he set out to show 'the excellency of Learning and Knowledge', and to 'deliver it from the discredits and disgraces which it hath received; all from ignorance; but ignorance severally disguised, appearing sometimes in the zeal and jealousy of Divines; sometimes in the severity and arrogancy of Politiques; and sometimes in the errors and imperfections of learned men themselves'. And then he explains these obstacles to knowledge (here quoting his observations only on the first kind): 'I hear the former sort say, that Knowledge is of those things which are to be accepted of with great limitation and caution, that the aspiring to overmuch knowledge was the original temptation and sin whereupon ensued the fall of man, that Knowledge hath in it somewhat of the serpent, and therefore where it entereth into a man it makes him swell; SCIENTIA INFLAT: that Salomon gives a censure, that there is no end of making books, and that much reading is weariness of the flesh, and again in another place, that in specious knowledge there is much consternation, and that he that increaseth knowledge increaseth anxiety, that St. Paul gives a caveat, that we be not spoiled through vain philosophy, that experience demonstrates how learned men have been arch-heretics, how learned times have been inclined to atheism, and how the contemplation of second causes derogate from our dependence upon God, who is the first cause.'
12 The Treaty of Ratisbon was a major affair, and one of the chief players in it was Pope Gregory XV. He helped Ferdinand II with money and diplomatic aid in the conquest of Bohemia and Moravia, and supported the savage repression of Protestantism there, sending Carlos Caraffa as nuncio to Vienna to advise on the best means to be used. Gregory was largely responsible for ensuring that Ferdinand's promise to Maximilian of Bavaria was kept in the matter of transferring the electorship of the Palatinate to him – both the electoral right and the territories – thereby securing a Catholic majority for elections to the Imperial throne. As a reward for Gregory's help, Maximilian gave him the Palatinate library of Heidelberg, 3,500 items strong, containing much occult literature. Pope Gregory immediately sent a deputation to transport the library back to Rome, where it was housed in the Vatican Library as the 'Gregoriana'. About a thousand of these books and manuscripts found their way back to Heidelberg in 1815 and 1816 as gifts from Pope Pius VII to mark the end of the Napoleonic Wars.
13 Baillet, pp. 51–3.
14 Ibid.
15 See A. C. Grayling, *Descartes: The Life and Times of a Genius* (London, 2005), ch. XX. Given the relevance of these conjectures to the current discussion, I here reprise some of my account of the evidence as given in my earlier book.
16 Quoted in Cole, pp. 25–6.
17 S. Gaukroger, *Descartes: An Intellectual Biography* (Oxford, 1995), p. 108.
18 The following account is taken from Baillet's report in Book II, ch. 1 of his *Life*, itself based directly on the lost notebook, and therefore in all probability almost a transcription of Descartes' own words.
19 On 'exploding head syndrome' see the article by Dr Joel Saper (Director of the Michigan Head Pain & Neurological Institute in Ann Arbor) in the *Detroit Free Press*, 24 October 2000. I also experience this syndrome, but only when excessively tired. Online at www.fasterdisaster.com/EAPstorypage.htm.
20 Yates, *The Rosicrucian Enlightenment*, p. 150.

21 Despite the immense care Descartes took always to soothe and placate Catholic, and especially Jesuit, opinion – or at least to try to – knowing that his views could so easily be branded as dangerous along with the rest, he was ultimately unsuccessful. For all his assiduity in orthopraxy and avowed orthodoxy, and for all his wooing of Jesuit opinion, his works ended on the *Index of Forbidden Books* – in company, it has to be said, with almost every other book of any interest ever written – and the universities were forbidden to teach his doctrines. But that lay in the future.

22 See A. C. Grayling, *Towards the Light* (London, 2007).

16. From Magic to Method

1 R. Allen, *The British Industrial Revolution* (Cambridge, 2009); B. Freese, *Coal: A Human History* (London, 2004).

2 Isaac Newton, *Philosophiae Naturalis Principia Mathematica* (1687), Book III, 'Rules of Reasoning in Philosophy', Rule IV, in a new translation and edition by I. Bernard Cohen, Anne Whitman and Julia Budenz, *The Principia: Mathematical Principles of Natural Philosophy* (Los Angeles, CA, 1999); C. R. Darwin, *The Autobiography of Charles Darwin, 1809–1882*, ed. Nora Barlow (London, 1958).

3 Francis Bacon, *Great Instauration*, 'Plan'. All of Bacon's works are online in the complete fifteen-volume edition edited by J. Spedding et al. which can be found at University of Pennsylvania University digital library.

4 Ibid.

5 Ibid.

6 Francis Bacon, *Novum Organum* (1620), in *The New Organon*, ed. Lisa Jardine and Michael Silverthorne (Cambridge, 2002), Aphorism 89.

7 Paolo Rossi, *Francis Bacon: From Magic to Science*, trans. from the Italian by Sacha Rabinovitch (London, 1968).

8 Quoted ibid., p. 19.

9 Ibid., p. 21.

10 Quoted ibid., pp. 29, 30.

11 Ibid., p. 31.

12 Bacon, *Redargutio philosophiarum*, Spedding Book III, p. 573.

13 A good example is *La Minera del Mondo* (*The Riches of the World*) by Maria Bonardo, described by Rossi as 'more like a collection of fairy tales' than a work of fact, which it presented itself as.

14 The names of his works say it all: *Apologia Compendiaria, Fraternitatem de Rosea Cruce suspicionis . . . maculis aspersam, veritatis quasi Fluctibus abluens* &c. (Leyden, 1616). Against Libavius, *Tractatus Apologeticus integritatem Societatis de Rosea Cruce defendens* &c. (Leyden, 1617).

15 William H. Huffman, *Robert Fludd and the End of the Renaissance* (London, 1988), and Allen G. Debus, 'The Chemical Debates of the 17th Century: The Reaction to Robert Fludd and Jean Baptiste van Helmont', in M. L. Righini Bonelli and W. R. Shea (eds), *Reason, Experiment, and Mysticism in the Scientific Revolution* (New York, 1975), pp. 19–47.

16 B. de Grammont, *Historiarum Galliae*, Book XVIII (Toulouse, 1643), iii, pp. 208–9. See also J. S. Spink, *French Free Thought from Gassendi to Voltaire* (New York, 1960), ch. 1 passim and pp. 28–33.

17 Grammont, *Historiarum Galliae*.

18 William L. Hine, 'Mersenne: Naturalism and Magic', in Brian Vickers (ed.), *Occult and Scientific Mentalities in the Renaissance* (Cambridge, 1984), pp. 165–76.

19 Didier Kahn, *Entre atomisme, alchimie et théologie: la réception des thèses d'Antoine de Villon et Etienne de Clave contre Aristote, Paracelse et les 'cabalistes' (24–25 août 1624)* (London, 2001), and see also Gaukroger, Descartes, p. 136.

20 René Descartes, *The Discourse on the Method of Rightly Conducting the Reason, and Seeking Truth in the Sciences* (1637), Part I. Available as a Gutenberg Project ebook at http://www.gutenberg.org/files/59/59-h/59-h.htm#part6.
21 Ibid., Part II.

17. The Birth of Science

1 While these pages were in proof there appeared D. Wootton's *The Invention of Science* (London, 2015), an extensive and comprehensive account which promises to be the standard text on the subject. In addition to M. Boas, *The Scientific Renaissance,* a guide to the origin of the scientific revolution is to be found in P. Dear's *Revolutionising the Sciences* (Princeton, 2001).
2 See W. McGucken, *The Jesuits and Education* (New York, 1932).
3 Angus Armitage, *Copernicus: The Founder of Modern Astronomy* (New York, 1990).
4 There is no good reason for anyone not to know in outline what contemporary science has to say about the world; many excellent popular introductions exist by leaders in their fields, and almost all of them discuss scientific method and outlook. See L. Krauss, *A Universe from Nothing* (New York, 2012) and R. Dawkins, *The Greatest Show on Earth* (London, 2009).
5 J. F. Heilbron, *Hume* (Oxford, 2010).
6 D. Sobel, *A More Perfect Heaven* (New York, 2011), passim; A. Chapman, *Stargazers* (New York, 2014), ch. 3 passim.
7 Chapman, *Stargazers*, ch. 11, Part II, passim.
8 Ibid.
9 Ibid.
10 Sobel, *A More Perfect Heaven*, ch. 7, pp. 1–4.
11 Ibid., ch. 8.3.
12 Isaac Newton, *Philosophiae Naturalis Principia Mathematica* (1687), Book II, Section IX.
13 John Gribbin, *Science: A History* (London, 2002), p. 118n.
14 David Hume, 'Whether the British Government Inclines More to Absolute Monarchy, or to a Republic', in Eugene F. Miller (ed.), *David Hume: Essays, Moral, Political, and Literary* (Indianapolis, 1987), Part I, Essay VII (LVII.5).
15 Unsurprisingly, Christian apologists claim variously that no such event occurred, or that it is not what it seems, that it was a local affair merely, that it was just Plato's Academy and it had run out of money . . . the main close-to-contemporary account of the closure is John Malalas, *Chronicle*, 18.47; see also Alan Cameron, 'The Last Days of the Academy at Athens', *Proceedings of the Cambridge Philological Society* 195 (1969), pp. 7–29, and P. Chuvin, *A Chronicle of the Last Pagans*, trans. B. A. Archer (London, 1990). For contrary views of a more scholarly kind than the apologetics of the Christian blogosphere, see Edward Watts, 'Justinian, Malalas and the End of Athenian Philosophical Teaching in AD 529', *Journal of Roman Studies* 94 (2004), pp. 168–82.
16 Lois Magner, *A History of Life Sciences* (New York, 2002), p. 119.
17 W. E. Knowles Middleton, *The Experimenters: A Study of the Accademia del Cimento* (Baltimore, 1971).
18 Elias Canetti's family lived in Ruschuk in Bulgaria. They went up the Danube to Vienna for such things as shopping and visiting the dentist and the doctor. When they did so they described it as 'going to Europe'.

18. War and Science

1 John Simkin, *First World War Encyclopedia* (Spartacus Educational ebook, 2012).

2 However much of a comedy of ideas it might be, the descriptions in Voltaire's *Candide* (1759) give a chilling picture of what it was like when an army passed through one's home area.
3 Geoffrey Parker, 'Why the Armada Failed', *History Today* 38:5 (1988), pp. 26–33; James McDermott, *England and the Spanish Armada* (New Haven and London, 2005).
4 Michael Roberts, *The Military Revolution 1560–1660* (London, 1967).

19. Society and Politics

1 See M. Goldie and J. Burne (eds), *The Cambridge History of Political Thought 1450–1700* (Cambridge, 1994).
2 J. Dunn, *The Political Thought of John Locke* (Cambridge, 1992); G. Rogers and A. Ryan, *Perspectives on Thomas Hobbes* (Oxford, 1996).
3 A. Gazier, *Bossuet et Louis XIV* (Paris, 1914), passim.
4 Ibid.
5 For the life and character of Louis XIV see I. Dunlop, *Louis XIV* (London, 1999); B. C. Smith, *Louis XIV* (Cambridge, 1992).
6 W. Beck, *Louis XIV and Absolutism* (London, 2012), passim.
7 R. Mousnier, *The Institution of France under the Absolute Monarchy 1598–1789* (Chicago, 1979), Vol. I ch. 4, passim.
8 T. Hobbes, *Leviathan* ed. R. Tuck. (Cambridge, 1996); online at Project Gutenberg www.gutenberg/files/3207/3207-h.htm. The following references are by section heading for use with the online version (which is unpaginated).
9 Ibid., 'The Definition of a Commonwealth'.
10 Ibid., 'Nothing Done To A Man'.
11 Ibid., 'These Rights are Indivisible'.
12 Ibid., 'The Preservation of the Good of the People'.
13 Scholars debate whether this is so. See Jean Hampton, *Hobbes and the Social Contract Tradition* (Cambridge, 1986); David Gauthier, *The Logic of Leviathan* (Oxford, 1969); Deborah Baumgold, *Hobbes' Political Theory* (Cambridge, 1988).
14 Quentin Skinner, *Hobbes and Republican Liberty* (Cambridge, 2008).
15 Isaiah Berlin,'Two Concepts of Liberty' in *Liberty* (Oxford, 2002).
16 J. Locke, *Two Treatises of Government*, Second Treatise, pp. 25–51 passim.
17 Ibid., ch. 2, passim.
18 Ibid.
19 Ibid.
20 Ibid.
21 Ibid.
22 See T. Harris, *Revolution: The Great Crisis of the British Monarchy 1685–1720* (London, 2007), Part 1, passim.
23 Not in the pejorative sense employed by the American political right wing, for whom 'liberal' is a surrogate for 'socialist', both terms of malediction in their lexicon.
24 See A. Apperly, 'Hobbes on Democracy' in *Politics* (1999) 19(3), pp. 165–171.
25 See S. James, *Spinoza on Philosophy, Religion and Politics* (Oxford, 2014), passim.

20. Language and Belief

1 See Jean-Jacques Demorest (ed.), *Studies in Seventeenth Century French Literature* (Ithaca, NY, 1962); J. Leslie Price, *Dutch Culture in the Golden Age* (London, 2011).

2 *The Cambridge History of English and American Literature: An Encyclopaedia in Eighteen Volumes* (Cambridge, 1907–21), vol. IV: *Prose and Poetry: Sir Thomas North to Michael Drayton*, entry on Translators §8: John Florio.
3 Thomas Sprat, *History of the Royal Society* (1667), p. 113.
4 Joseph Addison, *Spectator* No. 70 (21 May 1711), p. 181.
5 Racine, *Phèdre*, 1.1. My translation.
6 Christopher Marlowe, *Doctor Faustus*, Act I scene 1.
7 William Shakespeare, *The Tempest*, Act I scene 2.
8 John Milton, *Paradise Lost*, Book VIII, lines 65–70.
9 Another word for the outlook was 'Epicureanism', mistakenly applying Epicurus' view that goodness consists in pursuing pleasure and avoiding pain. Epicurus himself regarded drinking and whoring as painful, whereas pleasure was sitting under an olive tree sipping water and discussing philosophy. His ethics is the reverse of what latter-day 'Epicureans' think.
10 Revolutionary movements begin with works of description and persuasion; the resulting totalitarianisms that grow out of them, once the revolution is achieved, criminalise non-acceptance of the teachings thus purveyed, the revolutionary works themselves becoming holy writ. The model is not unique to religion.
11 Pascal is of course right on the score of probabilities. But note: there is as much probability that there is a God as that there are fifty or a million or any number of gods, and again as much probability as that there fairies and gnomes, or unicorns, or that Mars is populated by three-legged two-headed intelligent beings . . . namely, a vanishingly small probability which as such it is irrational to believe or act upon. The point is not probability, but rationality: 'ratio' means 'proportion', and one's beliefs and actions should be proportional to the evidence – and the probabilities it sustains – in order to be justifiable. Pascal's reference to infinitely small probabilities is reference to unjustifiable grounds for belief, even on his pragmatic and prudential ground.
12 G. N. Clark, *The Seventeenth Century* (Oxford, 2nd edn, 1947), p. 320.
13 Ibid., p. 321.

21. *Is It a Myth?*

1 See the *English Historical Review* (*EHR*) 129:541 (December 2014). In this journal there is a review of Anthony Pagden's *The Enlightenment and Why It Still Matters* (Oxford, 2013), criticising it for its normative claims about the significance of the Enlightenment, and for saying that science had 'marginalized theology'. It questions whether Pagden's chief claim, that the historical failure of Christianity is the same thing as the triumph of the modern, and that therefore 'the only possible just society must necessarily be a secular one' (Pagden, p. 344), cannot be 'historically demonstrated' (*EHR*, p. 1508). On the criticised points, Pagden is right; and that he is right – along with the Whiggish, meliorist, progressivist account contained in the present book – is what his book and this one demonstrate. It is impossible to look at the history of the last three to four centuries and understand how Professor J. C. D. Clark, author of the review, can say otherwise. Moreover it is important that one should recognise that the modern dismantling of the hegemony of Christianity over minds and states alike is what is required with regard to Islam in our own era if the same process of Enlightenment and its attendant enlightenment is to occur there.

Bibliography

Addison, Joseph, *Spectator* 70 (21 May 1711)
Agrippa, Cornelius, *The Occult Philosophy in Three Books*, Book I, translated by 'J.F.' (John French? J. Freake?) (London, 1651)
Auchincloss, L., *Richelieu* (London, 1972)
Ayers, M. and Garber, D. (eds), *The Cambridge History of Seventeenth Century Philosophy*, vol. I (Cambridge, 2003)
Bacon, Francis, *Great Instauration* (London, 1605)
—, *Novum Organum* (1620), in *The New Organon*, ed. L. Jardine and M. Silverthorne (Cambridge, 2002)
—, *Advancement of Learning* (London, 1623)
Ball, P., *The Devil's Doctor: Paracelsus and the World of Renaissance Magic and Science* (London, 2006)
Baillet, A., *La Vie de Monsieur Descartes* (Paris, 1693)
Baumgold, D., *Hobbes' Political Theory* (Cambridge, 1988)
Berkeley, George, *Notebooks*, ed. A. A. Luce (Oxford, 2010)
Berlin, I., *Two Concepts of Liberty* (Oxford, 1958)
Bireley, R., 'The Peace of Prague (1635) and the Counterreformation in Germany', *Journal of Modern History* 48:1 (March 1976)
Bonelli, M. L. Righini and Shea, W. R. (eds), *Reason, Experiment, and Mysticism in the Scientific Revolution* (New York, 1975)
Broydé, I. and Jacobs, J., 'Zohar', *The Jewish Encyclopedia* (New York, 1901–6)
Cambridge History of English and American Literature (Cambridge, 1907–21), vol. IV: *Prose and Poetry: Sir Thomas North to Michael Drayton*
Cameron, A., 'The Last Days of the Academy at Athens', *Proceedings of the Cambridge Philological Society* 195 (1969)
Childs, J., *Warfare in the Seventeenth Century* (London, 2001)
Chuvin, P., *A Chronicle of the Last Pagans*, trans. B. A. Archer (London, 1990)
Clark, G. N., *The Seventeenth Century* (Oxford, 2nd edn, 1947)
Cole J. R., *The Olympian Dreams and Youthful Rebellion of Rene Descartes* (Chicago, 1992)
Cope, Z., *William Harvey: His Life and Times: His Discoveries: His Methods* (London, 1957)
Cramer, K., *The Thirty Years War and German Memory in the Nineteenth Century* (Lincoln, NE, 2007)
Croxton, D. and Tischer, A., *The Peace of Westphalia* (Westport, CT, 2002)

Crump, Thomas, *A Brief History of Science: As Seen through the Development of Scientific Instruments* (London, 2001)

Darwin, Charles, *The Autobiography of Charles Darwin, 1809–1882*, ed. Nora Barlow (London, 1958)

Davies, N., *Europe* (London, 2014)

Dear, P., *Mersenne and the Learning of the Schools* (Ithaca, NY, 1988)

Debus, A. G., 'The Chemical Debates of the 17th Century: The Reaction to Robert Fludd and Jean Baptiste van Helmont', in M. L. Righini Bonelli and W. R. Shea (eds), *Reason, Experiment, and Mysticism in the Scientific Revolution* (New York, 1975)

Demorest, J-J. (ed.), *Studies in Seventeenth Century French Literature* (Ithaca, NY, 1962)

Descartes, René, *The Discourse on the Method of Rightly Conducting the Reason, and Seeking Truth in the Sciences* (1637), Gutenberg ebook at www.gutenberg.org/files/59/59-h/59-h.htm#part6

Dunn, R., *The Age of Religious Wars 1559–1715* (New York, 1979)

Evans, G. and Newnham, J., *The Dictionary of World Politics: A Reference Guide to Concepts, Ideas and Institutions* (Hemel Hempstead, 1990)

Evelyn, John, *Diaries*, available online

Ferguson, J., *Bibliotheca Chemica: A Catalogue of the Alchemical, Chemical and Pharmaceutical Books in the Collection of the Late James Young of Kelly and Durris* (London, 2010)

Gauthier, D., *The Logic of Leviathan* (Oxford, 1969)

Godfrey, E., *A Sister of Prince Rupert: Elizabeth Princess Palatine and Abbess of Herford* (London and New York, 1909)

Grafton, A., *Defenders of the Text: The Traditions of Scholarship in an Age of Science 1450–1800* (Cambridge, MA, 1991)

Grammont, B. de, *Historiarum Galliae* (Toulouse, 1643)

Grayling, A. C., *Berkeley: The Central Arguments* (London, 1986)

—, 'Modern Philosophy: Locke, Berkeley and Hume', in *Philosophy: A Guide through the Subject* (London, 1998)

—, *Descartes: The Life and Times of a Genius* (London, 2005)

—, *Towards the Light* (London, 2007)

—, 'The Enlightenment', in *Ideas That Made the Modern World* (London, 2008)

Gribbin, J., *Science: A History* (London, 2002)

Hampton, J., *Hobbes and the Social Contract Tradition* (Cambridge, 1986)

Harkness, D., *John Dee's Conversations with Angels: Cabala, Alchemy, and the End of Nature* (Cambridge, 1999)

Hays, J. N., *Epidemics and Pandemics: Their Impacts on Human History* (Santa Barbara, 2005)

Hill, C., *The Century of Revolution 1603–1714* (London, 1961, 2nd edn, 1980)

Hine, W. L., 'Mersenne: Naturalism and Magic', in Brian Vickers (ed.), *Occult and Scientific Mentalities in the Renaissance* (Cambridge, 1984)

Hobbes, Thomas, *Leviathan* (1651, revised 1668), full text available at ebooks.adelaide.edu.au/h/hobbes/thomas/h68l

Huffman, W. H., *Robert Fludd and the End of the Renaissance* (London, 1988)

Hume, David, 'Whether the British Government Inclines More to Absolute Monarchy, or to a Republic', in E. F. Miller (ed.), *David Hume: Essays, Moral, Political, and Literary* (Indianapolis, 1985)

Hunter, M. (ed.), *Robert Boyle by Himself and his Friends* (London, 1994)

Innocent X (Pope), *Zelo Domus Dei* (Rome, 1648)

Johnson, F. R. and Larkey, S. V., 'Thomas Digges, the Copernican System, and the idea of the Infinity of the Universe in 1576', *Huntington Library Bulletin* (1934)

Jones, J. R., *The Anglo-Dutch Wars of the Seventeenth Century* (London and New York, 1996)

Jue, J. K., *Heaven Upon Earth: Joseph Mede (1586–1638) and the Legacy of Millenarianism* (Dordrecht, 2006)

Kahn, D., *Entre atomisme, alchimie et théologie: la réception des thèses d'Antoine de Villon et Etienne de Clave contre Aristote, Paracelse et les 'cabalistes' (24–25 août 1624)* (London, 2001)
Kant, Immanuel, *Was ist Aufklärung* (1784), full text available at gutenberg.spiegel.de/buch/-3505/1
Kléber, P., *Solomon's Secret Arts: The Occult in the Age of Enlightenment* (New Haven and London, 2013)
Locke, John, *Two Treatises of Government* (London, 1689), full text available at www.gutenberg.org/ebooks/7370
Lockhart, P. D., *Sweden in the Seventeenth Century* (London, 2004)
McDermott, J., *England and the Spanish Armada* (New Haven and London, 2005)
Magner, L., *A History of Life Sciences* (New York, 1979)
Marlowe, Christopher, *Doctor Faustus* (first performed *c.* 1594, published 1604), full text available at www.gutenberg.org/ebooks/779
Middleton, W. E. Knowles, *The Experimenters: A Study of the Accademia del Cimento* (Baltimore, 1971)
Miller, Eugene F. (ed.), *David Hume: Essays, Moral, Political, and Literary* (Indianapolis, 1985)
Milton, John, *Paradise Lost* (1667), full text available at www.gutenberg.org/ebooks/20
Munck, T., *Seventeenth Century Europe* (London, 1990)
Necrometrics website, necrometrics.com/pre1700a.htm#30YrW
Newton, Isaac, *Philosophiae Naturalis Principia Mathematica* (1687), in *The Principia: Mathematical Principles of Natural Philosophy*, trans. and ed. I. Bernard Cohen, Anne Whitman and Julia Budenz (Los Angeles, CA, 1999)
Nischan, B., 'John Bergius: Irenicism and the Beginnings of Official Religious Toleration in Brandenburg-Prussia', *Church History* 51 (1982)
Nye, A., *The Princess and the Philosopher: Letters of Elisabeth of the Palatine to René Descartes* (Lanham, MD, 1909)
O'Hara, G., *Britain and the Sea since 1600* (Basingstoke and New York, 2010).
Ollard, R. L. and Tudor-Craig, P., *For Veronica Wedgwood These: Studies in Seventeenth-Century History* (London, 1986)
Onnekink, D. (ed.), *War and Religion after Westphalia* (London, 2013)
Osiander, A., 'Sovereignty, International Relations, and the Westphalian Myth', *International Organization* 55:2 (2001)
Pagden, A., *The Enlightenment and Why It Still Matters* (Oxford, 2013)
Pal, C., *Republic of Women* (Cambridge, 2012)
Parker, G., 'Why the Armada Failed', *History Today* 38:5 (1988)
—, *The Thirty Years' War* (New York, 1997)
—, *Global Crisis: War, Climate Change and Catastrophe in the Seventeenth Century* (London, 2014)
Parkinson, G. H. R., *Renaissance and 17th Century Rationalism* (London, 2003)
Pennington, D., *Europe in the Seventeenth Century* (London, 1989)
Peterson, G. D., *Warrior Kings of Sweden* (London, 2007)
Petit, L., *Descartes et la Princesse Elisabeth: roman d'amour vécu* (Paris, 1969)
Power, D., *William Harvey* (London, 1897)
Prak, M., *The Dutch Republic in the Seventeenth Century* (Cambridge, 2005)
Price, J. Leslie, *The Dutch Republic in the Seventeenth Century* (London, 1998)
—, *Dutch Culture in the Golden Age* (London, 2011)
Racine, Jean, *Phèdre*, full text available at abu.cnam.fr/cgi-bin/donner_html?phedre2
Roberts, M., *The Military Revolution 1560–1660* (London, 1967)
—, *Gustavus Adolphus and the Rise of Sweden* (London, 1973)
—, 'Isaac Newton's Occult Studies', in *The Esoteric Codex: Alchemy I* (lulu.com, 2013)
Rossi, P., *Francis Bacon: From Magic to Science*, trans. Sacha Rabinovitch (London, 1968)

Sangher, L., Review of P. Kléber, *Solomon's Secret Arts: The Occult in the Age of Enlightenment* in *English Historical Review* 129:541 (December 2014)
Saper, J., *Detroit Free Press*, 24 October 2000
Shakespeare, William, *The Tempest* (1611), full text available at shakespeare.mit.edu/tempest/full
Sharratt, M., *Galileo: Decisive Innovator* (Cambridge, 1994)
Simkin, J., *First World War Encyclopedia* (Spartacus Educational ebook, 2012)
Skinner, Q., *Hobbes and Republican Liberty* (Cambridge, 2008)
Spink, J. S., *French Free Thought from Gassendi to Voltaire* (New York, 1960)
Sprat, Thomas, *History of the Royal Society* (1667)
Stanford University Humanities Center, 'Mapping the Republic of Letters', republicofletters.stanford.edu
Syfret, R. H., 'The Origins of the Royal Society', *Notes and Records. Royal Society of London* 5 (1947–8)
Thomas, K., *Religion and the Decline of Magic* (London, 1997)
Treasure, G. R. R., *Seventeenth Century France* (London, 1981)
Trevor-Roper, H., *Crisis of the Seventeenth Century: Religion, the Reformation and Social Change* (London, 2001)
Turnbull, G. H., *Samuel Hartlib: A Sketch of his Life and his Relation to J. A. Comenius* (Oxford, 1920)
Vickers, B. (ed.), *Occult and Scientific Mentalities in the Renaissance* (Cambridge, 1984)
Voltaire, *Candide* (1759), any edition, available online
Wakeman, H., *The Seventeenth Century* (Quintessential Classics eBook, 2015)
Watts, E., 'Justinian, Malalas and the End of Athenian Philosophical Teaching in AD 529', *Journal of Roman Studies* 94 (2004)
Wedgwood, C. V., *The Thirty Years War* (London, 1938)
Westfall, R. S., *Never At Rest: A Biography of Isaac Newton* (Cambridge, 1983)
Wilson, P. H., *The Thirty Years War: Europe's Tragedy* (London, 2009)
Woolley, B., *The Queen's Conjuror: The Life and Magic of Dr Dee* (London, 2001)
Yates, F., *Giordano Bruno and the Hermetic Tradition* (London, 1964)
—, *The Rosicrucian Enlightenment* (London, 1972)
—, *The Occult Philosophy in the Elizabethan Age* (London, 1979)
Zilliacus, L., *From Pillar to Post: The Troubled History of the Mail* (London, 1956)

Index

Acknowledgments

I thank my colleagues and students at NCH, my outstanding editor Bill Swainson, Catherine Clarke, Dr Hannah Dawson, Nick Humphrey and Dr Ron Witton, for various inspirations, helps and encouragements, all greatly appreciated.

A Note on the Author

A. C. Grayling is Professor of Philosophy at, and Master of, the New College of the Humanities, London. He is a prolific author, whose books include philosophy, ethics, biography, history, drama and essays. He has been a regular contributor to *The Times*, *Financial Times*, *Observer*, *Independent on Sunday*, *Economist*, *Literary Review*, *New Statesman* and *Prospect*, and is a frequent and popular contributor to radio and television programmes, including *Newsnight*, *Today*, *In Our Time*, *Start the Week* and *CNN News*. Grayling chaired the judging panel of the Man Booker Prize, 2014. Among his recent books are *Towards the Light*, *Liberty in the Age of Terror*, *The Good Book: A Secular Bible* and *The God Argument*.

A Note on the Type

The text of this book is set in Adobe Garamond. It is one of several versions of Garamond based on the designs of Claude Garamond. It is thought that Garamond based his font on Bembo, cut in 1495 by Francesco Griffo in collaboration with the Italian printer Aldus Manutius. Garamond types were first used in books printed in Paris around 1532. Many of the present-day versions of this type are based on the Typi Academiae of Jean Jannon, cut in Sedan in 1615.

Claude Garamond was born in Paris in 1480. He learned how to cut type from his father and by the age of fifteen he was able to fashion steel punches the size of a pica with great precision. At the age of sixty he was commissioned by King Francis I to design a Greek alphabet; for this he was given the honourable title of royal type-founder. He died in 1561.